# REALIZING GENJŌKŌAN
## THE KEY TO DŌGEN'S SHŌBŌGENZŌ

# REALIZING GENJŌKŌAN

## THE KEY TO DŌGEN'S SHŌBŌGENZŌ

by Shohaku Okumura

foreword by Taigen Dan Leighton

Wisdom

Wisdom Publications
199 Elm Street
Somerville MA 02144 USA
www.wisdomexperience.org

*Library of Congress Cataloging-in-Publication Data*
Okumura, Shohaku, 1948–
  Realizing Genjōkōan : the key to Dōgen's Shōbōgenzō / by Shohaku Okumura.
    p. cm.
  Includes bibliographical references and index.
  ISBN 0-86171-601-9 (pbk. : alk. paper)
  1. Dogen, 1200–1253. Shobo genzo. 2. Spiritual life—Sotoshu. 3. Sotoshu—Doctrines. I. Dogen, 1200–1253. Shobo genzo. Genjo koan. English. II. Title.
  BQ9449.D654G4665 2010
  294.3'85—dc22

                        2010007994


ISBN 978-0-86171-601-2      ebook ISBN 978-0-86171-934-1


24 23 22 21
7  6  5  4


Appendix 3, "Dōgen's Life," is reprinted with permission from *Eihei Dōgen—Mystical Realist.*

Cover art by Eiji Imao: www.etima025.wixsite.com/mizunokioku
Cover design by JBTL. Interior design by Gopa & Ted2, Inc. Set in DGP 12/15.4.

Wisdom Publications' books are printed on acid-free paper and meet the guidelines for permanence and durability of the Production Guidelines for Book Longevity of the Council on Library Resources.

Printed in the United States of America.

Please visit fscus.org.

# Contents

# FOREWORD

THIS BOOK is a treasure. Shohaku Okumura has given us a work of great value for any student of Eihei Dōgen's teachings, for Zen practitioners, or for anyone interested in learning about Zen. The writings and teachings of the thirteenth-century Japanese Sōtō lineage founder Eihei Dōgen have been highly influential not only in the introduction of Zen to the West, but for Western interest in all of Buddhism. And of all Dōgen's profuse writings, none has likely been more frequently cited or more illuminating than this essay, Genjōkōan. Even though it was written originally as a letter to a lay practitioner, as is common for Dōgen's writings it is also highly dense and profound, and its subtleties of meaning are far from obvious. An old Zen slogan denigrates dependence on words and letters, instead emphasizing direct pointing to mind and awareness. So it is ironic that Zen has produced extensive libraries of writings, often composed of commentaries on previous writings like this one. But the point of such writing, as Dōgen specifically delineates in some of his essays, is the encouragement and refining of practice, rather than propounding theoretical philosophical positions. Genjōkōan is such a text, clarifying and supporting the actual unfolding practice of awakening. This extended and engaging commentary by Shohaku Okumura further reveals and supports the practical application of Dōgen's teaching, making it a great service both to new students as well as to those long familiar with Genjōkōan.

For new students of Zen meditation, many passages herein will be very helpful for finding the inner rhythm of Zen meditation and practice generally. For example, in chapter 5, "Realization beyond Realization," one finds varied useful accounts of how we create and are impacted by our mental maps of the world, the process of delusion that Dōgen clearly but subtly defines in Genjōkōan. Shohaku says, "Within this mental map there are things we think are good, useful, or valuable, such as flowers, and there are other things we think are bad, useless, or worthless, such as weeds. Usually we take it for granted that the fabricated picture of the world in our minds is the world itself." Our attachment to flowers and dislike of weeds is one of Dōgen's early images in Genjōkōan. The process of zazen helps us see through our usual graspings and rejections, and the resulting mischief in our lives. Shohaku provides practical elaboration. For example,

> The practice of zazen can help us understand that our pictures of the world and our values are biased and incomplete, and this understanding allows us to be flexible. Being flexible means that we can listen to others' opinions knowing that their biases are simply different from ours, according to the circumstances and conditions of their individual lives. When we practice in this way our view broadens and we become better at working in harmony with others. By continually studying the nature of reality, of the Dharma in its universal sense, and by awakening to our biases, we keep working to correct our distorted views. This is how letting go of thought in zazen informs practice in our daily lives.

Shohaku also clarifies the practical relevance of the study of the self and the dropping off of the body and mind of the self, which is described and encouraged by Dōgen in Genjōkōan. In clear language

Shohaku expresses his own letting go of self-identification in zazen as taking off the clothes of identity to reveal our naked being.

> We wear the clothing of occupations such as doctor, lawyer, mechanic, priest, student, teacher. But when we sit facing the wall and let go of thought, including comparing ourselves with others, we take off all this clothing. In zazen I am not a Japanese Buddhist priest; I am neither Japanese nor American. In zazen we are neither rich nor poor, neither Buddhist nor Christian. The terms "Japanese," "American," "Buddhist," "Christian," "man," and "woman" are only relevant when we compare ourselves with others. When I compare myself with Americans, I am Japanese, but before I knew of people who weren't Japanese I didn't know that I was Japanese. When we just sit facing the wall in zazen, we are neither deluded living beings nor enlightened buddhas; we are neither alive nor dead; we are just as we are. That's it. In zazen we take off all of our clothing and become the naked self.

Shohaku also shows how primary Buddhist teachings are embedded in the first paragraph of the Genjōkōan text, demonstrating that Zen and Dōgen's teaching are firmly rooted in the Buddha's teaching and the developments of Mahayana Buddhist philosophy. Shohaku interprets the first sentence in terms of some of Shakyamuni Buddha's basic teachings such as the four noble truths and the twelve links of causation. The second sentence, ". . . without [fixed] self, there is no delusion and no realization, no buddhas and no living beings, no birth and no death" is presented with extended commentaries on Madhyamika emptiness teaching, the Yogacara study of consciousness, as well as the Tathagata-garbha "Buddha-womb" branch of Mahayana thought. These are all expressed and compared in terms of the Heart Sutra, which is provided in Shohaku's translation in an epilogue. The third sentence, "Since the Buddha Way by nature goes beyond [the dichotomy of] abundance and deficiency, there is arising and perishing, delusion and realization, living beings and buddhas," Shohaku presents as Dōgen's own teaching, echoing Dōgen's commentary on the Heart Sutra, "Maka Hannya Haramitsu," also provided in Shohaku's translation in the epilogue. While providing this introduction to Buddhist teachings generally, Shohaku's discussions of Genjōkōan lead to comparisons with selections from many other writings of Dōgen, presented with Shohaku's translations and illuminating commentaries.

This book will be informative to new students of Zen and Dōgen, but it will also be helpful for the many Western Zen people who have long studied Genjōkōan. Many quite useful translations of this essay are already available, as well as helpful commentaries, but this book goes beyond. I have been considering Genjōkōan for thirty-five years, and still I enjoyed many helpful revelations in this book.

One example is that the fourth Chinese character or *kanji* used by Dōgen for the word Genjōkōan, the "an" of "kōan," differs slightly from the character more commonly used for the familiar term *kōan*, the encounter dialogue teaching stories, famous in Zen history and anthologized with extensive commentaries. Shohaku carefully analyzes the many fascinating implications of this different character used by Dōgen. These interpretations are supported by the important commentary of Dōgen's close disciple Senne, and include the nuances from using the "hand" radical, with meanings related to healing, as well as the variant character's meaning of caring for one's uniqueness or particularity. Thus the term Genjōkōan has connotations including the manifesting of the interaction of unity and uniqueness.

Perhaps the most renowned statement in all of Dōgen's writings is the Genjōkōan line, "To study the Buddha Way is to study the self." This kanji for "study" can mean, "to become intimate with." Shohaku further analyzes the meaning here in terms of this Chinese character's combining "self" and "wings of a bird," so that this study of the self advocated by Dōgen Shohaku likens to a baby bird learning to fly. The ensuing discussion is informative and colorful, including Shohaku's example for such study of using our interaction with a car as we drive. Shohaku's explications of the overtones of the kanji for "study" are highly suggestive. As Dōgen follows the above line with, "To study the self is to forget the self," we might view this "self with bird wings" as the self flying away, or perhaps the deeper self taking flight "to be verified by all things" and "let body and mind of the self and of others drop off," as Dōgen then adds.

Another example of the helpfulness of Shohaku's commentary includes his discussion of the Zen master who fans himself in the story near the conclusion of Genjōkōan, demonstrating how the wind of Dharma and its nature permeates everywhere. This teacher, Magu Baoche, is somewhat obscure in Zen history, but Shohaku provides three other relevant stories about him, including his encounters with the great master Linji (Jap.: Rinzai). These stories and the examination of Baoche's fanning himself lead to an informative discussion of the important teaching of Buddha nature, its complexities, and how it relates to Dōgen's emphasis on the importance of diligent practice.

I am honored to write this foreword, and I am privileged to have worked with Shohaku Okumura on three previous books of translations of Dōgen. When I lived in Kyoto from 1990 through 1992 I frequently traveled to the Kyoto Sōtō Zen Center at the temple outside Kyoto where Shohaku lived with his family, and then in late 1992 at his residence nearby in Kyoto. We translated Dōgen's important early writing Bendōwa with Uchiyama Roshi's engaging commentary for the book *The Wholehearted Way*. At the same time we were translating the collection of Dōgen's Chinese writings about monastic practice, Eihei Shingi, for the book Dōgen's *Pure Standards for the Zen Community*. Later, when Shohaku was living in San Francisco and working at the Sōtō Zen Education Center at Sōkōji in Japantown we had the opportunity to work together again. From November 1999 to February 2003 we translated Dōgen's massive work Eihei Kōroku, including most of what is known of the last decade of Dōgen's teaching, for the book *Dōgen's Extensive Record*.

Throughout the process of these translations I increasingly appreciated the consideration and thoroughness that Shohaku brought to the
study and translation of Dōgen. Dōgen's writing is famous for being
challenging, poetic, full of classic allusions to Buddhist and Chinese
terms, and suffused with extensive wordplay including puns and inten-
tionally tangled syntax, all directed at bringing forth the inner meaning
of Buddhist teachings. As we struggled together to clarify and express
in English Dōgen's meaning, Shohaku's patience and loyalty to Dōgen
was inspiring. When confronted by one of the many particularly difficult passages from Dōgen, we would often take several hours wrestling
with its meanings. At such times I would suggest plausible interpretations, but Shohaku would not settle for something uncertain, assidu-
ously pointing out how my suggestion was questionable or could not be
possible. Surprisingly often in such cases, when we returned after several hours to consider Dōgen's passage very literally, its meaning would
suddenly become apparent (or at least clear enough that we could note
possible alternatives in the footnotes). Shohaku's inspirational care
and faithfulness in conveying Dōgen's meaning is also apparent in this
translation and commentary on Genjōkōan.

This book, *Realizing Genjōkōan*, in many ways bears comparison with
*The Wholehearted Way*. The latter is a translation of the very early
Dōgen writing Bendōwa, which expresses the inner meaning of zazen
and is radically subversive to our usual human conceptualization, as
in Dōgen's remarkable, "mind-blowing" claim that when one person
performs upright sitting meditation, even for a short time, then "all
space in the universe completely becomes enlightenment." Genjōkōan
was one of Dōgen's very next writings, only two years after Bendōwa,
and is similarly decisive in presenting his basic philosophy, as in his
clear and helpful definition of the difference between delusion and
enlightenment, "Conveying oneself toward all things to carry out
practice-enlightenment is delusion. All things coming and carrying
out practice-enlightenment through the self is realization." Not surprisingly, Shohaku's commentary on this difference is revealing.

*The Wholehearted Way* also contains a translation of the commentary on Bendōwa by Shohaku's beloved teacher Kōshō Uchiyama Roshi. This commentary, given in 1978 and 1979, is down to earth, practical, lively, and very illuminating to the text and its practice. In *Realizing Genjōkōan*, Shohaku emulates his teacher by providing his own practical, insightful commentary to the Genjōkōan text, including many personal examples from Shohaku's own life. Shohaku Okumura is a very quiet man, and one of the greatest models I have ever met of true, deep humility. So he would probably object to my saying that in this book I believe Shohaku Okumura has fulfilled the traditional recommendation for Zen disciples to surpass their teacher. At the very least, Shohaku certainly has provided a helpful practical commentary on Dōgen for this time in America, as Uchiyama Roshi did for his time in Japan.

Finally, I want to address directly one portion of Shohaku's commentary that might be controversial for some American Zen people. In relation to the important Genjōkōan line, "To be verified by all things is to let the body and mind of the self and the body and mind of others drop off," Shohaku discusses the phrase frequently cited by Dōgen, "dropping body and mind," *shinjin datsuraku* in Japanese. For Dōgen this phrase, which he heard at least some version of from his Chinese teacher, Rujing, is a synonym for both zazen and for enlightenment itself. There is a popular story about Dōgen that goes back to a hagiographical, nonhistorical work about the whole Zen lineage leading to Dōgen written by his third generation successor Keizan. This story, which has become enshrined in Sōtō legend, claims that Dōgen had a dramatic awakening experience (Jap.: *kenshō* or *satori*) related to hearing the phrase about "dropping body and mind" from Rujing. Shohaku Okumura disputes that story, which Dōgen himself never mentioned. Shohaku cites several highly respected modern Japanese Sōtō scholars who agree, and he concurs with them that Dōgen never advocated or understood dropping body and mind as some sudden or special psychological experience or condition. Certainly dramatic opening experiences can occur in practice, historically and still today, and may be helpful in shifting life perspectives. Some approaches to Zen have even emphasized such experiences as the goal of practice. But Dōgen is very clear that the awakening he speaks of is an ongoing vital process, and dramatic experiences are not the point of practice. Even in traditions that promote kenshō, it is not seen as the ultimate conclusion of practice. For example, the great eighteenth-century Rinzai master Hakuin had many dozens of such experiences. And modern Rinzai adepts have clarified that kenshō is not some experience to acquire, but a way of actively seeing into any or all of experience. For Dōgen, dropping off body and mind is zazen itself, and the "deep awareness of the fact that the existence of the self is not a personal possession."

For all people interested in Zen, this book on Genjōkōan will be a valuable and illuminating resource. Please enjoy it.

Taigen Dan Leighton

TAIGEN DAN LEIGHTON is a Zen priest and author of *Visions of Awakening Space and Time: Dōgen and the Lotus Sutra* and of *Faces of Compassion: Classic Bodhisattva Archetypes and Their Modern Expression*, and has co-translated many works by Dōgen, as well as *Cultivating the Empty Field: The Silent Illumination of Zen Master Hongzhi*.

# Preface

ENJŌKŌAN IS ONE of the best known chapters of Dōgen
Zenji's Shōbōgenzō. It is the best text to use in beginning a
study of Dōgen's teachings, and understanding it is essential
to developing an understanding of zazen and our daily activities as
bodhisattva practices.

Since philosophical and intellectual study alone can provide only
a limited understanding of Zen, Dōgen wrote many instructions for
daily activities, the core of Zen practice. He wrote Fukanzazengi
(Universal Recommendations for Zazen) to give instructions for sitting zazen, and he wrote Fushukuhanpō (Dharma for Taking Meals)
to instruct practitioners in eating formal meals in the meditation
hall. Dōgen also gave instructions for working in a Zen kitchen in
Tenzo-Kyōkun (Instructions for the Cook). These works contain
concrete instructions for behavior in every aspect of our daily lives,
and they show us the proper attitude to maintain toward our lives in
general. Although these teachings were originally written for people
practicing in Zen monasteries many years ago, Dōgen's writings are
still vividly relevant to the lives of modern practitioners in today's
society.

Genjōkōan is the first chapter of Shōbōgenzō, the work in which

Dōgen expressed the foundational philosophy supporting the many concrete instructions he gave to his students. Genjōkōan presents in a precise and concrete way Dōgen's philosophy that we should approach everything we do as bodhisattva practice.

Although Genjōkōan is one of Dōgen's most widely read writings, and is a foundational text, it is nonetheless very difficult to understand. Rather than simply explaining Buddhist teachings, Dōgen uses poetic and precise language to express an understanding born of his own profound insight and experience. In Japan the Shōbōgenzō is studied with the aid of commentaries written by Sōtō Zen masters, but often these are as difficult to understand as Dōgen's original words. Ultimately, though we can greatly benefit from commentaries, we must also read Dōgen's writings with the aid of our own experiences of zazen and daily life practice. This is how I have come to the understanding of Genjōkōan that I am offering to you now. So please do not take my words at face value; please study this text in the context of your own experience and practice. This is the way the Buddha Dharma has been transmitted for generations.

Before we begin exploring Dōgen, let me tell you about how I came to be writing this book, and how this book came to be.

I read Kōshō Uchiyama's first book, *Jiko* (Self), in the fall of 1965, the year of the book's initial publication. I was a seventeen-year-old high school student living in Ibaraki, a town located between Ōsaka and Kyōto. Soon I became very interested in his way of life and wanted to become his disciple, although at the time I did not completely understand why. As a result of my connection to Uchiyama Rōshi's teachings, I wanted to learn about Dōgen Zenji, the founder of the Japanese Sōtō Zen tradition and source of inspiration for Uchiyama Rōshi's way of life.

Although it was my treasure-house of knowledge and wisdom, the small library of the public school I attended contained very few books written by or about Dōgen, no doubt due in part to the fact specific religious education was prohibited in public classrooms at that time.

I was able to find *Shōbōgenzō* and *Zuimonki* in the *Iwanami Bunko*, a collection of classic books from Japan, China, and the West, but even *Zuimonki*, simpler of the two texts, was too difficult for a high school student to read because, of course, it was written in thirteenth-century classic Japanese with many Buddhist and Zen terms. Trying to read it was perhaps akin to an American high schooler trying to read Chaucer.

I found only one book written about Dōgen. It contained a brief biography and the author's commentaries on *Shōbōgenzō Bendōwa* (Talk on Wholehearted Practice of the Way), *Genjōkōan* (Actualization of Reality), and *Shōji* (Life and Death). Because I had no knowledge whatsoever of Buddhism, even the commentaries in modern Japanese were difficult for me. I understood almost nothing I read in this book, but the beauty of Dōgen Zenji's writing impressed me, especially in Genjōkōan. It seemed like a poem to me, and I copied the entire text in my notebook. The beginning of Genjōkōan, in which Dōgen Zenji discusses Buddha Dharma, the Buddha Way, realization and delusion, practice and enlightenment, and life and death, was incomprehensible to me. Yet, like many teenagers, I considered myself a poet (although I quit writing poems when I began practicing zazen), and I appreciated the poetic beauty of the second half of the text, especially Dōgen's images of a bird flying in the sky and a fish swimming in the ocean.

One of the few sentences I did understand that affected me deeply read: "Therefore, if there are fish that would swim or birds that would fly only after investigating the entire ocean or sky, they would find neither path nor place." As I write in chapter 11 of this book, I was exactly like that fish who wants to understand the ocean before swimming, or a bird who needs a reason to fly before flying. This was the only part of Genjōkōan that I understood, but it taught me first of all I needed to begin doing *something* in my life. So in 1968 I went to Komazawa University to study the teachings of the Buddha and of Dōgen Zenji. There I met some people who were practicing zazen sincerely, and I began sitting with them. Later, in January 1969, I went to Antaiji in Kyōto to participate in a five-day *sesshin*, the intensive meditation retreat in the Zen tradition.

Less than two years later, on December 8, 1970, I received *tokudo*—novice ordination as a Zen monk—at the age of twenty-two. At that time, I formally became Uchiyama Rōshi's disciple. The next day my teacher said to me, "Before the ceremony yesterday your father asked me to take care of his son. However, I cannot take care of you. If you want to be my disciple, you must walk with your own feet in the direction I am walking." That was the first personal instruction I received on how to swim in the ocean of Buddha Dharma.

I was still a university student at that time, and I wanted to quit school so I could practice at Antaiji, but Rōshi encouraged me to complete my education. So I went back to Komazawa University for another year, graduating in the spring of 1972, and began my practice at Antaiji soon after. I stayed there until Uchiyama Rōshi retired in 1975. In February of that year, shortly before his retirement, I received Dharma transmission from him. After I spent six months training at Zuiōji monastery as a requirement to be affirmed as a teacher in the Sōtō Zen tradition, I went to Massachusetts to practice at Pioneer Valley Zendō. I lived there for five years, wholeheartedly and thoroughly practicing zazen in Uchiyama Rōshi's style of *shikantaza*, just sitting. I was extremely fortunate that in my twenties I could sustain that rigorous practice.

In my early thirties I developed physical problems due to the hard work I performed at Valley Zendō, and I had to return to Japan in 1981. In Kyōto my teacher encouraged me to translate Dōgen Zenji's teachings into English. He hoped that I would create a place to practice zazen, continue translating, and study the teachings I translated with people from other countries. I listened repeatedly to Uchiyama Rōshi's recorded *teishōs*—his formal Zen talks—and I occasionally visited him at his residence in Uji, near Kyōto. From 1984 to 1992 I practiced at the Kyōto Sōtō Zen Center with the support of Rev. Yūho Hosokawa of Sōsenji. During that time I held a monthly five-day sesshin and with the help of Western practitioners produced five books of translations. It was then, during my thirties, that I discovered my full life's work. Thus I resolved to continue my teacher's lifelong vow of transmitting zazen practice to the next generation and producing Dharma teaching texts understandable to modern readers. Having married at age thirty-five, I now swam the Dharma ocean primarily with Westerners and my family.

In my forties I began to practice in America as a teacher. In 1993 I moved to Minneapolis to teach at the Minnesota Zen Meditation Center, whose founder, Dainin Katagiri Rōshi, had passed away in 1990. I taught as the interim head teacher there until 1996, and I remained a part-time teacher there for another year. As part of the study program at MZMC, I had the good fortune to hold a Genjōkōan study group with several of Katagiri Rōshi's senior students, including Steve Hagen, Jōen Snyder O'Neal, Michael O'Neal, Norm Randolph, Zuiko Redding, and Karen Sunna. Sten Barnekow from Sweden also participated during his stay in Minneapolis. The English translation of Genjōkōan used in this book is a result of our practice in that study group.

When I completed my term as head teacher of MZMC in 1996, I formed Sanshin Zen Community with the help of practitioners from across the United States and around the world, and, full of hope, we began to search for a suitable location for a new practice center. The search was postponed, however, when in the summer of 1997 I moved to California and took a job as director of the Sōtō Zen Education Center (currently known as the Sōtō Zen Buddhism International Center) that had been newly formed by the Japanese Sōtō school. The Sōtō Zen Education Center was located at Zenshuji in Los Angeles, where for about a year I gave monthly lectures on Genjōkōan. The center moved to San Francisco in 1999, and as part of my responsibility as its director, I traveled to various Zen centers across the United States, sitting zazen and sharing Dōgen Zenji's teachings with many practitioners. I was then in my fifties, and the range of my Dharma swimming had grown very wide, extending from California to New England and from Alaska to Florida.

In 2003 I moved to Bloomington, Indiana, to establish Sanshinji, Sanshin Zen Community's practice center, and I am now working as part-time director with the Sōtō Zen Buddhism International Center. Since establishing Sanshinji, more than ten people have become my disciples, and many lay practitioners have been joining me in the practice that I learned from Uchiyama Rōshi. I am grateful to all the people practicing shikantaza with me who support this simple and yet infinitely deep way of life based on the teachings of Dōgen Zenji. Without all those practitioners, I could not continue swimming the Dharma ocean.

This is my sixtieth year of life, and over forty years have passed since I first felt the desire to become Uchiyama Rōshi's disciple after reading his book *Jiko*. For most of my life I have been swimming this one particular way of zazen practice in the boundless, great ocean of Buddha Dharma, where the route of any bird or fish is traceless. Although I am a slow swimmer, I feel fortunate that I have been able to continuously swim the great ocean, and I am extremely grateful for my teacher, Dharma brothers, and friends who have supported my practice. Numberless others have helped me sustain this narrow yet boundless way as well. The generosity of thousands of people in Japan, for example, who made donations in response to my practice of *takuhatsu*, a monk's begging rounds, enabled me to continue to sit zazen and do translation work. Those people supported me without knowing who I was or what I was doing in my life, and without them, I could not have continued to practice.

The lectures that were to become the heart of this book were recorded at the Sōtō Zen Education Center and kindly transcribed by Rev. Chiko Corona. Rev. Corona was at that time a disciple of Kenkō Yamashita Rōshi, who served as the abbot of Zenshuji and the Bishop of North America for many decades. (And after her teacher's death, she became my disciple.) I also wrote a series of articles on Genjōkōan for the center's newsletter, *Dharma Eye*. Rev. Chiko Corona, Rev. Koshin Steve Kelly, and Rev. Daigaku Rummé then edited my very

Japanese English into real English. This process continued for several years.

Then, another disciple of mine, Rev. Shoryu Bradley, worked several years on revising the series of articles into a single book. Molly Whitehead kindly offered her time in reviewing the entire manuscript and offered many valuable suggestions for improving its readability. Rev. Jisho Warner of Stone Creek Zen Center also reviewed it and offered many valuable suggestions. I am grateful to Josh Bartok of Wisdom Publications for his kind advice, support, and encouragement, and to Sōtōshū Shūmuchō and the Sōtō Zen Buddhism International Center for granting me permission to publish this material with an American publisher.

A special thanks goes to Mr. Eiji Imao who kindly gave me permission to use his painting of *iwana* (char) swimming in infinite space and time. Since my first viewing of his paintings of swimming fish, they have been inscribed in my mind as images from Dōgen's Genjōkōan. I believe the beautiful painting used for this book conveys Dōgen's deep message as well as any words I have written.

Without the generous support, advice, and work of these many people, all of it rooted in the love of Dharma and practice as taught by Dōgen Zenji, this book could not have evolved into its current form, truly a manifestation of the reality of interdependent origination as expressed by many practitioners from the East and the West.

Finally, I would like to express my appreciation to my wife, Yuko, for her continuous support for me and our children over the last twenty-five years. My daughter, Yoko, is now twenty-one years old and my son, Masaki, is seventeen, the age I was when I first read Uchiyama Rōshi's book. I hope they both will find their own unique ways of swimming this boundless ocean.

—Shohaku Okumura

# THE TEXT

# GENJŌKŌAN

(1) When all dharmas are the Buddha Dharma, there is delusion and realization, practice, life and death, buddhas and living beings.

(2) When the ten thousand dharmas are without [fixed] self, there is no delusion and no realization, no buddhas and no living beings, no birth and no death.

(3) Since the Buddha Way by nature goes beyond [the dichotomy of] abundance and deficiency, there is arising and perishing, delusion and realization, living beings and buddhas.

(4) Therefore flowers fall even though we love them; weeds grow even though we dislike them. Conveying oneself toward all things to carry out practice-enlightenment is delusion. All things coming and carrying out practice-enlightenment through the self is realization. Those who greatly realize delusion are buddhas. Those who are greatly deluded in realization are living beings. Furthermore, there are those who attain realization beyond realization and those who are deluded within delusion.

(5) When buddhas are truly buddhas they don't need to perceive they are buddhas; however, they are enlightened buddhas and they continue actualizing Buddha. In seeing color and hearing sound with body and mind, although we perceive them intimately, [the perception] is not like reflections in a mirror or the moon in water. When one side is illuminated, the other is dark.

(6) To study the Buddha Way is to study the self. To study the self is to forget the self. To forget the self is to be verified by all things. To be verified by all things is to let the body and mind of the self and the body and mind of others drop off. There is a trace of realization that cannot be grasped. We endlessly express this ungraspable trace of realization.

(7) When one first seeks the Dharma, one strays far from the boundary of the Dharma. When the Dharma is correctly transmitted to the self, one is immediately an original person.

If one riding in a boat watches the coast, one mistakenly perceives the coast as moving. If one watches the boat [in relation to the surface of the water], then one notices that the boat is moving. Similarly, when we perceive the body and mind in a confused way and grasp all things with a discriminating mind, we mistakenly think that the self-nature of the mind is permanent. When we intimately practice and return right here, it is clear that all things have no [fixed] self.

(8) Firewood becomes ash. Ash cannot become firewood again. However, we should not view ash as after and firewood as before. We should know that firewood dwells in the dharma position of firewood and has its own before and after. Although before and after exist, past and future are cut off. Ash stays in the position of ash, with its own before and after. As firewood never becomes firewood again after it has burned to ash, there is no return to living after a person dies. However, in Buddha Dharma it is an unchanged tradition not to say that life becomes death. Therefore we call it no-arising. It is

the established way of buddhas' turning the Dharma wheel not to say that death becomes life. Therefore, we call it no-perishing. Life is a position in time; death is also a position in time. This is like winter and spring. We don't think that winter becomes spring, and we don't say that spring becomes summer.

(9) When a person attains realization, it is like the moon's reflection in water. The moon never becomes wet; the water is never disturbed. Although the moon is a vast and great light, it is reflected in a drop of water. The whole moon and even the whole sky are reflected in a drop of dew on a blade of grass. Realization does not destroy the person, as the moon does not make a hole in the water. The person does not obstruct realization, as a drop of dew does not obstruct the moon in the sky. The depth is the same as the height. [To investigate the significance of] the length and brevity of time, we should consider whether the water is great or small, and understand the size of the moon in the sky.

(10) When the Dharma has not yet fully penetrated body and mind, one thinks one is already filled with it. When the Dharma fills body and mind, one thinks something is [still] lacking. For example, when we sail a boat into the ocean beyond sight of land and our eyes scan [the horizon in] the four directions, it simply looks like a circle. No other shape appears. This great ocean, however, is neither round nor square. It has inexhaustible characteristics. [To a fish] it looks like a palace; [to a heavenly being] a jeweled necklace. [To us] as far as our eyes can see, it looks like a circle. All the myriad things are like this. Within the dusty world and beyond, there are innumerable aspects and characteristics; we only see or grasp as far as the power of our eye of study and practice can see. When we listen to the reality of myriad things, we must know that there are inexhaustible characteristics in both ocean and mountains, and there are many other worlds in the four directions. This is true not only in the external world, but also right under our feet or within a single drop of water.

(11) When a fish swims, no matter how far it swims, it doesn't reach the end of the water. When a bird flies, no matter how high it flies, it cannot reach the end of the sky. Therefore, since ancient times, no fish has ever left the water and no bird has ever left the sky. When the bird's need or the fish's need is great, the range is large. When the need is small, the range is small. In this way, each fish and each bird uses the whole of space and vigorously acts in every place. However, if a bird departs from the sky, or a fish leaves the water, it immediately dies. We should know that [for a fish] water is life, [for a bird] sky is life. A bird is life; a fish is life. Life is a bird; life is a fish. And we should go beyond this. There is practice-enlightenment—this is the way of living beings.

(12) Therefore, if there are fish that would swim or birds that would fly only after investigating the entire ocean or sky, they would find neither path nor place. When we make this very place our own, our practice becomes the actualization of reality (*genjōkōan*). When we make this path our own, our activity naturally becomes actualized reality (*genjōkōan*). This path, this place, is neither big nor small, neither self nor others. It has not existed before this moment nor has it come into existence now. Therefore [the reality of all things] is thus. In the same way, when a person engages in practice-enlightenment in the Buddha Way, as the person realizes one dharma, the person permeates that dharma; as the person encounters one practice, the person [fully] practices that practice. [For this] there is a place and a path. The boundary of the known is not clear; this is because the known [which appears limited] is born and practiced simultaneously with the complete penetration of the Buddha Dharma. We should not think that what we have attained is conceived by ourselves and known by our discriminating mind. Although complete enlightenment is immediately actualized, its intimacy is such that it does not necessarily form as a view. [In fact] viewing is not something fixed.

(13) Zen Master Baoche of Mt. Magu was waving a fan. A monk approached him and asked, "The nature of wind is ever present and permeates everywhere. Why are you waving a fan?"

The master said, "You know only that the wind's nature is ever present—you don't know that it permeates everywhere."

The monk said, "How does wind permeate everywhere?"

The master just continued waving the fan.

The monk bowed deeply.

The genuine experience of Buddha Dharma and the vital path that has been correctly transmitted are like this. To say we should not wave a fan because the nature of wind is ever present, and that we should feel the wind even when we don't wave a fan, is to know neither ever-presence nor the wind's nature. Since the wind's nature is ever present, the wind of the Buddha's family enables us to realize the gold of the great Earth and to transform the [water of] the long river into cream.

The First Chapter of
Shōbōgenzō (The True Dharma Eye Treasury)
Genjōkōan (Actualization of Reality)

> This was written in mid-autumn in the first year of Tenpuku era [1233] and given to my lay disciple, Yō Kōshū, who lived in Chinzei (Kyūshū).

> Compiled in the fourth year of Kenchō [1252]

—Translated by Shohaku Okumura

# DŌGEN ZENJI'S LIFE
## AND THE IMPORTANCE OF GENJŌKŌAN

DŌGEN ZENJI was born in the year 1200 in Kyōto, which
was then the capital city of Japan. He was born into a high-
society family, and some believe his father was the emperor's
secretary and Dōgen was the grandson of the prime minister. Dōgen's
father is believed to have died when Dōgen was two years old, and
his mother is believed to have died when he was eight. It is said that
it was his mother's death that prompted Dōgen, of his own accord, to
resolve to become a Buddhist monk. At thirteen Dōgen was ordained
at Enryakuji monastery on Mt. Hiei, near Kyōto, in the Tendai tradition, one of the two major Buddhist schools at that time. Yet Dōgen
became unhappy with the practice at Mt. Hiei and left there when
he was seventeen. Dōgen left the monastery, at least in part, because
he was unable to find anyone there who could give him a satisfactory
answer to a very important question that arose in his practice.

According to his biography, Dōgen's question related to the primary
Mahayana teaching of Buddha nature, an especially important teaching in the Tendai school of his time. The *hongaku-hōmon* (dharma
gate of original enlightenment) teaching of the Tendai school states
that all living and nonliving beings are already enlightened buddhas,
since they all have Buddha nature. But Dōgen questioned why it was

necessary for all buddhas to arouse the way-seeking mind and practice if they were already enlightened buddhas. In the Buddhist traditions of India, China, and other countries practice was always very difficult. But why did even the ancient masters, who possessed great capability, have to practice so hard to attain enlightenment if they were inherently enlightened? Why do any of us have to study and endure such difficult practice if we are already buddhas?

This was the great question that Dōgen asked as a teenager and kept asking until he found its answer years later.

Dōgen visited many Buddhist teachers, but none gave him a satisfactory answer. According to the traditional account, however, one of the teachers he visited, Venerable Kōin, told Dōgen that he would find the answers to this deep question only through practicing in the Zen tradition. Kōin also encouraged Dōgen to visit China, which was then considered to be the home of authentic Zen practice. Following Kōin's recommendation, at age seventeen Dōgen left the Tendai monastery at Mt. Hiei and joined the community of monks at Kenninji, founded in 1202 as the first Zen monastery in Japan. The founder of Kenninji, Master Eisai (1141–1215), was the first Japanese Buddhist priest to transmit Rinzai Zen teachings from China to Japan. Dōgen began practicing at Kenninji after Eisai had already died, but he studied there with Eisai's direct disciple, Myōzen (1184–1225), for seven years until Dōgen reached the age of twenty-three.

In Dōgen's time Zen was new to Japan, and since Dōgen and Myōzen wanted to study authentic, traditional Chinese Zen, together they traveled to China in 1223. Dōgen studied there for five years until he was twenty-seven, but unfortunately Myōzen, Dōgen's first Zen teacher, died before he could return to Japan.

Upon his arrival in China, Dōgen practiced at Tiantong Monastery under the guidance of its abbot, Wuji Liaopai (Jap.: Musai Ryōha, 1149–1224), a Rinzai Zen master. When Liaopai passed away the next year, Dōgen left Tiantong to visit a number of other monasteries. During this time Dōgen met several Zen masters who were all, as far as we know, members of the Rinzai tradition that was so popular in Chinese Zen communities of the day. It is therefore evident that Dōgen spent the first ten years of his association with Zen practicing in the Rinzai tradition. Yet Dōgen felt that none of the masters he met during this period was his true teacher. Just as Dōgen was planning to give up his search and return to Japan in disappointment, he heard that a great master had been appointed abbot of Tiantong Monastery. In the summer of 1225 Dōgen returned to that monastery, where he met Tiantong Rujing (Jap.: Tendō Nyojō, 1163–1228), knowing from their first meeting that he had found the true teacher he had spent so many years searching for. It was in the same month of this auspicious meeting that Dōgen's first Zen teacher, Myōzen, passed away at Tiantong Monastery. Dōgen continued to practice with Rujing for two years, returning to Japan in 1227 after receiving Dharma transmission from him in the Sōtō lineage.

Dōgen again practiced at Kenninji after returning to Japan. Yet he left the monastery in 1230, because he found that its Rinzai style did not allow him to practice and teach in his own way, and he also felt that the practitioners at Kenninji had lost the genuine spirit of Zen practice established there by Eisai. After leaving Kenninji Dōgen lived and practiced alone for several years at a small hermitage in Fukakusa, a village then on the outskirts of Kyōto.

In keeping with his vow to help all people learn to practice zazen, Dōgen wrote Fukanzazengi in 1227, immediately after his return from China. Fukanzazengi is an essay presenting the essential meaning of zazen and practical instructions for sitting. Three years later while living in his hermitage, the thirty-one-year-old Dōgen wrote Bendōwa (Talk on the Wholehearted Practice of the Way), a presentation of eighteen questions and answers discussing the practice of zazen within the context of Buddhist teachings.

The year 1233 was a very important and productive year for Dōgen. People gradually began to come to practice with him, and finally in 1233 he founded his own monastery, Kōshōji. In 1233 he also rewrote

Fukanzazengi, and that original manuscript is still stored at Eiheiji as a national treasure. During Kōshōji's first *ango*, or summer practice period, Dōgen composed Maka Hannya Haramitsu (Skt.: Maha Prajna Paramita), a short commentary on the Heart Sutra (Skt.: Maha Prajna Paramita Hridaya Sutra). It was later in the fall of 1233 that Dōgen wrote Genjōkōan for a lay practitioner.

I believe it was through these two short writings, Maka Hannya Haramitsu and Genjōkōan, that Dōgen expressed his basic understanding of Buddhist teachings. For him the practice of zazen is the practice of Maha Prajna Paramita (Great Perfect Wisdom), a philosophy he expressed poetically in Genjōkōan. I am not certain if my English translation communicates its poetic tone, but the original Japanese version is beautiful.

Dōgen Zenji practiced at Kōshōji for ten years until moving his assembly to Echizen, where he founded Daibutsuji (later renamed Eiheiji) in 1243. He worked another ten years to establish his own monastery in the remote mountains of Echizen, and he composed many writings until the end of his life in 1253. The postscript to Genjōkōan says that the text was compiled in 1252, the fourth year of the Kenchō Era and the year before Dōgen's death. Scholars differ in their opinions concerning the meaning of this word "compile" (Jap.: *shūroku*). Some think that it refers to Dōgen's placing of Genjōkōan as the first chapter of his Shōbōgenzō. In any case, it is likely that in 1252 Dōgen rewrote Genjōkōan, originally composed when he was young, before introducing it as the first chapter of Shōbōgenzō.

Several versions of Shōbōgenzō exist, numbering between twelve and ninety-five chapters. Traditionally, a seventy-five-chapter version is considered to be Dōgen Zenji's original collection, and some scholars think that he later wrote the contents of the twelve-chapter version as an addition to that compilation. In the Tokugawa era (1603–1868) Sōtō scholars found several more chapters and published them along with already known chapters to make a ninety-five-chapter version. Today, one group of scholars believes that Dōgen was unsatisfied with his seventy-five-chapter version of Shōbōgenzō and planned to rewrite the text as a hundred-chapter collection. These scholars consider the twelve-chapter version to be the only portion of this revision that Dōgen was able to complete before his death.

# THE MEANING OF "GENJŌKŌAN" 2

THE EXPRESSION *genjōkōan* is used many times in Shōbō-genzō, especially in the seventy-five-chapter version. The compound appears twenty-five times in various chapters, and the Japanese word *genjō* by itself is used more than three hundred times in sixty-three chapters. Understanding the meaning of *genjō*, as well as the meaning of *kōan*, is crucial to the study of Dōgen Zenji's teachings in Shōbōgenzō.

In Chinese characters, or rather in the Japanese system of characters known as *kanji*, *genjōkōan* is written as 現成公案. *Gen* (現) means "to appear," "to show up," or "to be in the present moment." It can also be a noun for something unseen that now can be seen. *Shutsugen* (出現), for example, can refer to the appearance of the moon from behind the clouds or to a person appearing from within a house (*shutsu*: "to come out"; *gen*: "to appear"). Also, *genzai* (現在) in Japanese means "present moment" and *gendai* (現代) means "modern times." So *gen* can be a kind of manifestation or actualization of something potential into something actual. *Jo* (成), in Japanese, means "to become," "to complete," or "to accomplish." As a verb the compound term *genjō* means "to manifest," "to actualize," or "to appear and become." As a noun it refers to reality as it is actually happening in the present moment. The meaning of the word *kōan*, however, is more difficult to explain.

There are two different sets of *kanji* that are read *kōan* in Japanese, 公案 and 公按. As I will discuss later, it is debatable whether or not a distinction can be made between these two, but in any case, *kōan* is a very famous word in Zen. It is especially significant in the Rinzai Zen tradition of kōan practice. In this practice students work with ancient stories or sayings of Chinese masters that are considered to be expressions of truth, Zen teachings, or reality. The word *kōan* has been used in this way since the Sung dynasty in China (eleventh to thirteenth c.) when Zen masters began to give kōans to their students as practice questions to work with. Japanese Rinzai masters, especially Hakuin Zenji (1685–1768), developed a system of kōan practice that was later introduced to Westerners by D. T. Suzuki (1870–1966). In this usage of the word, *kōan* carries the connotation of both a truth and a question. The kanji for this common usage of *kōan* is 公案.

*Kōan* is also commonly understood as referring to a public document placed on the desk of a government office, and in ancient China it referred to a law issued by the emperor. Such a law was unchangeable and unquestionable, applying to all the nation's subjects. Chinese emperors had absolute authority, and subjects were required to adhere to all the emperor's edicts in all circumstances. In the Zen tradition, people thought that kōan stories and sayings, like those government documents, expressed something unchangeable; Zen kōans are thus taken to be an expression of unchangeable truth or reality.

The *kō* (公) of the word *kōan* means "to be public." "To be public" in this context means "to equalize inequality," and this equalizing is a reference to the duties of government officials in ancient China. When dealing with disputes between citizens, these officials had to think of the people involved as equals, and they had to try to find fair and unbiased solutions to people's problems. To make something public therefore meant to make something equal. So *kō* in this broader sense means to equalize the unfair or unequal situations among beings that arise in this world of disorder and discrimination.

As mentioned above, there are two ways of writing *kōan* with Chinese characters, and the character for *an* (案 or 按) is what differs in the two spellings. In Dōgen Zenji's original text of Shōbōgenzō, he used the less common kanji (公按) for the word *kōan* rather than the commonly used characters—which is to say he used 按 for *an* rather than the kanji 案 for *an* as it is used in "kōan (公案) practice." This less commonly used character (按) is also pronounced *an*, and if you look carefully you may be able to see that part of the kanji is the same in both characters (安). Yet the more common character for *an* (案) contains a part that means *wood* or *tree* (木), though its original meaning was *desk*. So here *an* referred to a place to think, read, and write, and this *an* could also be used as a word for a paper or document placed on a desk. In the other *an* (按) that Dōgen used in the word *kōan*, part of the kanji (手) means *hand*, with the literal meaning of the character being "to press" or "to push with a hand or a finger." For example, *massage* in Japanese is *an-ma* (按摩). So the *an* of this word literally means "to push," "to press," or "to massage for healing." In a broader sense, the meaning of *an* is "to investigate in order to fix something that is out of order," in the way a massage is given to heal the body or put it back in order.

Now let us turn to the subject of why Dōgen used the alternative kanji for *kōan*. In Shōbōgenzō, Dōgen Zenji used 按 for the *an* in *kōan*, but in Japanese we may interpret the two different kanji for *kōan*, 公案 and 公按, as the same word. Even Zen dictionaries such as *Zengaku-dai-jiten* make no distinction between the two versions, and so it is debatable whether or not Dōgen meant to make a distinction between them. However, in the beginning of the commentary by Senne (about whom, more below) on Genjōkōan, the oldest of its kind, Senne and his disciple Kyōgō defined the word *kōan* based on the kanji 按, saying, "*Kō* (公) means to be public, to equalize inequality. *An* (按) means to keep one's lot."

Senne's definition of the word *kōan* is important, since he lived and practiced with Dōgen for many years and was his direct disciple. Senne once served as Dōgen's *jisha* (personal attendant), and he compiled volumes 1, 9, and 10 of Eihei Kōroku (Dōgen's Extensive Record), the collection of Dōgen's formal Dharma discourses. Senne founded Yōkōji temple in Kyōto after Dōgen Zenji's death, and with his own disciple Kyōgō he wrote the first commentary on the seventy-five-chapter version of Shōbōgenzō. Senne's and Kyōgō's commentary is commonly called *Okikigakishō*, or simply Goshō. Goshō has been considered the most authoritative commentary on the seventy-five-chapter version of Shōbōgenzō since the Tokugawa period (seventeenth c.). We may therefore conclude that Senne's definition of kōan is likely the one Dōgen himself intended.

Senne's definition of *an*, "keeping one's lot," had a very significant meaning for people in Dōgen's time. Each person in Japanese society had different responsibilities depending on his or her occupation. The emperor, ministers, upper-class officers, lower-class officers, merchants, farmers, teachers, and all others had a certain place in society. "Keeping one's lot" meant recognizing one's place in society and performing one's duties and responsibilities within that place, but it also refers to the individuality of people. It means recognizing that we all have our own particular personality traits and capabilities that make us unique; we can't trade places with anyone else in this life. In this sense "to keep one's lot" also means "to be private."

When we read the word *kōan* in this way, we see that it refers both to the equality of all things (*kō*) and to the uniqueness or particularity of each and every being (*an*); *kō* and *an* are in opposition to one another. In Goshō we read, "Kōan refers to Shōbōgenzō itself." The word "Shōbōgenzō" means "True-Dharma-eye-treasury," the treasury that in the Zen tradition is said to have been transmitted from the Buddha to the ancestors of every generation. In other words, we can simply say that Shōbōgenzō is a name for the true reality of all beings. So according to Goshō, the word *kōan* expresses the reality of our own lives; we are the intersection of equality (universality, unity, oneness of all beings) and inequality (difference, uniqueness, particularity, individuality). Reality, or emptiness, includes both unity and difference.

I often use the example of a hand in speaking about emptiness; we can call it a hand or we can call it a collection of five fingers. As a collection of five fingers, each finger is independent and has a different shape and function. We cannot exchange the little finger with the thumb because each has its own function, shape, and unique way of being. A thumb cannot do precisely what a little finger does and a little finger cannot do what a thumb does. Each finger is truly independent. And yet, from another perspective as one hand, all five fingers function together, and there is no separation between them. When we see the fingers in this united way, there is really just one hand.

Each one of us can be viewed in the same way. We are both universal and individual, and this universality and individuality are not two separate aspects of our being; each of them is absolute. One hand is 100 percent one hand. Five fingers are 100 percent five fingers. This whole universe is one universe; there is no separation within it. And yet, this universe is a collection of unique individual beings. These beings cannot be the same because each has its own particular time, position, and causal history. We cannot alter this reality because each and every thing is completely independent. And yet this whole world, this whole universe, and all of time from beginningless beginning to endless end, are one. We cannot separate ourselves or anything else from this unity; we really all exist in only one time and one space.

So we may view reality as a collection of independent things or we may view it as one vast seamless whole. The fact of these two ways of viewing reality is important in Buddhist philosophy. In Mahayana Buddhist philosophy these two aspects of the reality of life are called the Two Truths: absolute truth and relative or conventional truth.

For example, in the Heart Sutra emptiness is considered to be absolute truth in which there is no separation between the things of this world. For living beings, there are no eyes, no ears, no nose, no tongue, no hand, no nothing because this reality is just functioning without any fixed entity; it is empty. And as living beings we are interconnected completely, living with all other beings; we are all one whole, all living the same life. In this way the whole universe is just one thing, as five fingers are just one hand. Yet, eyes are eyes, a nose is a nose, a tongue is a tongue, and this person, Shohaku Okumura, is Shohaku Okumura. I'm not you and you are not me; when you eat food my stomach is not filled, and so on. In Zen these two realities are called *sabetsu* (distinction, inequality) and *byōdō* (equality). Viewed from one side everything is different, and viewed from another side everything is the same. To see one reality from both sides is the basic viewpoint of Mahayana Buddhism, including Zen. This is expressed, for example, in the Heart Sutra as "form is emptiness and emptiness is form." As form, everything is different, and yet these forms are empty. "Empty" means there is no difference, and yet this emptiness is form. In this way we see one reality as an intersecting or merging of oneness and uniqueness.

In the famous piece called Sandōkai (Merging of Difference and Unity), a traditional Zen poem composed by Zen master Shitou Xiqian (Jap.: Sekitō Kisen; 700–790), the author refers to these two sides of reality as difference and unity. In that poem, the true nature of reality is described as the merging of these two sides, with darkness representing unity and light representing discrimination. Light represents discrimination because when it is bright outside we can see that things have different forms, colors, names, and functions. But when it's completely dark, even though things still exist, we cannot distinguish between them, just as we cannot distinguish between beings when we see them from the viewpoint of unity. So light and darkness are two aspects of one reality, as difference and unity are two aspects of one reality. This view of reality is basic to Buddhism and Zen, and understanding it is essential to a study of Zen literature or Buddhist philosophy.

Dōgen, however, said that to see one reality from two sides is not enough; he said we should also *express* these two sides in one action. In the Heart Sutra, for example, these two sides of reality are expressed as "form is emptiness and emptiness is form." But in Shōbōgenzō Maka Hannya Haramitsu, Dōgen writes, "Form is form. Emptiness is emptiness." In other words, when we say "form is emptiness and emptiness is form" there is still a separation of form and emptiness because of the dualistic nature of language. If form really is emptiness and emptiness really is form, we can only say "form is form and emptiness is emptiness." This is so because when we say "form," emptiness is already there, and when we say "emptiness," form is already there. If we understand this basic point, we can understand the first three sentences of Genjōkōan (which we will explore in more depth in the next chapter):

(1) When all dharmas are the Buddha Dharma, there is delusion and realization, practice, life and death, buddhas and living beings.
(2) When the ten thousand dharmas are without [fixed] self, there is no delusion and no realization, no buddhas and no living beings, no birth and no death.
(3) Since the Buddha Way by nature goes beyond [the dichotomy of] abundance and deficiency, there is arising and perishing, delusion and realization, living beings and buddhas.

When we study and practice according to Dōgen Zenji's teachings, it is important that we have more than just an intellectual understanding of these two aspects of reality; we should actually manifest these views with our actions. This is an important yet difficult point that appears throughout Dōgen's work. In Tenzo-Kyōkun (Instructions for the Cook), for example, Dōgen said that as the cook of the community we have complete responsibility for the way we work, since our cooking is our own personal practice. Yet this personal practice is more than just a personal activity since it also has a function within the community. We cannot say, "This is my practice so I can just do whatever I want to do," because there is a certain way the food should be prepared and a certain time it should be ready. The cook prepares food that nurtures the entire community's practice, so cooking is a practice of both the whole community and of the cook.

Just as the cook must actualize both individual practice and community practice, all of us must aim to manifest with our own bodies and minds a personal practice that is at the same time a practice for the community. We must say to ourselves, "This is my own practice, no one can perform my practice for me"; but we must also say, "This practice is actually not just for me but for the whole community." We have to find how we can best serve the whole community, yet we must do this through our own personal action and responsibility. We are completely independent while at the same time we are fully part of the community. So, how can we actualize both sides of our lives within one action? This is really the basic point of our lives. It is true for all beings, but especially important for us to recognize since personal independence is emphasized so much in today's society.

If we think of ourselves only as independent persons and do not consider others, we cannot live in harmony with other people. On the other hand, if we undervalue individuality in our community, this is also unhealthy. In ancient Japanese society, for example, social units such as families, schools, communities, and countries were more important than the people living in them. This is an example of the opposite extreme of individualism—this kind of collectivism is also very unhealthy. But if we only see our independence and think, "I can do whatever I want to do," we become isolated and egoistic. These two extremes are sicknesses caused by misguided views of one reality. In actuality we are living both as independent, unique people and as parts of the whole community. To be healthy we must live within both aspects of this truth. When we grasp only one aspect and live accordingly, we become sick, either through collectivism or through egoism. We have to live together, and in order to live together we must, in a sense, put aside our uniqueness. The most important teaching of the Buddha is that we must find the middle way; so we must avoid the extremes of egoism or collectivism and practice with reality as the middle way. We have to create our own way; there is no fixed middle way in every situation. We must try to see the whole of every situation and find the healthiest, happiest way of life in each circumstance. This is the essential point of both Buddha's and Dōgen's teachings.

In Genjōkōan, Dōgen created a metaphor to express the reality of individuality and universality. He said that individuality can be expressed as a drop of water and universality or equality as moonlight. He said that this universal moonlight is reflected in even the smallest drop of water. This is the reality of our life; we are individual and yet universal. The vast, boundless moonlight is reflected in our lives, and through our practice we can keep awakening to the reality of both individuality and universality. When we think about reality, we tend to go to one extreme or the other. Thinking comes out of our experience, that is, our karma. Depending upon our past experiences, we have the tendency to think that one side of life should be more important than another, and we lose sight of reality as a whole. When we are grounded in zazen practice, each and every activity we perform in our daily lives is an opportunity to practice and awaken to the reality of the individual and the universal. Being free from the extremes of either side of reality lets us find the middle path of embracing both individuality and universality as the most vivid way of life.

In my understanding, this teaching of individuality and universality is the essence of the title *Genjōkōan*. Genjō is nothing other than kōan, and kōan is nothing other than genjō: *Genjō* means "reality actually and presently taking place," and *kōan* means "absolute truth that embraces relative truth" or "a question that true reality asks of us." So we can say that *genjōkōan* means "to answer the question from true reality through the practice of our everyday activity."

# Buddhist Teachings from Three Sources: Is, Is Not, Is

B EFORE BEGINNING my discussion of the body of Genjōkōan, I present a brief overview of the main themes of each section of the text (section numbers are in parentheses in the translation above).

1–3   Dōgen Zenji's understanding of Buddhist teachings are summarized.

4   Delusion and realization are defined as being dependent upon the relationship between self and myriad dharmas (all beings or all things).

5   Buddhas practice wholeheartedly without perceiving themselves as buddhas.

6   Studying the Buddha Way is studying the self, and studying the self is forgetting the self.

7   Studying the Buddha Dharma in relation to space is compared to sailing in a boat.

8   Life and death are discussed in terms of time, using the analogy of firewood and ash.

9   The relationship between the individual and realization is compared to a drop of dew and boundless moonlight.

10    Practice is an endless inquiry into the characteristics of the myriad dharmas.

11    The relationship between self and environment is compared to a fish swimming in water and a bird flying in the sky.

12    Finding one's place and path.

13    As the story of Magu Baoche tells, although the wind's nature is always present, to "feel the wind" we must "wave a fan."

So, now let us turn our attention to the first three sections of the text:

(1) When all dharmas are the Buddha Dharma, there is delusion and realization, practice, life and death, buddhas and living beings.
(2) When the ten thousand dharmas are without [fixed] self, there is no delusion and no realization, no buddhas and no living beings, no birth and no death.
(3) Since the Buddha Way by nature goes beyond [the dichotomy of] abundance and deficiency, there is arising and perishing, delusion and realization, living beings and buddhas.

These first three sentences of Genjōkōan present essential Buddhist teachings from three different sources. The first sentence summarizes the teachings of Shakyamuni Buddha, the second conveys an essential teaching of Mahayana Buddhism from the Heart Sutra, and the third contains Dōgen's own teachings.

## WHEN ALL DHARMAS ARE BUDDHA DHARMA: THE FOUR DHARMA SEALS

The Buddha's basic teachings, such as the Four Noble Truths and the twelve links of causation, centered on cause and effect. One of the best-known summaries of Shakyamuni Buddha's teachings, represented in the first sentence of Genjōkōan, is the teaching of the four Dharma seals (Jap.: *shihōin*).

In Japan, a seal is a stamp that functions like a person's signature in the United States. Such a seal certifies that a document, painting, or work of calligraphy was rendered by a particular person. Similarly, if a teaching contains the four Dharma seals, it can be said to be Buddha Dharma, or a teaching of the Buddha.

The first of the four seals says that everything in this life contains suffering (*issai kaiku*). The second says that everything is impermanent (*shogyō mujō*). The third says that everything lacks independent existence or fixed self (*shohō muga*), and the fourth says that nirvana is tranquility (*nehan jakujō*).

These four essential points make up a message from Shakyamuni Buddha to us. The message is that we can live our lives in one of two ways: we can live within samsara (the first seal) or within nirvana (the fourth seal). Whether we live within samsara or nirvana depends upon whether or not we awaken to the reality of impermanence (the second seal) and lack of independent existence (the third seal).

### Impermanence and Lack of Independent Existence

First I will discuss the second and the third Dharma seals, impermanence and lack of independent existence. These seals express the reality of human life and the reality of all beings (*shohō jissō*). In Mahayana Buddhism, the reality that all things are impermanent and without independent, fixed existence is referred to as *emptiness*. When we see the reality of emptiness, we see that sooner or later we must die, and we see that nothing, including ourselves, possesses an unchanging nature. The body and mind are simply a collection of five *skandhas*, or aggregates (form/materiality, sensation, perception, mental formations, and consciousness), the basic constituents of all things. The Buddha taught that these five skandhas, which are neither permanent nor substantial themselves, are constantly changing from the moment we are born, so there is no permanent owner/operator that is the essence of a human being. Yet somehow we assume that there is something within us that does not change, and this assumption is the foundation of self-identity.

My physical and mental conditions have constantly changed from infancy through adolescence, and they continue to change at my present age. Yet in some way I believe that I am the same person as that baby and teenager. We think that there is something that does not change in us—something that owns and controls our bodies and minds, in much the same way as a person owns and operates a car. This something that doesn't change is called *ga* in Japanese or *atman* in Sanskrit. The Buddhist definition of atman, somewhat equivalent to the idea of *self*, as it is sometimes called in English, is *jō-itsu-shu-sai*. *Jō-itsu-shu-sai* means "the permanent (*jō*) and only (*itsu*) owner of the body and mind (*shu*), which controls and operates the body and mind (*sai*)."

The Buddha taught that the atman or self does not ultimately exist. He said that everything living or existing is a collection of different elements that are constantly changing. Our lives are dependent on other beings and elements that allow us to be alive as the person we are in this moment. So if one of these things that we depend on changes, whether it is within or outside us, we also must change. This is in fact what the Buddha meant when he said that everything is impermanent and without essential existence. This is the basic reality of our lives, but it is difficult for us to accept.

The teachings of impermanence and lack of independent existence are not difficult to understand intellectually; when you hear these teachings you may think that they are quite true. On a deeper level, however, you probably still identify yourself as "me" and identify others as "them" or "you." On some level you likely say to yourself, "I will always be me; I have an identity that is important." I, for example, say to myself, "I am a Buddhist priest; not a Christian or Islamic one. I am a Japanese person, not an American or a Chinese one."

If we did not assume that we have this something within us that does not change, it would be very difficult for us to live responsibly in society. This is why people who are unfamiliar with Buddhism often ask, "If there were no unchanging essential existence, doesn't that mean I would not be responsible for my past actions, since I would be a different person than in the past?" But of course that is not what the Buddha meant when he said we have no unchanging atman or essential existence.

To help us understand this point, we can consider how our life resembles a river. Each moment the water of a river is flowing and different, so it is constantly changing, but there is still a certain continuity of the river as a whole. The Mississippi River, for example, was the river we know a million years ago. And yet, the water flowing in the Mississippi is always different, always new, so there is actually no fixed thing that we can say is the one and only Mississippi River. We can see this clearly when we compare the source of the Mississippi in northern Minnesota, a small stream one can jump over, to the river's New Orleans estuary, which seems as wide as an ocean. We cannot say which of these is the true Mississippi: it is just a matter of conditions that lets us call one or the other of these the Mississippi. In reality, a river is just a collection of masses of flowing water contained within certain shapes in the land. "Mississippi River" is simply a name given to various conditions and changing elements. Since our lives are also just a collection of conditions, we cannot say that we each have one true identity that does not change, just as we cannot say there is one true Mississippi River. What we call the "self" is just a set of conditions existing within a collection of different elements. So I cannot say that there is an unchanging self that exists throughout my life as a baby, as a teenager, and as it is today. Things that I thought were important and interesting when I was an elementary or high school student, for example, are not at all interesting to me now; my feelings, emotions, and values are always changing. This is the meaning of the teaching that everything is impermanent and without independent existence.

But we still must recognize that there is a certain continuity in our lives, that there is causality, and that we need to be responsible for what we did yesterday. In this way, self-identity is important. Even though in actuality there is no unchanging identity, I still must use expressions like "when *I* was a baby . . . , when *I* was a boy . . . , when *I* was a teenager. . . ." To speak about changes in our lives and communicate in a meaningful way, we must speak as if we assumed that there is an unchanging "I" that has been experiencing the changes; otherwise, the word "change" has no meaning. But according to Buddhist philosophy, self-identity, the "I," is a creation of the mind; we create self-identity because it's convenient and useful in certain ways. We must use self-identity to live responsibly in society, but we should realize that it is merely a tool, a symbol, a sign, or a concept. Because it enables us to think and discriminate, self-identity allows us to live and function. Although it is not the *only* reality of our lives, self-identity is *a* reality for us, a tool we must use to live with others in society.

### The First Dharma Seal: Everything Contains Suffering

"Everything contains suffering" means that we suffer when we don't recognize the reality of impermanence and lack of independent existence. If we cling to our sense of independent self as if it were permanent and make self-centered desires the priority of our lives, then life as a whole becomes suffering. "Everything contains suffering" refers even to pleasure, happiness, and success, since both the positive and negative things we experience become part of the cycle of suffering.

When we live based on self-centered desire and the idea of permanence, we grasp at things that we like and try to push away things that we don't like. We may think that if we try hard enough we can make our lives into something permanently agreeable. We cling to what is "good" in our lives and expect it not to change. We try to protect our egos and make them important and powerful by becoming better than others. Sometimes we succeed and are happy, and sometimes we fail and feel terrible; this is samsara. *Samsara* is a Buddhist term that usually refers to the "cycle of existence," the transmigration or rebirth of a person through the six realms of existence: hell, the hungry ghost realm, the animal realm, the realm of fighting spirits, the human realm, and the realm of heavenly beings.

However, here I interpret samsara as the emotional "up-and-down" quality of our lives; sometimes we are as happy as heavenly beings but in the next moment descend into the misery of a hell dweller. We create samsara in an unending cycle as we attempt to protect our egos. In this cycle we feel we are sometimes in heaven and sometimes in hell, but no condition lasts forever because everything is always changing. This is transmigration; our lives go up and then fall down, up and down and up and down. Even happiness, pleasure, and success become part of suffering if we live based on our egocentricity. This is so because sooner or later we will lose whatever we accomplish, since everything is always changing and nothing lasts forever. No matter how successful we are, someday, even if it is not until we die, we must give up everything; we will have to open the hand of thought whether we want to or not. The sense of independent self that today we grasp with our thoughts as the center of the world will someday perish.

"Opening the hand of thought" is an expression my teacher, Kōshō Uchiyama Rōshi, coined for the process of letting go of thought in zazen. When we think, we grasp "things" with the "hand" of thought, believing them to actually be the concepts we have made of them. In our zazen practice, we open the hand of thought that grasps objects, and these concepts fall away from us.

If we are not successful in fulfilling our desires or in avoiding unpleasant things, our lives become painful. But even if we are successful and happy, that happiness or success is still centered on our mistaken sense of permanence and independence. Since those agreeable things are based on the hope that they will be permanent and will fulfill our self-centered desires, often we fear the loss of everything that our happiness depends upon. And since other people want to have happiness or success, life becomes a competition with others. If we are happy, others may try to take our happiness from us in order to gain their own happiness. Competition makes society a realm of the fighting spirits (*asuras*) in which some people are happy and some are unhappy.

I think this is the meaning of "everything contains suffering."

When we hear these words we may feel that Buddhism is pessimistic, but this is not the case. What this means is that even what we consider the positive side of our lives lies within the realm of samsara; everything is part of the cycle of suffering. "Everything" means *everything*—not only pain, sickness, and death, but pleasure, happiness, and success as well.

### The Fourth Dharma Seal: Nirvana

Nirvana is the way of life that is based on awakening to the reality of impermanence and lack of independent existence. It is not a special stage of practice, nor is it a certain condition of mind; it is simply the way to live one's life in accordance with reality. When we truly see impermanence and lack of independent existence, we understand deeply that we cannot hold on to anything; nothing lasts forever. Seeing reality encourages us to stop clinging to our lives and their contents and gives us the chance to open the hand of thought before life forces us to open it. This seeing, accepting, and letting go is Buddhist practice.

When we deeply understand this reality, and practice in accordance with it, we no longer believe we need to compete with others or with ourselves. We no longer struggle to be more important or powerful than others, and we no longer strive to be who we want to be. This practice of awakening, which is itself nirvana, allows us to settle into the reality of impermanence and lack of independent existence. We then begin to live more peacefully.

Nirvana is not a fantastic state of mind like an LSD trip, and it is not a special trance or escape from life. Nor is nirvana a state in which a person no longer experiences pain and sorrow. The Buddha, for example, was enlightened when he was thirty-six years old. At that time he entered nirvana, and yet his life was not an easy one; he traveled all over India in a time when travel was difficult, for instance, he experienced pain, and eventually he died. But because the Buddha had been released from egocentricity, his hard times were no longer transmigrations in samsara. Pain was simply pain, pleasure was simply pleasure; for him they were no longer part of the cycle of suffering. Within nirvana we can appreciate both positive and negative experiences as simply the scenery of our lives.

"The scenery of life" is another expression Uchiyama Rōshi used to explain our zazen practice. He said that even when we adopt the bodhisattva path and practice zazen, letting go of thought, we still experience many different conditions in all aspects of our lives: some are painful, some are pleasing, and some are neither. Yet all these different conditions are simply the scenery of our lives, and we should keep working and studying, regardless of the circumstances we encounter, so we can investigate the myriad dharmas (all beings and things). In nirvana we can accept all conditions and even enjoy them in a sense, but, of course, acceptance requires our effort in practice, and we must still work to develop ourselves and to relieve the suffering of others. If we open the hand of thought that grasps "this person" (that is, our self) as the center of the world, then our lives broaden and our hearts open to all beings. This is the basic teaching of Shakyamuni Buddha.

In sum, the four Dharma seals contain Buddha's basic message of cause and effect, and Dōgen Zenji refers to this basic message in the first sentence of Genjōkōan. When he wrote, "There is delusion and realization, practice, life and death, buddhas and living beings," he was presenting a view of reality from the perspective of individuality and cause and effect.

## WHEN THE TEN THOUSAND DHARMAS ARE WITHOUT FIXED SELF: MAHAYANA BUDDHISM

### Madhyamika, Yogacara, and Tathagata-garbha

The second sentence of Genjōkōan presents a perspective of reality that developed out of a continued effort to understand certain important philosophical points in the teachings of the Buddha. Mahayana Buddhism, a result of this effort, is thought to have begun around the

first century BCE. Various groups within different movements created the Mahayana sutras, including the various versions of the Maha
Prajna Paramita Sutra, the Lotus Sutra (Saddharma Pundarika Sutra),
the Flower Ornament Sutra (Avatamsaka Sutra), the Pure Land Buddhist sutras, and others.

Around the second or third century CE, the great Mahayana Buddhist master Nagarjuna, who is considered the founder of many
Mahayana schools, established a philosophical system based on the
emptiness teachings of the Prajna Paramita sutras, of which the Heart
Sutra is the most well known. Nagarjuna was the author of important Mahayana texts such as his Maha Prajna Paramita Sastra, a commentary on the Prajna Paramita Sutras in one hundred volumes, and
Mulamadhyamakakarika, an exposition of his own philosophical
thought. The Madhyamika school, formed during the fourth to fifth
centuries, was based on the teachings of Mulamadhyamakakarika,
and it engaged in continuous debate with another Mahayana school,
the Yogacara.

The Yogacara school analyzed human consciousness to try to
explain how the individual creates suffering. Yogacara philosophers
such as Asanga and Vasubandhu thought that human consciousness
was made up of eight "layers," with each layer existing deeper in our
being. The first five layers were said to be connected to phenomena
that happen when human sense organs meet their corresponding
sense objects—and we'll look at the other three slightly out of order.
These philosophers said that everything we experience is stored in
*alaya*, the eighth and deepest consciousness, which acts as a "storehouse" for the seeds of our experiences and is the source of our karma.
Even things we have forgotten are "stored" in this consciousness. So
when we encounter circumstances, certain seeds come up from the
alaya consciousness and prompt us to behave in a certain way. Yogacara philosophers thought that the seventh consciousness, *manas*,
clings to alaya, believing that what it presents is true reality. Manas
interprets the experiences of this life as "me." The sixth consciousness,

*mano-vijinana*, is our usual psychological consciousness, which is influenced by manas. This is why our thinking is distorted so that we cannot see the reality of emptiness and lack of independent existence, resulting in our lives becoming confused and full of suffering. This is a basic teaching of the Yogacara school. (And while the Yogacara also taught how one can be free from egocentricity, these teachings are not so relevant to the present topic, so I will not discuss them here.)

Another Mahayana philosophy, *Tathagata-garbha*, offers one explanation of how it is possible for ordinary beings to change their lives from samsara to nirvana. Tathagata-garbha theory says that we can do this because all living beings have Buddha nature; all of us are basically Buddha's children, so we inherently have the possibility to awaken to the reality of our true nature and live within nirvana. This theory enabled Mahayana Buddhists to have faith in our ability to someday become buddhas, asserting that if we follow Buddha's teachings lifetime after lifetime, even though we are presently deluded, we can progress through the fifty-two stages of a bodhisattva and someday reach buddhahood. Although a school based on Tathagata-garbha theory never developed, Tathagata-garbha teachings are an important element in Mahayana Buddhism. Vasubandhu's *Thesis on Buddha Nature*, for example, had an important influence on the formation of Chinese Mahayana Buddhism.

So we can see that the teachings of emptiness of the Madhyamika school, the theory of consciousness-only of the Yogacara school, and the theory of Tathagata-garbha, as well as other Mahayana schools and philosophies, evolved as a result of their effort to explain various points of the Buddha's teaching of cause and effect. Through this process, however, the Mahayana movement in general eventually developed what may appear to be a fundamentally different teaching from that of early Buddhism.

In the second sentence of Genjōkōan, Dōgen Zenji presents this fundamental teaching of Mahayana Buddhism, creating a pronounced contrast to the first sentence. This essential Mahayana

teaching appears in the basic message of the Heart Sutra, which we
will now briefly examine.

### The Heart Sutra

Mahayana Buddhists say that the Heart Sutra (see appendix 1) pres-
ents the true teachings of the Buddha, but if we do not read the Heart
Sutra carefully, we may come to the conclusion that it negates all of
Buddha's teaching.

Early Buddhist teaching maintained that the whole world is made
up of only five skandhas (aggregates): form, sensation, perceptions,
mental formations, and consciousness. The Buddha taught these five
skandhas describe everything that exists. In human beings, only the
first skandha, form (Skt. and Pali: *rupa*), is a material aggregate; the
other four are mental aggregates. So the Buddha taught that human
beings are really only made up of body and mind; there is no such
thing as a fundamental essence, soul, or atman that exists apart from
the body and mind.

But the beginning of the Heart Sutra in fact negates all of the
skandhas, the elements of being. It says that there are no five skandhas
because they, like everything else, are empty. In this sense the Heart
Sutra does negate the Buddha's teaching; this is a main difference
between early Buddhism and Mahayana Buddhism.

The Heart Sutra also says, "There is no ignorance, nor extinction of
ignorance; there is no old age and death nor extinction of old age and
death." This is a reference to the teaching of the twelve links of causation. Ignorance is the first link in the chain, and old age and death
are the last. So the statement negates the first and last links and all
of the ten links between them, yet it also says that there has been no
extinction of those links. So the Heart Sutra is saying that there is no
such thing as the twelve links of causation and yet they have never
disappeared.

"No suffering, no origination, no stopping, no path. . . ." This is the
negation of suffering, the cause of suffering, the cessation of suffering
(nirvana), and the path to nirvana. In other words, this is a negation

of the Four Noble Truths. It is clear in this passage that the Heart Sutra negates what Shakyamuni Buddha taught.

If those who created the Heart Sutra wanted to negate Buddha's teaching, they would not have claimed to be followers of the Buddha, but these in fact were. And the Heart Sutra states that it contains the true teaching of the Buddha even though a "no" appears before all of the basic teachings of Shakyamuni Buddha in the text. It is therefore very important that we understand what these negations mean. These negations were written to help us realize the freedom that the Buddha taught of: freedom from attachment, in this case attachment to concepts that narrow our ability to respond to reality as it unfolds. The Heart Sutra says that even the teachings of Buddhism are empty and should not be clung to as irrefutable truths.

## THE BUDDHA WAY: DŌGEN ZENJI'S TEACHINGS

### Maka Hannya Haramitsu

The third sentence of Genjōkōan presents Dōgen Zenji's own teaching concerning Buddhist practice. We can study Dōgen Zenji's understanding of traditional Mahayana teachings, which he refers to as the Buddha Way, by examining his commentary on the Heart Sutra, Maka Hannya Haramitsu (see appendix 2), the second chapter of Shōbōgenzō. Maka Hannya Haramitsu and Genjōkōan were written within a few months of each other, and they are closely connected. As I said, in Maka Hannya Haramitsu Dōgen expressed his understanding of Mahayana teachings by commenting on the Heart Sutra, while in Genjōkōan he expressed his understanding using his own poetic words.

To begin with, let us turn our attention to Maka Hannya Haramitsu. It begins as follows:

> The time of Avalokiteshvara Bodhisattva practicing profound prajna paramita is the whole body clearly seeing the emptiness of all the five aggregates.

"Aggregates" is the English translation of *skandhas*. It's very clear that this sentence is a paraphrase of the first sentence of the Heart Sutra. He adds only one word, "whole body."

> The five aggregates are form, sensations, perceptions, mental formations, and consciousness; this is the fivefold prajna.

The Heart Sutra said these five skandhas are empty, but here Dōgen says they are "the fivefold prajna"; they are themselves prajna paramita, or wisdom.

> Clear seeing is itself prajna. To unfold and manifest this essential truth [the Heart Sutra] states that "form is emptiness and emptiness is form." Form is nothing but form, emptiness is nothing but emptiness—one hundred blades of grass, ten thousand things.

Here Dōgen seems to be saying something different from the Heart Sutra, but he is actually clarifying an important point within the sutra. He is showing us that "form is emptiness and emptiness is form" captures only part of the truth. There are two parts to this statement that we say are one: "form" and "emptiness." But if those two parts really are the same, we don't need to say "form is emptiness" because form is itself emptiness. When we say "form," emptiness is already included, so to say "form is emptiness" is in a sense to try to add something extra that isn't needed or to try to separate something that is inseparable and then try to put it together again. This is why Dōgen clarifies that "form is form and emptiness is emptiness."

"Form is emptiness and emptiness is form" is still a product of the process of thinking. This process presents both "form" and "emptiness" as concepts within the mind, and then it says that these two concepts are one thing. But Dōgen Zenji points to the reality of form and emptiness within our actual lives, and this reality includes much more than just mental processes or conceptual views. Each one of the myriad things is a form. All things are themselves empty, and yet when we say, "all things are themselves empty," we produce a thought; we connect two concepts.

These concepts and our thoughts about them are creations of our minds. This is the way we fail to see the actual reality, the emptiness of things. Dōgen cautions us not to live our lives according to our thinking; he admonishes us rather to just see and to just live. To live in this way means that we just see and experience what we encounter in our lives without saying it is empty, even though it truly is empty. That's it. We don't need to say "This is empty" if it really is empty. Dōgen placed importance on the true reality of each being (*shohō-jissō*) rather than on any conceptual reality we might have of it. He saw that true reality does not dwell within our thinking; it is every one of myriad things. This is why Dōgen said,

> Form is nothing but form, emptiness is nothing but
>    emptiness.
> One hundred blades of grass—ten thousand things.

"One hundred blades of grass" and "ten thousand things" mean "everything." In other words, everything is prajna paramita because everything is empty. Prajna is not a personal, individual wisdom we can possess; rather, each thing is itself reality and each thing is itself prajna, or wisdom.

> The twelve sense fields are twelve instances of prajna
> paramita.

"Twelve sense fields" refers to the eyes, ears, nose, tongue, body, and mind, and each of the six types of sense objects that interact with those sense organs. The Heart Sutra says that these twelve fields do not exist, but Dōgen says that they are twelve instances of prajna paramita.

Also, there are eighteen instances of prajna: eye, ear, nose, tongue, body, mind; sight, sound, smell, taste, touch, objects of mind; as well as the consciousnesses of eye, ear, nose, tongue, body, and mind.

Again, the Heart Sutra says these things do not exist, but Dōgen Zenji says that these things are in fact prajna exactly because they *are* empty, because they *are* impermanent and lack independent existence. Everything is prajna itself.

Also there are four instances of prajna: suffering, its cause, cessation, and the path [to cessation]. Also there are six instances of prajna: generosity, pure precepts, calm patience, diligence, quiet meditation, and wisdom.

These are the six paramitas. The Sanskrit word *paramita* can be translated as "perfection" or "(crossing the river) to reach the other shore." The second translation indicates that these six practices allow bodhisattvas to cross the river that lies between samsara and nirvana, leaving "this shore" and reaching "the other shore."

There is also a single instance of prajna manifesting itself right now—unsurpassable, complete, perfect awakening.

"Unsurpassable, complete awakening" is a translation of *anuttara-samyak-sambodhi*. *Anuttara* means "unsurpassable" or "beyond comparison." *Samyak* means "true," "right," "genuine," or "authentic." *Sambodhi* means "awakening" or "realization." This phrase is an epithet for Shakyamuni Buddha's awakening under the bodhi tree.

Also, there are three instances of prajna: past, present, and future.

Past, present, and future (the three times; *sanze*) are all instances of prajna. Here Dōgen refers to time (the three times) because the Heart Sutra says that "All buddhas of past, present, and future rely on prajna paramita." He says that these three times are also prajna paramita. In section 8 of Genjōkōan (and also in the entire chapter of Shōbōgenzō Uji), Dōgen discusses the nature of time, drawing on his profound and unique insight that "time is being and being is time." (I discuss Dōgen's teachings about time in chapter 8 of this volume.)

> Also, there are six instances of prajna: earth, water, fire, wind, space, and consciousness.

According to traditional Buddhist teachings, these six elements are the constituents of all beings and things. The four great elements (*maha bhuta*) are: First, the earth element: the solidity that keeps things together. In the human body, bone is considered to be the earth element. Second, the water element: humidity. Blood and other liquids that protect the human body from drying up are water elements. Third, the fire element. The body's warming heat is considered part of the fire element. Fourth, the wind element. In the body, this is the movement that enables growth. Fifth, the space element. Mahayana Buddhists added this to the original four. It is the element in which the other four elements exist. Sixth, the conscious element.

> Also, four instances of prajna are going on daily: walking, standing, sitting, and lying down.

Everything we do is prajna. Walking, standing, sitting, and lying down are the four conducts (*si-igi*), and they encompass all states of bodily activity. All of our actions, including walking to a destination and lying down to sleep, are included as times of practice, twenty-four hours a day.

Although it is true that in studying Dōgen Zenji's Maka Hannya

Haramitsu we find a Buddhist teaching different from the Heart Sutra, upon reflection we see that the essential teachings of Shakyamuni Buddha, the teachings of the Heart Sutra, and the teachings of Maka Hannya Haramitsu are exactly the same. Even though differences in expression between these three can seem contradictory, the reality they reveal is the same.

Early Buddhism shed light upon this reality with teachings such as the four dharma seals, the Four Noble Truths, and the twelve links of causation. According to the primary message of these teachings, if we free ourselves of ignorance and ego-attachment, we can transform our lives from the suffering of samsara to the cessation of suffering that is nirvana. Realization of this transformation occurs through embracing the eightfold noble path and other practices.

Mahayana teachings such as the Heart Sutra, however, emphasize a different expression of reality. From the perspective of prajna, if we think there are fixed places or conditions called "samsara," "nirvana," "delusion," and "enlightenment," our practice becomes merely an attempt to escape from what we think is undesirable. In this situation we cannot be released from samsara and delusion, because in trying to escape them we actually create them. The negative expression of reality contained in the Heart Sutra is a guideline for liberation from even the desire to escape from samsara and enter nirvana; it tells us that samsara and nirvana are exactly the same.

Dōgen inverts the teachings of the Heart Sutra and returns to positive expressions of reality. He says that the five aggregates are not obstacles to awakening, because they are themselves manifestations of impermanence and lack of independent existence; they express the reality of all beings and are therefore prajna. One must accept the body and mind as a collection of the five aggregates that are prajna, according to Dōgen, and use the body and mind to practice; there is no escaping the body, the mind, no escaping the five aggregates.

The characteristic theme of Dōgen Zenji's teaching is "action rather than thinking is practice"; in Maka Hannya Haramitsu Dōgen encourages us to actively encounter everything in our lives as prajna:

> Therefore, Buddha Bhagavat is itself prajna paramita. Prajna paramita is nothing other than all beings. All these things are empty in form, without arising or extinguishing, neither defiled nor pure, neither increasing nor decreasing.

Here Dōgen says that all things are prajna paramita because each and every thing is empty. He tells us that we therefore cannot hold on to concepts such as "good," "bad," "defiled," "pure," "increasing," or "decreasing." We cannot control the myriad dharmas, grasp them, or cling to them; we just have to open the hand of thought.

> Actualizing this prajna paramita is to actualize Buddha Bhagavat.

We should actualize this prajna paramita, and this actualization is the actualization of Buddha's Dharma body, or reality itself. The word *actualizing* here is a translation of *genjō*, and we can therefore see a close connection between Maka Hannya Haramitsu and Genjōkōan. *Genjōkōan* (to actualize *kōan*) is equivalent to actualizing (practicing and manifesting) prajna paramita, and this is the way Buddha Bhagavat reveals itself.

> Inquire into it! Practice it! Making offerings and prostrations [to prajna paramita] is attending and serving Buddha Bhagavat.

Since everything is prajna paramita, we should inquire into everything. "To inquire into everything" means to try to see the reality of each and every being. In other words, prajna paramita is reality itself; prajna paramita is Buddha Bhagavat, and we must inquire into the nature of reality and practice with it. How can we awaken to the reality of impermanence and lack of independent existence that is emptiness? How can we actualize this reality through practice and through our actions in each situation of our daily lives? This is precisely what we must inquire into.

In this book, I am communicating through this writing, and I hope my communication is an expression of impermanence and lack of independent existence. But if I mistakenly cling to my egocentric ideas and write about my understanding only in order to convince others of my views, I am not expressing prajna. My communication becomes only an expression of my self-centered desire. (I try not to do this, but I am not sure that I am truly expressing prajna—so please don't trust me!) You must be really free from what I say and you must inquire into prajna and practice prajna yourself. What I can communicate to you is only my own understanding from my reading, my practice, and my daily life; I cannot communicate an understanding of the reality of your life. You must inquire into your life for yourself.

The final sentence of Maka Hannya Haramitsu reads:

"Attending and serving [all beings] is itself Buddha Bhagavat." Here "attending to all beings" means that whatever we encounter is our practice. When we prepare meals, cooking is our expression of prajna. Water, fire, and ingredients are all prajna. They are all Buddha's Dharma body, just like everything else that we meet in our lives. Dōgen teaches us that we must deeply revere everything we encounter. Prajna is not only practicing zazen and studying Dharma; the work we do and all our other activities should be expressions of prajna paramita as well. This is the essence of Dōgen's teaching.

### Genjōkōan

Let us return again to the first sentences of Genjōkōan. In the first sentence Dōgen Zenji writes:

> When all dharmas are the Buddha Dharma there is delusion and realization, practice, life and death, buddhas and living beings.

As we have seen, this is what Shakyamuni Buddha actually taught: the Dharma based on cause and effect and presented from the view of individuality. Dōgen said we must inquire into it, understand it, and accept it. The second sentence reads:

> When the ten thousand dharmas are without [fixed] self, there is no delusion and no realization, no buddhas and no living beings, no birth and no death.

As I explained earlier, this is the message of the Heart Sutra based on the teachings of emptiness and presented from the perspective of absolute unity. Next we read:

> Since the Buddha Way by nature goes beyond [the dichotomy of] abundance and deficiency, there is arising and perishing, delusion and realization, living beings and buddhas.

I believe this sentence represents Dōgen's own way of teaching the Buddha Dharma.

We usually think of abundance (arising, realization, buddhas) as positive, and we consider deficiency (perishing, delusion, and living beings) as negative. When we understand Buddha's teaching in this commonsense way, it seems that we should escape from samsara, which is something bad, in order to reach nirvana, which is something good. We think nirvana is a goal we can achieve in the same way that a poor person can work hard and become rich. We may think that practice is a way to reach nirvana in the same way that working hard is a way to attain wealth.

The common understanding of Buddha's teaching is that since ignorance turns the lives of deluded beings into suffering, we should eliminate our ignorance so we can reach nirvana. If we simply accept that teaching and devote our lives to the practice of eliminating our ignorance and egocentric desires, we will find that it's impossible to do. Not only is it impossible, but it actually creates another cycle of samsara. This happens because the desire to become free from delusion or egocentricity is one of the causes of our delusion and egocentricity. And the idea that there is nirvana or samsara existing separately from each other is a basic dualistic illusion; the desire to escape from this side of existence and enter another side is another expression of egocentric desire.

When we are truly in nirvana we awaken to the fact that nirvana and samsara are not two separate things. This is what Mahayana Buddhism teaches, especially through the Prajna Paramita Sutras; it teaches that samsara and nirvana are one. If we don't find nirvana within samsara, there is no place we can find nirvana. If we don't find peacefulness within our busy daily lives, there is no place we can find peacefulness. This is why the Heart Sutra "negates" the Buddha's teaching; it attempts to release us from dichotomies created in our thoughts. If we understand Buddha's teaching with our common-sense, calculating way of thinking, we create another type of samsara. Eventually we feel more pain as our desire to reach nirvana creates more difficulty in our lives. This desire to end our suffering is another cause of suffering, and the Heart Sutra presents the Buddha's teachings in a negative way in order to avoid arousing this desire.

We do have to be free from this desire for nirvana. But if we use our egocentric, calculating mind to deal with this Mahayana teaching, we may come to the conclusion that there is simply no need to practice. We may say to ourselves, "If samsara and nirvana are really one thing, why do I have to practice?" This is another misguided idea derived from a misunderstanding of Mahayana teaching: because reality includes all things and because everything in the world has Buddha nature, everything is simply all right; there is no problem and nirvana is just living however we want to live. That's it.

This is not the meaning that Mahayana teachers meant to communicate. Yet such ideas were very popular in Japan in Dōgen Zenji's time, and in fact Dōgen himself questioned the teaching of Buddha nature. As I explained in an earlier chapter, his question was: "If all beings have Buddha nature, why did buddhas and ancestors have to arouse bodhi-mind and practice? Why does anyone have to practice?" This question was very important in the development of Dōgen's practice and teaching.

Dōgen's answer to this question was "just practice"; not because we want to escape from samsara, not because we want to reach nirvana, but just practice right now, right here without any agenda. With this kind of practice, nirvana is already here. Of course when we practice in this way, samsara is still here too. So within this practice, at this moment, both nirvana and samsara are present.

This is the meaning of "just practice" and "just sit." In Japanese the expression *shikan* (as in *shikantaza*) means "just do it," without the thought "I don't like samsara so I'm practicing to reach nirvana in the future." Such goal-oriented thinking is just a story we create. As long as we practice within that story, we will never reach nirvana. When we just open the hand of thought and face whatever we are facing, we can truly find peace. We don't need to escape and go somewhere else; we just live right now, right here, with mindfulness. This is how we can find a way to live in nirvana within samsara.

In the first two sentences of Genjōkōan Dōgen equates the terms "all dharmas" and "ten thousand dharmas" to "Buddha Dharma" and "without fixed self," but in the third sentence he simply uses "Buddha Way. " One way we can view that is this: "Buddha Dharma" and "without [fixed] self" refer to the teachings of Shakyamuni Buddha and Mahayana Buddhism respectively, while "Buddha Way" refers to our practice in everyday life.

One might ask why only the first of these three sentences contains the word "practice," but if we carefully examine the other two sentences, I think it becomes apparent that they are about practice as well. The second sentence, for instance, is presented from the perspective of prajna paramita, and prajna paramita is equivalent to practice. That prajna is practice—not something to be gained as the result of practice—is evident in the first line of the Heart Sutra:

"Avalokiteshvara Bodhisattva when deeply practicing prajna paramita clearly saw that all five aggregates are empty." This sentence says that in practice, Avalokiteshvara's whole body and mind (a collection of the five aggregates) saw that all five aggregates (the whole body and mind) are empty; the whole body and mind saw the emptiness of itself in practice. Because the second sentence of Genjōkōan is written from this perspective of prajna paramita, it is a statement that can only be realized within practice. Similarly, the subject of the third sentence of Genjōkōan, the Buddha Way, is equivalent to practice. I think this is why Dōgen Zenji does not use the word "practice" in either the second or third sentences of this piece.

Wholehearted practice in everyday life was essential to Dōgen's teachings. Dōgen was not concerned with developing philosophical systems to be studied only by scholars or privileged practitioners; instead he wanted to show people how to practice the teachings of Buddhism within their day-to-day lives. In section 4 of Genjōkōan, which I will discuss in the next chapter, Dōgen Zenji begins to explain how we can realize awakening within our daily practice.

# FLOWERS FALL, WEEDS GROW

(4) Therefore flowers fall even though we love them; weeds grow even though we dislike them. Conveying one-self toward all things to carry out practice-enlightenment is delusion. All things coming and carrying out practice-enlightenment through the self is realization. Those who greatly realize delusion are buddhas. Those who are greatly deluded in realization are living beings. Furthermore, there are those who attain realization beyond realization and those who are deluded within delusion.

## OUR LIVES ARE THE INTERSECTION OF SELF AND ALL THINGS

To DISCUSS the relationship between delusion and enlightenment and living beings and buddhas, Dōgen Zenji discusses the relationship between *jiko*, the self, and *banpō*, all beings (*ban* means ten thousand, myriad, or numberless; *po* means beings or things). According to Dōgen, delusion and enlightenment lie only within the relationship between self and others. Delusion is not some fixed thing within our minds that, if eliminated, will be replaced by enlightenment.

In the statement "Flowers fall even though we love them and weeds grow even though we dislike them," "we" refers to *jiko* (self) and flowers and weeds are examples of *banpo*, or the myriad things. Flowers simply grow, bloom, and fall; weeds also grow, luxuriate, and wither. Neither flowers nor weeds are inherently good or bad; they simply grow and live. And yet we human beings are usually not neutral in our relationship to things. Since we enjoy flowers, we love it when they bloom, and since we don't like weeds, we are unhappy when they appear. And though we love flowers, they still fall, and we feel sad and disappointed. As for weeds, they grow quickly and spread, and we become angry.

Weeding is one of the main jobs of Buddhist priests in Japanese temples, especially in the summer, and the weeds grow so quickly! In the middle of August, Japanese Buddhist temples have the *O-bon* ceremony, which lasts for a week and is one of their primary annual events. Before O-bon begins, temple priests have to weed the grounds, clean the buildings in their temple compounds, and do many other chores in preparation for this very important event. Weeding is a major task, and by the time we finish, new weeds are already growing where we began, so we must start all over again. Since weeds are stronger than we are, we can never get rid of them all, and this sometimes makes us angry or sad, just as working with our delusions can make us frustrated or hopeless. If we are not actually doing the weeding, we can be "objective" and say "weeds are just weeds," while we claim to neither like nor dislike weeds. Yet when we have to do the work of weeding, it is difficult to say that weeds are just weeds. This is because as long as we are alive, we exist only within relationship to everything that we encounter in our lives. We cannot see things as observers from outside the world, as we might imagine that God does.

In section 4 Dōgen Zenji is discussing this relationship between the self and all beings. He is pointing out that we like things we think are useful, meaningful, or valuable, but we dislike or ignore things that do not suit us. This evaluation occurs within the relationship between self and the myriad dharmas, but there is no such dichotomy within the reality of the myriad dharmas. Within the relationship between self and all beings, there is good and bad, positive and negative, right and wrong. We don't really see the myriad dharmas as they are. We think about things we encounter and name them, assign value to them, and put them into categories such as good or bad, valuable or worthless, likable or unlikable. Our life is actually formed by what we encounter because we create our own world of likes and dislikes based on how we categorize the things we meet. Within this world of likes and dislikes, we do not perceive the myriad dharmas as they really are. Things we like and things we hate look much bigger than they are, and things we are not interested in become small or invisible to us. The world we live in is the world we create based on how our mind encounters the myriad dharmas. We cannot prevent our mind from creating our world as it does, but it is possible to realize that the world of our creation does not reflect true reality. Practicing with this realization and letting go of rigid belief in the narratives and preferences of our minds is, again, opening the hand of thought.

## SELF AND ALL THINGS

This relationship between self and all beings is expressed in the philosophy of every Buddhist tradition. For example, early Buddhist teachers used the twelve sense fields, or *jūnisho* in Japanese, to explain the relationship between self and all dharmas. *Jūnisho* was defined as the six sense organs (eye, ear, nose, tongue, body, and mind) and the six objects of each sense organ (form or color, sound, smell, taste, touch, and objects of mind). Early Buddhist teachings about the twelve sense fields explain that our relationship with the myriad dharmas is created through our sense organs and their objects. In other words, we see color and shape with our eyes, we hear with our ears, we smell with our noses, we taste with our tongues, and we sense touch with our bodies. "Objects of mind" refers to memories, images, or concepts we can "see" or "hear" or think about without actually using our sense organs. So what we perceive is actually a kind of stimulation that happens within our bodies and minds; we do not directly perceive the things (dharmas) themselves.

*Jūhachi-kai*, or the eighteen elements, was also a part of early Buddhist thinking. The eighteen elements consisted of the six sense organs, the six objects of each sense organ, and the six individual elements of consciousness associated with each sense organ (*roku shiki*). This teaching says that the meeting of a sense organ and an object causes a certain type of consciousness to arise in the mind. Eye-consciousness, for example, arises from the meeting of the eye with color or shape, and taste-consciousness arises when a flavor contacts the tongue.

Early Buddhists analyzed life in this way to show that beings have no permanent essence such as an atman or soul that can exist outside of the relationship between the body/mind and its objects. They showed that our lives consist only of these eighteen elements, including numberless relationships between our sense organs, their objects, and each sense consciousness.

The eighteen elements appear in the Heart Sutra with the word *mu* (meaning "no") placed before each element. This is because even though early Buddhists used the elements to negate the existence of atman, the Heart Sutra negated even the fixed existence of the eighteen elements. It showed that the elements also have no substance; they are just phenomena. In this way the Heart Sutra gives us the meaning of emptiness.

As I mentioned earlier, the first two sentences of Genjōkōan contain teachings of early Buddhism and the Heart Sutra. The first sentence corresponds to the eighteen elements as taught in early Buddhism. The second sentence negates these elements, as the Heart Sutra does, saying that although the sense organs, their objects, and sense consciousness exist, they are all actually empty. This is what Mahayana Buddhism teaches in order to help us free ourselves from attachment to the self and all objects.

## Dōgen Zenji's Comments

Let us again return to Dōgen's teachings on the Heart Sutra, Maka Hannya Haramitsu. Here, you will recall, Dōgen says,

> The twelve sense fields are twelve instances of prajna paramita. There are eighteen instances of prajna: eye, ear, nose, tongue, body, mind; sight, sounds, smell, taste, touch, objects of mind; as well as the consciousnesses of eyes, ears, nose, tongue, body, and mind.

Again, we see that Dōgen expresses the teaching of emptiness in a positive way, changing the teaching as it is presented in the Heart Sutra. The Heart Sutra says that the eighteen elements don't exist because they are empty, but Dōgen says that the elements do exist and they are themselves prajna. Prajna means "wisdom which sees emptiness," but prajna is not a function of our minds but rather the reality of each thing as it is. By saying that the eighteen elements are instances of prajna, Dōgen is expressing the reality of all beings which includes being and nonbeing, form and emptiness.

Recognition of this reality is the reason Dōgen says in Maka Hannya Haramitsu, "Form is nothing but form; emptiness is nothing but emptiness." Again, when we say form is emptiness, in our minds there are two things, form and emptiness, and we say those two things are one. This is the way we usually experience things in our daily lives. When we see a flower, for example, the flower is really there and we may think, "This flower is now in front of my eyes. It is very beautiful, but it will wither and fall someday." Although we believe this thought, in undeniable reality as we see the flower there is only the flower blooming; there is no falling. But we may think, "This flower is blooming now but in the past it was a seed, and it will fall someday to form seeds for the next generation of flowers." Or we may think, "This flower is here but it is empty, impermanent; there is no fixed substance to this flower." This is how we think and understand the Buddha's teaching when we study it. But what Dōgen teaches is that at the actual moment of its blooming, the flower is just a flower. He doesn't say, "We should know that the flower is empty," because the flower is actually empty even when we don't say so. For Dōgen, when we see a flower and think, "This flower is empty," we separate ourselves from the flower.

Prajna is not a way of thinking or understanding; it is the flower itself, and the flower is revealing actual emptiness. That is why Dōgen says,

> Form is nothing but form, emptiness is nothing but emptiness—one hundred blades of grass, ten thousand things.

"One hundred blades of grass, ten thousand things" are banpō, or the myriad dharmas, things as they are without being processed by the thinking mind. Our desires and aversions and all the things happening within us and outside of us are in reality the manifestation of one real life: Buddha-mind or the Buddha's life. This is the message that Dōgen Zenji delivers to us in Genjōkōan, and he shows us how to see true reality and how to live our lives in accordance with this reality. We usually think of the self as subject and banpō as object. We assume that the subject thinks about and evaluates the object. But this common way of understanding our lives is not necessarily true. According to the Buddha Dharma, this is not reality. The reality is that the self is part of the myriad dharmas; we are part of nature and the world. The myriad dharmas are everything, including the self. When we say "all dharmas," the self is already included. If we leave "all dharmas," we cannot live. If fish leave the water or birds leave the sky, they will die. It is the same with us; sky and water are banpō and the self is like the fish and bird. This is an important point because our basic way of thinking is based on separation between subject and object. We think, "I am the subject and everything outside of me is an object." But this is not the actual truth.

> Conveying oneself toward all things to carry out practice-enlightenment is delusion. All things coming and carrying out practice-enlightenment through the self is realization.

In this sentence from Genjōkōan Dōgen Zenji presents definitions of delusion and enlightenment. "Realization" is a translation of *satori* (悟り) and "delusion" is a translation of *mayoi* (迷い). Both satori and mayoi exist only within the relationship between self and others. Actually, "delusion" is probably not a good translation of the Japanese or Chinese character for *mayoi*, which is also pronounced *mei* (迷). *Mei* is a psychological condition caused by the delusion that is a product of consciousness. Within consciousness reality is distorted; we don't see things as they are, and that is delusion. Mayoi is not this delusion itself but a psychological condition *caused by* the delusion; it is a type of confusion caused by the inability to see things as they are. When we don't see things clearly, we cannot make good judgments and are unsure which way to go. So mayoi is comparable to being lost. The root of the kanji is written 米 and has the sound "*mei*." It looks like an intersection, perhaps one in which we don't know which way to go. The lower part of the kanji means "walking." When we walk, our destination should be clear. If our destination is not clear, we will become lost in confusion and anxiety, make bad decisions, and have many other problems. This is the condition of suffering in samsara.

In the condition of mayoi we are always uncertain, never knowing which way to go or which action to take. We cling to what we wrongly believe is true of a situation and act according to our mistaken ideas. As a result, we fall into a much more difficult condition. This is what Dōgen Zenji is saying in the sentence "Conveying oneself toward all things to carry out practice-enlightenment is delusion." This means we take our distorted ideas and desires and move toward the world trying to find truth or reality. We try to see and capture reality with our minds, abilities, willpower, and effort; we try to become enlightened in order to put everything under the control of the self so that our life is stable and peaceful. This attitude, according to Dōgen, is delusion.

> All things coming and carrying out practice-enlightenment through the self is realization.

The subject of practice is not the personal self but all beings. To practice is to awaken to the self that is connected to all beings, or the ten thousand dharmas. Dōgen says that these myriad dharmas are themselves Buddha Dharma, and the reality of all dharmas is the Dharma body of Buddha—the dharmakaya—or Buddha itself. Since we are part of all dharmas, the foundation of our practice must be our awakening to the reality that we are indeed part of all dharmas, or part of Buddha. In other words, it is not I who practice, but rather Buddha carries out Buddha's practice through me. In our zazen practice and in our daily activity of bodhisattva practice, it is not a matter of individual actions based on individual willpower and effort. It is rather the myriad dharmas, or all beings, that carry out practice through our individual bodies and minds.

For this reason Dōgen taught that zazen is not a practice meant to make human beings into buddhas; zazen is itself Buddha's practice. Dōgen defined Buddha as *Jin Daichi*, "whole great earth." This is an expression for the self that is together with all beings. Yet even though we share this connection with all beings, we still think in deluded, self-centered ways. Our thoughts about reality are upside down; we think, "I am the center of the world" or "These things are my possessions." We often think that everything in this world exists in order to make us happy. This may be the basis for views and values in modern society, but the teachings of the Buddha and Dōgen show us that this is an inverted way of viewing things. Our practice of zazen enables us to see clearly that we are part of the world, part of nature, and part of Buddha. It lets us see that we don't need to personally become a buddha, but rather we need to awaken to the reality that from the beginning we are living Buddha's life.

By letting go of our thoughts, of our consciousness, we actualize the self that is connected with all dharmas. This is not the self awakening to reality, but zazen awakening to zazen, Dharma awakening to Dharma, and Buddha awakening to Buddha. Zazen practices zazen; it is not that a separate individual practices zazen to become enlightened. This is the meaning of Dōgen Zenji's expression "practice and enlightenment are one." It is through this practice that universal and interpenetrating reality manifests itself. This is the meaning of genjōkōan in my understanding.

# Realization beyond Realization 5

## Buddhas and Living Beings

L ET'S LOOK FURTHER into the section we began exploring in the previous chapter:

(4)[ . . . ] Those who greatly realize delusion are buddhas. Those who are greatly deluded in realization are living beings. Furthermore, there are those who attain realization beyond realization and those who are deluded within delusion.

In stating that "those who greatly realize delusion are buddhas" Dōgen points to a basic truth of practice. If we are truly honest and sincere with ourselves, we will find that no matter how hard we practice, our motivation for practice is still based in some amount of self-centeredness. Dōgen said that those who recognize this self-centered basis of their practice are buddhas. This means that the act of truly seeing our self-centeredness is itself Buddha, and when we see this self-centeredness we must bring repentance[1] (about which, more below) into our practice to work to free ourselves from our selfish motivations. Our practice, the awakening that allows us to see our own self-centeredness and let go of it, is Buddha. So to awaken to this reality of our delusion, the reality that we are almost always self-centered and unable to see the truth of impermanence and lack of independent existence, is itself Buddha. This is what Dōgen means when he says that to realize delusion is to be a buddha.

Repentance has been practiced throughout the history of the Buddhist sangha. On days of the full and new moon (the first day and the fifteenth day of the lunar calendar), monks gather in the practice of *uposadha* (Ch.: *busa*; Jap.: *fusatsu*). In the early days of Buddhism, the sangha leader recited the monks' precepts on this occasion, and any participant who had violated the precepts admitted doing so before the assembly. Repentance had deep significance for all Sangha members, since all had adopted the Buddhist precepts as their guidelines for living; to violate the precepts was a deviation from their life vows. When members realized they had strayed, they repented and returned to their vows. The *fusatsu* gathering still continues in many Buddhist traditions, and *ryaku-fusatsu* (modified *fusatsu*) is still practiced twice a month in Sōtō Zen monasteries, although the gathering has become very ceremonial.

In Mahayana Buddhism, repentance is always a part of practicing with the bodhisattva vows. Our vows are expressions of our determination to walk the bodhisattva path, and when we become aware that we have strayed from the right track, we offer repentance by returning to the path. This awakening to the incompleteness of one's practice and returning to one's path is the meaning of repentance in Mahayana Buddhism.

> Those who are greatly deluded in realization are living beings.

It's essential here to recognize that buddhas and living beings are not two separate groups of people; all beings are part of one universal reality, and in this sense there is no separation between buddhas and living beings. This is the meaning of the phrase "no buddhas and no living beings" in the second sentence of Genjōkōan. We practice

within the universal reality of no separation, so there is no separation between us, our practice, and Buddha. In this view of reality, we
actually are buddhas. We live as part of the universal reality of life,
whether we know it or not, and there is no separation between self and
other, even though we separate them in our minds. No matter how
self-centered our ideas, we always live within the network of interdependent origination and are connected with and supported by all
beings in the whole world. "Network of interdependent origination"
is an expression I use to refer to the reality of interconnectedness. It
is similar to Indra's Net, an analogy used in Mahayana Buddhism in
which all things of the universe are depicted as knots or nodes in the
limitless net of reality.

Yet we are capable of seeing universal reality from another point
of view. Even though we are living out universal reality with all living
beings, from this other point of view we are still self-centered and we
often lose sight of reality. Our self-centeredness causes many problems
for us and for others, so we must practice in order to live naturally
and peacefully in accordance with reality. The desire to rid ourselves
of self-centeredness and live in accordance with reality gives us the
energy to practice zazen and study Buddha Dharma. So in a sense,
our delusions, our view that we are separate from universal reality and
our desire to change, is very important because it is a motivating force
in our lives that enables us to practice.

In our zazen, we let go of our ego-centered selves and become
one with the total interpenetrating reality that is universal reality,
or absolute reality. We cannot see this absolute reality as an object
of our discriminating minds, but when we let go of our relative, self-
centered way of viewing things, we are naturally a part of absolute
reality. Because it includes *everything*, this absolute reality does not
exclude our relative views and discriminating minds, including our
deluded relative views. If it did not include our relative views, it
would not be truly absolute. So we cannot be an observer of absolute
reality because we ourselves are part of the total movement of that
reality. In the same way that a person cannot step outside of his or

her own body and observe the body with a separate set of eyes, we cannot step outside of ourselves and observe absolute reality. Since we cannot take an absolute position as individuals, we hold a certain position within absolute reality as a karmic self, a limited, individual self that is born, lives, and dies according to changing causes and conditions. Our point of view is based in this karmic self, so we see the world from a limited perspective, a small part of a much greater reality. Our narrow perspectives as individual, relative, karmic beings are the source of our delusion.

Though we are deluded as individual karmic beings, we are still living within the absolute, universal reality that is Buddha Dharma, and even though we are living within this universal reality, we are still deluded as individual karmic selves. This is the reality of human life. In other words, we are deluded within realization, and in practice we realize, or awaken to, the reality that we are deluded; we are therefore not deceived by our delusion. Yet the "subject" that practices Dharma is not this individual karmic self, it is not the "I"; it is rather universal reality that is itself practicing and manifesting reality. This shift in the "subject" of practice from the individual to universal reality is essential to Dōgen Zenji's teaching in Genjōkōan.

> Furthermore, there are those who attain realization beyond realization ...

There are some people who realize reality within practice and go beyond. In Shōbōgenzō Daigo (Great Realization), Dōgen Zenji writes:

> Therefore we should study the reality that no sentient or insentient beings are without knowledge from the time of birth. When there is innate knowledge, there is innate realization, innate verification, and innate practice. Thus, the buddha-ancestors, being already the good trainers[2] of beings, have been respectfully considered as "[the men of]

innate realization." This is because they are born holding realization. They are people with innate realization being filled with great realization. They are thus because they study holding realization. Therefore, we realize great realization by holding the triple world, realize great realization by holding the hundreds of grasses, realize great realization by holding the four great elements, realize great realization by holding the buddha-ancestors, and realize great realization by holding reality (*kōan*). All these are holding great realization and further realizing great realization. The very moment to do this is just now.[3]

Here Dōgen says that all beings are born within the network of interdependent origination that is itself great realization, that is itself prajna. Buddha-ancestors and all of us are born, live, and die within this great realization. Our practice is to realize great realization within this great realization, moment by moment; or perhaps it is better to say that great realization realizes great realization through our practice. This is what Dōgen Zenji meant in saying that there are those who attain realization beyond realization.

. . . and those who are deluded within delusion.

Dōgen also writes about this delusion within delusion in Shōbōgenzō Keisei-sanshoku (Sounds of Valley Streams, Colors of Mountains):

People nowadays rarely seek genuine reality. Therefore, though they are deficient in practice with their bodies and deficient in realization with their minds, they seek the praise of others, wanting others to say that their practice and their understanding accord with each other. This is exactly what is called delusion within delusion. You should immediately abandon such mistaken thinking.

This is the meaning of Dōgen Zenji's expression "delusion within delusion." Even though we are born, live, and die in the midst of great realization (*daigo*), within our minds we create our own pictures of the world and our own value systems, and we pursue only the values that we have created within our own systems. We may cultivate, for example, our reputation as a sincere and virtuous practitioner, instead of simply practicing sincerely and nurturing our virtues. In our minds we are able to create a very complicated fantasy of who we are, a fantasy in which we usually consider ourselves heroes or heroines.

Yet in true reality, the relationship between the self and all things is made up of numberless conditions, and these conditions are, as my teacher Uchiyama Rōshi said, simply the scenery of our lives. So it is most important as practitioners of the bodhisattva path to keep awakening to this reality that exists, before we fabricate any fantasy about it within our minds.

## Buddha Actualizing Buddha without Thinking So

(5) When buddhas are truly buddhas they don't need to perceive they are buddhas; however, they are enlightened buddhas and they continue actualizing Buddha. In seeing color and hearing sound with body and mind, although we perceive them intimately, [the perception] is not like reflections in a mirror or the moon in water. When one side is illuminated, the other is dark.

"When buddhas are truly buddhas" means that when we are actually practicing and living as a part of interpenetrating reality, we cannot see that we are really living out absolute reality. This is so because when we are living in harmony with absolute reality, there is no separation between absolute reality and us. When we truly practice, there is no separation between subject and object or between the self and all beings. Conditions in the world create the individual, and the individual creates conditions in the world. The world and individuals are working together as one total reality, so we cannot see "self" as subject and "the world" as object. There is no way to judge a situation or a person as good or bad from the perspective of total reality, because "good" and "bad" are terms that only have relevance when we separate reality into subject and object.

However, as individuals living within total reality, we do see ourselves as subject and view things outside us as objects. We continually judge, act, and choose according to our preferences and the conditions of our environment. As individuals, we see things as good or bad, and we choose the good and avoid the bad. To do this, we create a copy of reality to guide our minds, although we still continue living within absolute reality, beyond thought. Our thoughts about reality are like an atlas of the earth. An atlas shows us a likeness of the earth, but it is not possible to make an atlas that perfectly represents the earth. This is so because the earth has three dimensions and the sheet of paper on which the atlas is made has only two dimensions. Thus the size, shape, or directional representation of the earth must be distorted to make an atlas. On some atlases, for example, Greenland is bigger than North America.

In the same way, a human being's mental picture of the world cannot be a perfect copy of reality. Within this mental map there are things we think are good, useful, or valuable, such as flowers, and there are other things we think are bad, useless, or worthless, such as weeds. Usually we take it for granted that the fabricated picture of the world in our minds is the world itself. We think "my system of values is right and others' values are distorted." This is our basic delusion. This delusion, which may be called ignorance, causes many problems when we encounter people with different systems of value and different views of the world. I believe this is the reality of the human condition that Yogacara Buddhist philosophers addressed in proposing that everything we experience is consciousness only.

In zazen, our practice is to let go of our fabricated mental map, to open the hand of thought, and thereby sit down on the ground of reality. Thinking can only produce a distorted mental copy of the world, and this copy is based on karmic experiences. But when we let go of thought, we understand that the copy in our minds is not reality itself. Then we no longer have to blindly trust our thoughts and we can instead inquire further into the nature of reality.

Our zazen is not a method of correcting the distortion of our "conceptual maps." Instead we just let go of the map and sit down on the earth of reality. Letting go is, on the one hand, the complete rejection of any thought based on our limited karmic experiences. Yet on the other hand, letting go is the acceptance of all thoughts as mere secretions of the mind and elements of an incomplete map of reality. We just let thoughts come up and we just let them go away. We neither negate anything nor affirm anything in zazen. We can do this because we are simply sitting facing the wall without any of the direct interactions we normally have with other people, beings, and objects. So our zazen practice both goes beyond and yet includes the complete rejection and the complete acceptance of thought.

When we sit facing the wall in zazen there is no separation between subject and object, yet many things still come up in the mind. We often think of something and then start to interact with our thoughts as objects. But in zazen, with only the wall in front of us, it is easy to see that thoughts are illusions. This is so because when we let go, those thoughts and judgments disappear, leaving only the wall. This is an important point in our practice of zazen; it is dropping off body and mind. Yet immediately thoughts come back in our sitting, so our practice is simply to continue to let go of whatever comes up.

When thoughts, judgments, or evaluations arise in zazen and we engage with them, there is separation between subject and object. When we let go of thought, subject and object are one; there is no one to evaluate and nothing to receive evaluation. At that time only manifesting reality exists, and manifesting reality includes our delusions. When we sit in the upright posture, keeping the eyes open, breathing through the nose, and letting go of thoughts, reality manifests itself. This is *genjōkōan* (actualization of reality).

In our daily lives, however, we cannot simply keep letting go of thought in this way. In order to live we must make choices using our incomplete conceptual maps of the world, and to make choices we must distinguish positive from negative. Yet the practice of zazen can help us understand that our pictures of the world and our values are biased and incomplete, and this understanding allows us to be flexible. Being flexible means that we can listen to others' opinions knowing that their biases are simply different from ours, according to the circumstances and conditions of their individual lives. When we practice in this way our view broadens and we become better at working in harmony with others. By continually studying the nature of reality, of the Dharma in its universal sense, and by awakening to our biases, we keep working to correct our distorted views. This is how letting go of thought in zazen informs practice in our daily lives.

Whether practicing in daily life or zazen, there is no way to conceive of being a buddha or being enlightened. There is no way we can judge ourselves because we cannot step outside of ourselves into objectivity. This is so because there is no separation between subject and object in the actualization of reality. So without worrying about becoming a buddha or attaining enlightenment, we just keep trying to settle ourselves more deeply into immeasurable reality.

Zazen itself is this immeasurable reality that is the foundation for our practice in the zendo and in daily life. In zazen we don't grasp or engage anything; we just are as we are, that's all. Through the practice of shikantaza, we simply sit without doing anything, and there is no way to judge whether the zazen I sit today is good or the zazen I sat yesterday was bad. Whether the mind is busy or calm, we just keep letting go of whatever comes up. We keep the same posture through all mental conditions without being pulled this way or that, so there is no good or bad zazen. Zazen is always zazen.

Maintaining the zazen posture through all conditions is a very important part of our practice. Keeping this posture is, as Dōgen says in Fukanzazengi, "the Dharma-gate of peace and joy" that is itself realization, the actualization of reality in practice. Yet if we cling to favorable conditions and try to avoid difficult conditions, we create the cycle of suffering, of samsara, within our zazen practice. This cycle may begin if we seem to succeed in making our zazen pleasurable. Although such success initially makes us happy, sooner or later conditions change and our success disappears, making us miserable. If we keep struggling, our zazen becomes a cycle of "transmigration," shifting between realms of happiness and misery, and our practice is then no longer Buddha's practice.

> When buddhas are truly buddhas they don't need to perceive they are buddhas; however, they are enlightened buddhas and they continue actualizing Buddha.

This sentence means that we cannot judge whether we are buddhas or not because true reality is beyond such judgments. Still, the simultaneous existence of individuality and universality in our lives is the truth of our existence. This truth is itself "Buddha constantly manifesting Buddha," and when we awaken to this truth moment by moment, Buddha is manifest. We cannot say that any of us as individuals are buddhas because we are living beings who are interdependent with all beings and given life by all beings. No one can truthfully say "I have become a buddha" because there is no such thing as an independent "I" that can do things outside of its connection to others. Yet when we place ourselves on the ground of reality, letting go of our individuality within practice, *our practice* manifests Buddha.

However, although we are living within Buddha's life and our practice can manifest Buddha, we are still deluded beings and we ourselves create the cycle of suffering in samsara. This is, as Uchiyama Rōshi said, the scenery of our lives. We must therefore accept that we are deluded so that we can practice with the reality of our lives.

## THE MOON IN WATER

> (5)[ . . . ] In seeing color and hearing sound with body and mind, although we perceive them intimately, [the

perception] is not like reflections in a mirror or the moon in water.

Usually we think we see things in the same way that a mirror reflects an image of an object. We think the object is reflected in our eyes and that our eyes see the object. Yet "seeing color and hearing sounds with body and mind" means that our lives and our bodies do not function in such a disjointed way. It is really true that we see things not only with our eyes and hear things not only with our ears. The whole body and mind are involved in the activities of seeing objects, hearing sounds, smelling fragrances, tasting flavors, and feeling sensations.

When having a meal, for example, all our senses are engaged. We see the food's color and shape with the eyes, smell and taste the food, and even hear the sound of our biting and chewing. When we swallow, we experience satisfaction in feeling the food move down the throat until it settles in the stomach. We may think of how delicious the food is and experience gratitude for those who prepared the meal, and we may think appreciatively of the immeasurable work that was involved in growing, harvesting, and transporting the food. These experiences of the meal are not simply discrete products of individual sense organs and their separate objects; we experience a meal engaging the entire body and mind.

The analogies of a mirror and its reflection, and the moon's reflection in water, illustrate the unity of the self and all things. This is one of two ways that Dōgen uses these images in Genjōkōan. In the present instance he is saying that a mirror and reflecting water are not separate from the objects whose images they reflect. In other words, there is no separation between the person who experiences and the objects that are experienced. The subject of experience, the object of experience, and the experience itself are all truly one reality.

I remember an experience when the unity of subject and object became very apparent to me. I lived in Massachusetts from 1975 to 1981 working to establish a small Zen community with two of my Dharma brothers. We had bought about six acres of land in a wooded area in western Massachusetts, and our conditions were so primitive that we didn't even have water when we first moved there. First we built a small house where we sat zazen, slept, cooked, and lived, and since we had no outside financial support, we had to work to support ourselves. When we got part-time jobs in a tofu factory a few years after moving into the house, our employer regularly gave us leftover pieces of tofu that were too small to sell. We ate tofu almost every day and it became our main source of protein. One day when I was shopping at a natural food store with a practitioner from our zendo, we saw a poster that read, "We are what we eat." In response I said, "If that is so, we are tofu!"

Of course, the sign was saying that since our health depends upon eating wholesome foods, we should eat in a healthy way. But later I discovered that the German materialist philosopher Ludwig Andreas Feuerbach (1804–72) was the author of this saying. Coming from a materialist, I think the phrase "we are what we eat" might be a criticism of the saying found in the Bible "Man does not live by bread alone." This well-known Christian saying means that people need spiritual nourishment from the word of God in addition to physical nourishment. So I think Feuerbach was saying that people actually do not need "spiritual nourishment" because human life depends solely on material conditions such as food. For Feuerbach, "we are what we eat" implied that human beings are comprised solely of physical elements.

In Buddhist teachings, "we are what we eat" has a deep meaning. When I hold a glass of water, for example, the water is there and I am here. But, wondrously enough, when I drink the water it becomes part of me. When I breathe, part of the air becomes part of me. We are what we eat, drink, breathe, hear, smell, taste, and see. There is no "me" that exists other than the things that make up my body and mind. We are intimately connected to things in our environment, so much so that they are actually part of us. We *are* all the things that we experience; we are created by them. Without this relationship with all things, we could not exist even for one moment. In reality "I," "you," and all other beings do not exist at all; only relationships and interactions exist.

Even from a conventional perspective, individuals must live within a community in order to survive. Our ability to think, use language, and make decisions are all gifts received from the community and culture in which we were born and educated. We are created by the world and by society, and we collectively create society and influence the world. The world and the self are truly one thing. When we function harmoniously as a part of this network of all things, as part of immeasurable or universal reality, our individual lives become healthy and wholesome.

Yet we are capable of functioning in a way that is not healthy and not in accord with the well-being of universal reality. In fact, human society can have the same relationship to this earth that cancerous cells have to their host. Cancer is a paradoxical phenomenon. Although cancerous cells are part of a host body, they do not follow the directives of that body. If not successfully treated, the cancer grows of its own accord until the body dies, and when the body dies the cancer dies. I think that civilization, created out of humanity's desire for happiness and prosperity, has begun to function in nature as cancerous cells function in the body. Although human beings are part of nature, they have produced a society that has begun to grow out of harmony with nature. This disharmony is a result of the attempt to manipulate the natural world into conforming to the agenda of human desires. We have killed numberless living beings and destroyed huge parts of natural ecosystems in order to build cities, and we call this "development." We have regarded human beings as the masters of nature, and our societies have struggled hard to make this world a "better" place for us.

Until I was a teenager at least, the basic message from the Japanese educational system and from Japanese society in general was "We are making the world better with the use of scientific knowledge and technology." But eventually people began to see that science and technology used in the service of human desires have caused many problems for people and for the natural world. We once thought that the human race was the most important part of a world in which everything belongs to us, yet in truth we are just a tiny part of nature. Human beings have finally begun to realize that we will perish if the natural environment perishes, just as cancer cells die when their host dies. We have begun to see that we share one life with nature and with all beings. In this way, society is awakening to the reality of interdependent origination, the truth that the Buddha taught. By correcting our inverted views of the world we can live naturally and wholesomely in harmony with all beings. This is the "right view" that the Buddha spoke of in the eightfold noble path. For Dōgen, zazen is the pivotal point in our practice of rectifying our inverted views. He saw that rooting our views in the reality of zazen allows our views to become rooted in the awareness of interdependence, enabling us to live in accordance with reality. This is a very simple yet profound and endless practice.

Dōgen describes this reality of interdependence in Genjōkōan. He says that to convey the self toward all things and to try to control things is to be deluded. If we practice to become a great person, for example, we may find ourselves competing with others and even using our knowledge of the Buddha's teachings to appear superior. In this case we end up simply imposing our own limited, self-centered concepts of practice onto the world around us. But when we drop our self-centered motivations and allow all things to come toward us to carry out practice, that is realization. This means that we cannot practice by ourselves; the subject of practice is not one particular person, it is all things carrying out practice/realization through the individual's body and mind. This is dropping off body and mind. Dropping off body and mind means we participate with the whole universe as it practices through our individual bodies and minds. We don't practice individually to improve ourselves; rather, we settle down peacefully within the network of interdependent origination and allow the universal life force to practice *through us* for all beings.

When one side is illuminated, the other is dark.

Here Dōgen Zenji is discussing enlightenment and delusion according to the relationship between the self and all things. The self is not separate from all beings, the myriad dharmas. The self is a part of all beings. Each of us is living together with all things within the network of interdependent origination, and there is no separate self that exists outside this network.

Although this is the basic reality of our lives, we usually don't see it. We create a personal picture of the world that is based on our limited life experiences and other conditions that obscure our objectivity. To take our own personal picture of the world as true reality is delusion. It is delusion because our personal views place us at the center of the universe as the all-important subject, and treat things "other" than us as objects to be manipulated. From this view we desire things we think will make us happy and satisfied, and we push away things we judge as inferior and undesirable.

Yet in the reality of Buddha's life, we are connected with and supported by all things. The self is not the subject of reality and other things are not its objects; we are in fact one with all things in the entire universe, and this reality is itself enlightenment. Enlightenment is not something we can possess or experience. We cannot, because of a certain experience that happened under certain conditions, say, "I am an enlightened person." If we judge an experience and say "I had an enlightenment experience," we have already separated "I" from the reality of all things, when in fact there is no "enlightenment" that is separate from this reality. Rather than striving for a particular experience or goal, we should simply keep practicing without judgment or evaluation. This means approaching all that we do without selfish desire, without even the desire for enlightenment; to practice in this way is to manifest universal reality. This is difficult, of course, because even when we are helping others or making sacrifices for them, we can usually find, if we search our hearts and minds deeply enough, an ego-centered motivation for our activity. This is true even in our zazen practice.

What complicated beings we are! It is impossible to make simple judgments about the egocentricity of our actions. Yet as the Buddha's children practicing with our bodhisattva vows, we must keep trying to help others and to free ourselves of selfishness. Try as we may, however, we will never be able to declare, "Now I am completely free from selfish desires." All we can do is to try in each moment, whatever we are doing, to practice the Buddha Way; we just keep opening the hand of thought and continuing to practice. There is no time when one can say, "I'm finished—now I have finally reached the level of an enlightened person." As Dōgen Zenji says, our practice is endless.

From one perspective, we are always living within the enlightenment of Buddha. From another perspective, no matter how hard or how long we practice in this lifetime, we will still be limited individuals. The reality of these two simultaneously true perspectives is truly wondrous. At all times we have the potential to act with either magnanimity or egocentricity, to do either right or wrong. Both Buddha and demons are living within us, so we need to live our lives moment by moment, being led by vow and repentance.

"When one side is illuminated, the other is dark" means that we are living as a part of the entirety of all things. We can refer to this entire reality as "self" (*jiko*), or we can call it "all things" (*banpō*). When we see reality as a whole, we see that the self includes the whole world because it is connected with all things (this view can also be expressed by saying the self does not exist). We can use either "self" or "all things" to name reality because when we say "self," all things are included in that "self," and when we say "all things," the self is included in that "all things." In Buddhism, this one total reality can be viewed from two sides: reality as a collection of numberless individual things (relative truth), and reality as one universal entirety containing no individuality (absolute truth). From this perspective, our lives are at once both individual and universal. So "when one side is illuminated, the other is dark" means that when we say "self," although "all beings" are included, "all beings" are in the dark and do not appear in our minds and speech. When we say "all things," "self" is still there but it is in the dark and so it does not appear in our minds and speech. When the self is illuminated, all things are in the dark, and when all things are illuminated, the self is in the dark. This is the way Dōgen Zenji expresses this wondrous reality of interdependent origination.

# Dropping Off Body and Mind

(6) To study the Buddha Way is to study the self. To study the self is to forget the self. To forget the self is to be verified by all things. To be verified by all things is to let the body and mind of the self and the body and mind of others drop off. There is a trace of realization that cannot be grasped. We endlessly express the ungraspable trace of realization.

## To Study the Buddha Way Is to Study the Self

THIS IS THE most essential point in the teachings of both Shakyamuni Buddha and Dōgen Zenji. In the Dhammapada, one of the earliest Buddhist scriptures, the Buddha said, "The self is the only foundation of the self."[4]

But what does this really mean? When someone says, "I study the Buddha Way," that person likely thinks that he or she, one certain individual, studies some objective thing called "the Buddha Way." In this case "I" is the subject and "the Buddha Way" is the object; this person called "I" wants to understand and possess "it." This is our common understanding of "I study it."

The original Japanese word translated as "study" in these sentences is *narau* (習う). *Narau* originated from the word *nareru* (慣れる) which means "to get accustomed to," "to become familiar with," "to get used to," or "to become intimate with." So *narau* refers to more than simply the intellectual study of something.

The Chinese character for *narau* is 習. The upper part of this kanji (羽) is the symbol for the wings of a bird, and the lower part (白) means "self." So *narau* means to study something in the way a baby bird "studies" flying with its parents. From birth a baby bird possesses the potential to fly, but it must watch its parents to learn how to actually perform the action of flying. The baby watches and tries again and again until finally it can fly like its parents. This is the original meaning of "to study" as it is used in Dōgen's "to study the self." This type of study is not simply an intellectual study, although of course human beings do use the intellect in the process of learning. But the accumulation of knowledge alone is not enough to allow us to learn to fly—that is, not enough for us to live truly and genuinely. In the same way that flying is the essential activity that enables a bird to be a bird (except for birds such as penguins or ostriches), studying the self is the essential activity that allows us human beings to be human. A human being is a living being who needs to study the self in order to thoroughly become human.

When we study the self in this way, we cannot see ourselves as the object of our study; we must rather "live out" our selves. We must practice with our entire body and mind; and intellectual investigation, though important, is only a small part of this study.

Even when we say, "I study the Buddha Way," there is still a subject and an object that are separate. But this is a mistaken way of thinking and a basic problem that keeps us human beings from seeing reality as it actually is. When we truly practice the Buddha Way or study the self, there is no separation between "I," "the self," "the Buddha Way," "study," and "practice." When we genuinely study the self, "I" is the self, and there is no "I" apart from the activity of studying. Subject, object, and activity are completely one thing. Yet when we think or speak, we use concepts and we must therefore say, "I study the self," or "I study the Buddha Way." So the important point is that we should just study and just practice. Within the action of just practicing and just studying, both "the self" and "the Buddha Way" are manifested. Keep studying, practicing, manifesting. This is what Dōgen Zenji meant when he wrote in section 5:

> When buddhas are truly buddhas they don't need to per-ceive they are buddhas; however, they are enlightened buddhas and they continue actualizing Buddha.

It works within the sphere of our daily lives to say, "I drink water"; this is how we communicate with others. When I say, "I want to drink a cup of water," I have expressed what I want and someone may bring a cup of water. There is no problem with this communication on the ground of conventional life within society. But when we speak in terms of Buddha Dharma, it does not work. This is because to real-ize Buddha Dharma we must go beyond words, concepts, language, and logic in order to be free from the problem of separation between subject, object, and activity. But this does not mean that we must stop thinking and see things in some unusual and mysterious way. In other words, the reality of our life is a very obvious and ordinary thing, but once we start to talk about this reality we lose its true, vivid, and immediate nature.

In our practice we just sit with our bodies and minds in the zendo, and we aim to practice the Buddha Way in our activities outside the zendo as well. In practicing the Buddha Way there is no separation between the self that is studying the self and the self that is studied by the self; self is studying the self, and the act of studying is also the self. There is no such thing as a self that is separate from our activity. Dōgen Zenji defined this self as *jijuyu-zanmai*, a term that Sawaki Kōdō Rōshi described as "self 'selfing' the self."[5]

To illustrate this point we can think of the relationship between a runner and the act of running. When we think of this, we realize that no runner is separate from the act of running; a runner and running are the same thing. If the runner becomes separate from running, then the runner is not running. If this is the case, the runner can no longer be called a runner since a runner is defined as "one who runs." The great ancient Indian master Nagarjuna presented this example as part of his illustration of emptiness and the negation of a fixed, permanent, fundamental essence that "owns" the body and mind.

Running as well as sitting, eating, drinking, and breathing are very ordinary things. But when we say, "There is no 'I' other than running" or "running without a runner," we think we are discussing something mysterious. But this view of the teachings of people such as Nagarjuna or Dōgen is mistaken. These teachers are trying to express a very ordinary thing in a truly realistic way without fabrication. To do this they use words that negate themselves in a way that reveals the reality beyond our thoughts.

When we practice the Buddha Way, there is no self, no Buddha Way, and no others. This is because self, Buddha Way, and others work together as one. What we call "our actions" are actually the work done by both self and other beings and objects. For example, when a person drives a car, the person thinks "he" as subject drives "the car" as object. But in reality we cannot drive without the car; we can only become a driver or be driven with the aid of the car, and the car can only express its full function as a vehicle of transportation when someone drives it. Our cars affect us both psychologically and materially as well. We will drive different cars in different ways, for example, depending upon the style or quality of the car. The feelings and attitude of a person driving a cheap old truck carrying a load of junk will likely be totally different from the feelings and attitude that person will have driving a luxurious new car carrying a VIP. A car can also provide us with the ability to travel quickly and conveniently, yet if it breaks down, we may have to make more effort than usual to get where we need to go. Repair, fuel, and insurance costs can exert an added financial stress on our lives and can even feel burdensome. So in a sense the car own us and shapes us as much as we own and control it, and the action of driving can actually be manifested only by a person and a car working together. This reality of mutual influence and interconnectedness is true not only for a "special" practice done by a group of people called "Buddhists"; in truth this is the way all beings are working within the circle of interdependent origination.

The Buddha Way includes both self and objects. The Buddha Way includes both people sitting and the sitting they do. They are actually one thing. This is very difficult to explain, yet it is an obvious reality of our lives. This reality is not some special state or condition that is only accomplished by so-called "enlightened" people. Even when we don't realize it, self, action, and object are working together as one reality, so we don't need to train ourselves to make them into one thing in our minds. If self, action, and object were really three separate things, they could not become one. The truth is that they are always one reality, regardless of what we do or think.

To study the self is to forget the self.

When we study ourselves as the Buddha Way, we find that there is no self that is separate from others because the self is connected with all beings. We see that the self does not really exist. It is, as the Diamond Sutra says, like a dream, a phantom, a bubble, a shadow, a drop of dew, or a flash of lightning. The self is empty in its self-being, so we must forget the self. Even the self that is studying the Buddha Way should be forgotten; the self forgets the self in studying the self. This is what we do in our zazen when we open the hand of thought. In zazen, we let go of everything that comes up from the self, including all thoughts, feelings, and emotions. We let go of truly everything, including both our selfish ideas and our understanding of the Dharma. Zazen, or just sitting (*shikantaza*), is from one perspective the complete negation of the limited, conditioned, karmic self that lives being led around by its own desires. Yet from another perspective, within this letting go, everything is accepted and nothing is negated; in zazen everything is just as it is. Letting go of thought is not killing thought; thoughts come up moment by moment, but we just let them go. Thoughts are there, but in our zazen we don't think, we just sit. Within just sitting everything is just as it is. Nothing is negated and nothing is affirmed. This just sitting is the prajna (wisdom) that sees emptiness without the separation of subject and object. Zazen is not a kind of method of contemplation through which "I" (subject) see "emptiness" (object); rather the practice of just sitting is itself prajna. This is why Dōgen Zenji said in Shōbōgenzō Zanmai-o-zanmai, "Sitting is itself Buddha Dharma," and in Shōbōgenzō Zuimonki, a record of Dōgen's informal talks presented to his assembly at Kōshōji, "Sitting is itself the true form of the self."

To forget the self is to be verified by all things.

"To be verified by all things" has the same meaning as "all things coming and carrying out practice-enlightenment through the self." By genuinely just sitting, we root our whole being in the ground of interdependent origination.

Shikantaza, zazen as Dōgen Zenji teaches it, is a unique practice—even compared to other meditation practices within the various traditions of Buddhism. When practicing shikantaza, we do nothing but sit with the whole body and mind. We do nothing with the mind, so this is not actually a meditation practice. In this zazen we don't practice with a mantra or contemplate anything. We don't count or watch the breath. We don't try to concentrate the mind on any particular object or use any other meditation techniques; we really just sit with both body and mind. With the eyes open, we simply sit in an upright posture and breathe deeply, quietly, and smoothly through the nose and from the abdomen. When we sit in this posture, even though we are still, the vital organs continue to function; the heart keeps beating and the stomach keeps digesting. Each and every organ in our body continues working in zazen, and there is no reason that our brains should stop working when we sit. Just as the function of a thyroid gland is to secrete hormones, the function of a brain is to secrete thoughts, so thoughts well up in the mind moment by moment. Yet our practice in zazen is to refrain from doing anything with these thoughts; we just let everything come up freely and we let everything go freely. We don't grasp anything; we don't try to control anything. We just sit.

Sitting zazen is a very simple practice, but simple does not necessarily mean easy. Yet it is a very deep practice. In zazen we accomplish nothing; as Sawaki Kōdō Rōshi said, zazen is good for nothing. But zazen is itself Buddha Dharma, and when we refrain from "doing" in this practice, the self is illuminated and verified by all things. Shikantaza is not a practice carried out by the individual. It is, rather, a practice in which we let go of the individual karmic self that is constantly seeking to satisfy its own desires. In zazen the true self, the self that is one with the entire universe, is manifest.

## DROPPING OFF BODY AND MIND

> To be verified by all things is to let the body and mind of the self and the body and mind of others drop off.

"Dropping off body and mind" is a translation of *shinjin-datsuraku* (身心脱落). This is a key word in Dōgen Zenji's teachings. This expression was originally used in the teachings of Dōgen's teacher, Tiantong Rujing (Jap.: Tendō Nyojō). In *Hōkyōki* (Record in the Hōkyō Era), Dōgen's personal record of his conversations with Zen Master Rujing at Tiantong Monastery, shinjin-datsuraku is a frequent topic of discussion between Dōgen Zenji and his teacher. Here is one of those discussions:

> Rujing said, "Sanzen[6] is dropping off body and mind. We don't use incense burning, making prostrations, *nembutsu* (reciting the Buddha's name), the practice of repentance, or reading sutras. We only engage in just sitting."
>
> Dōgen asked, "What is dropping off body and mind?"

Rujing said, "Dropping off body and mind is zazen. When we just practice zazen, we part from the five desires and remove the five coverings."

Dōgen asked, "If we part from the five desires and remove the five coverings, we follow the same teachings as those of the teaching schools and are therefore the same as practitioners of the Mahayana and of the Hinayana."

Rujing said, "The descendants of the ancestor [Bodhidharma] should not dislike the teachings of the Mahayana and Hinayana. If a practitioner is against the sacred teachings of the Tathagata, how can such a person be the descendant of buddhas and ancestors?"

Dōgen asked, "In recent times, some skeptical people say that the three poisonous minds are themselves Buddha Dharma and that the five desires are themselves the Way of the Ancestors. They say eliminating them is equal to making preferences and therefore the same as Hinayana practice."

Rujing said, "If we don't eliminate the three poisonous minds and the five desires, we are the same as the non-Buddhists in the country of King Bimbisara and his son Ajatasattu [during the time of Shakyamuni Buddha]. For the descendants of buddhas and ancestors, removing even one of the five coverings or one of the five desires is of great benefit; it is meeting the buddhas and ancestors."

Here Rujing says that "sanzen is dropping off body and mind" and "dropping off body and mind is zazen." He also says that in dropping off body and mind, we are freed from the five desires and eliminate the five coverings. The five desires are desires that arise in the mind as a result of contact with objects of the five sense organs. When we see, hear, smell, taste, or touch an object, we may enjoy the sensation and desire more of it; this is attachment. Or if the sensation is unpleasant our desire is to avoid it, and since this often is impossible, we become frustrated or angry. So we can see that the five desires are the source of greed as well as the source of anger.

The five coverings are hindrances that prevent the mind from functioning in a healthy way. These five coverings of the mind are greed, anger (hatred), sleepiness or dullness, distraction, and doubt.[7] The five desires and five coverings were originally discussed as obstacles to meditation in the Daichidoron (Mahaprajnaparamita-sastra), Nagarjuna's commentary on the Mahaprajnaparamita Sutra. Tiantai Zhiyi (Jap.: Tendai Chigi), the great philosopher of the Chinese Tiantai (Tendai) school, also mentioned them in his meditation manual, Makashikan (Ch.: Mohezhiguan) (Larger Book of Shamatha and Vipassana).[8] Zhiyi said that practitioners should part from the five desires and eliminate the five coverings in a meditation practice called *shikan* (shamatha and vipassana, "stopping" and "seeing"). As I mentioned in chapter 1, Dōgen Zenji was originally ordained as a Tendai monk in Japan. He was familiar with the teachings and meditation practice of the Tendai tradition, and he began to practice Zen because he was not satisfied with Tendai practice. So we see that in this conversation Dōgen was questioning Rujing to see if Zen teachings about the five coverings and five desires differed from Tendai teachings. Until this conversation Dōgen had been looking for teachings that differed from those of the Tendai school, yet here Rujing says that zazen practice should not differ from the Buddha's teachings that were recorded in the sutras and systematized in the philosophical teaching schools.

Rujing and Dōgen continued their conversation on this topic as follows:

> Rujing said, "The descendants of the buddhas and ancestors first eliminate the five coverings and then remove the six coverings. The six coverings consist of the five coverings plus the covering of ignorance. Even if a practitioner only eliminates the covering of ignorance, that practitioner will be freed of the other five coverings. Even if a practitioner eliminates the five coverings, if ignorance is not removed,

the practitioner has not yet reached the practice of the buddhas and ancestors."

Dōgen immediately offered a prostration and expressed gratitude for this teaching. Placing his hands in *shashu*[9] he said, "Until today, I have not heard of an instruction such as the one you have just given me, teacher. Elders, experienced teachers, monks, and Dharma brothers here do not at all know of this teaching; they have never spoken in this way. Today it is my good fortune to have received your great compassion through teachings that I have never before heard. This good fortune is a result of my connections to the Dharma in previous lives. And yet I would like to ask you another question; is there any secret method one can use to remove the five coverings or the six coverings?"

The teacher smiled and said, "To what practice have you been devoting your entire energy? That practice is nothing other than the Dharma that removes the six coverings. The buddhas and ancestors have not set up classifications in practice. They directly show us and singularly transmit the way to depart from the five desires and six coverings and the way to be free from the five desires. Putting one's effort into the practice of just sitting and dropping off body and mind is the way to depart from the five coverings and the five desires. This is the only method of being free from them; there is absolutely none other. How can there be anything that falls into two or three?"

This is Tiantong Rujing's explanation of dropping off body and mind (*shinjin-datsuraku*), and to understand this term, we should study his teachings since he originated the expression. According to Rujing, dropping off body and mind is freedom from the six coverings, which basically are the same as the three poisonous minds. The three poisonous minds are the cause of transmigration in samsara, and in zazen we let go of the three poisonous minds. This is why Dōgen

Zenji said that zazen is not a practice of human beings; it is the practice of buddhas.

In his instruction to Dōgen, Rujing also says that "the buddhas and ancestors have not set up classifications in practice" and that there is nothing "that falls into two or three." These sayings are from Tendai teachings that originated in the Lotus Sutra. In the Lotus Sutra we read:

> In the buddha-lands within the ten directions
> There is only the Dharma of One-Vehicle,
> Neither a second nor a third,
> Except the skillful teachings of the Buddha.[10]

This means that in reality, there are no such classifications as the three vehicles (*shravaka, pratyekabuddha,* and bodhisattva); they are simply tentative skillful means. Rujing uses these expressions to show that his zazen practice is not one of the three expedient means but is the practice of the Dharma of One-Vehicle. Dōgen echoes this teaching in Shōbōgenzō Zuimonki:

> Sitting itself is the practice of the Buddha. Sitting itself is non-doing. It is nothing but the true form of the Self. Apart from sitting, there is nothing to seek as the Buddha Dharma.

In *Hōkyōki*, Dōgen recorded one more conversation with his teacher concerning dropping off body and mind:

> Rujing said, "The zazen of arhats[11] and pratyekabuddhas[12] is free of attachment yet it lacks great compassion. Their zazen is therefore different from the zazen of the buddhas and ancestors; the zazen of buddhas and ancestors places primary importance on great compassion and the vow to save all living beings. Non-Buddhist practitioners in India

also practice zazen, yet they have the three sicknesses, namely attachment, mistaken views, and arrogance. Therefore, their zazen is different from the zazen of the buddhas and ancestors. Sravakas[13] also practice zazen, and yet their compassion is weak because they don't penetrate the true reality of all beings with wisdom. They practice only to improve themselves and in so doing cut off the seeds of Buddha. Therefore, their zazen is also different from the zazen of the buddhas and ancestors. In buddhas' and ancestors' zazen, they wish to gather all Buddha Dharma from the time they first arouse bodhi-mind. Buddhas and ancestors do not forget or abandon living beings in their zazen; they offer a heart of compassion even to an insect. Buddhas and ancestors vow to save all living beings and dedicate all the merit of their practice to all living beings. They therefore practice zazen within the world of desire,[14] yet even within the world of desire they have the best connection with this Jambudvipa.[15] Buddhas and ancestors practice many virtues generation after generation and allow their minds to be flexible."

Dōgen made a prostration and then asked, "What does 'allowing the mind to be flexible' mean?"

Rujing said, "Affirming the dropping off body and mind of the buddhas and ancestors is the flexible mind. This is called the mind-seal of the buddhas and ancestors."

Dōgen made six prostrations.

This is Dōgen's personal record of these conversations.

Traditionally, it is said that Dōgen Zenji had an enlightenment experience when Rujing, scolding a monk who was sitting next to Dōgen, said, "Zazen is dropping off body and mind. Why are you just sleeping?" This story originally appeared in Dōgen's biography as part of Keizan Jokin Zenji's Denkōroku (Transmission of Light).

Today some Dōgen scholars, such as Sugio Genyū of Yamaguchi

University and Ishii Shūdō of Komazawa University, think Keizan invented this story. Otherwise, they say, Dōgen's criticism of practice aimed at attaining *kensho* becomes a contradiction to his own practice experience. Professor Ishii has said that the fictitious story of Dōgen's enlightenment experience has caused more misunderstanding of Dōgen's teachings than any other fabricated portion of Dōgen's biography. Dōgen Zenji himself never wrote of a definitive enlightenment experience in any of his writings. In his lecture on Bendōwa (Talk on the Wholehearted Practice of the Way) published in Eiheiji's magazine Sanshō in July 1999, Suzuki Kakuzen Rōshi agreed with Professor Sugio and Professor Ishii: "In the case of Dōgen Zenji, his religious experience is not attaining some sudden and special psychological satori experience. Dōgen never talked about such an experience in Shōbōgenzō. In his teachings, realization is a deep awareness of the fact that the existence of the self is not a personal possession of the self."

I agree with these scholars because I think it is best to trust Dōgen's own account of his conversations with Rujing concerning dropping off body and mind, rather than give authority to an account apparently invented after Dōgen died.

In his conversations with Dōgen, Rujing said, "Sanzen is dropping off body and mind" and "dropping off body and mind is zazen." In other words, dropping off body and mind is not some special psychological condition resulting from zazen practice; rather, zazen is itself dropping off body and mind. About thirty years ago when I was a student at Komazawa University, Takasaki Jikidō raised a question about Dōgen's understanding of dropping off body and mind, or *shinjin-datsuraku*. In his book *Kobutsu no Manebi* (Imitation of Ancient Buddhas), Dr. Takasaki suggested that Dōgen possibly misunderstood the Chinese expression that Rujing used in his famous conversations with Dōgen. He suggested that Rujing said "dropping off mind dust" (心塵脱落) rather than "dropping off body and mind" (身心脱落), and that Dōgen misunderstood Rujing's words because both phrases are pronounced *shinjin-datsuraku*. Other scholars disagree, arguing that although the character combinations 心塵 and 身心 are each pronounced *shinjin*, they are pronounced with different tones in Chinese, and Dōgen would therefore not have confused them. My thought is that if Dōgen Zenji had heard Rujing use the expression only once, as he did in the fictitious story that appears in Denkōroku, it might be possible that he misunderstood. But according to Hōkyōki, written by Dōgen himself, Dōgen discussed the expression *shinjin-datsuraku* with Rujing at least three times. We know from Hōkyōki that Dōgen used the expression in speaking to Rujing, and it seems certain that Rujing would have corrected Dōgen if he had made a mistake in its pronunciation. For these reasons, I don't think it is possible that Dōgen made such a mistake in understanding these key words.

Let us take a closer look at this expression, *shinjin-datsuraku*, that is so widely discussed as an essential point in Dōgen's teachings. The literal meaning of the Chinese character *datsu* (脱) is "to take off" or "slough off," and *raku* (落) means "to drop off," "cast off," or "fall down." The scholar Carl Bielefeldt translates this expression as "slough off body and mind," emphasizing the first half of the compound, *datsu* (脱). The translations "dropping off body and mind" and "casting off body and mind" emphasize the second half of the compound, *raku* (落). But what does shinjin-datsuraku really mean for us in our practice?

Throughout our lives, from the time we are born until we die, we wear some kind of clothing. Clothing gives an indication of social class and occupation, and it may communicate cultural and religious background. Monks wear monks' robes, an emperor wears regal garments, farmers wear farm clothes, and soldiers wear uniforms according to their rank. Rich people wear luxurious garments and poor people wear inexpensive ones. Chinese people wear Chinese clothes, the Japanese wear Japanese clothes, Americans dress like Americans. When we see people's clothing, we see who those people are in society.

We wear other kinds of clothing. Social position and status are types of clothing that define us. We wear the clothing of poverty, wealth, or the middle class; we wear the clothing of occupations such as doctor, lawyer, mechanic, priest, student, teacher. But when we sit facing the wall and let go of thought, including comparing ourselves with others, we take off all this clothing. In zazen I am not a Japanese Buddhist priest; I am neither Japanese nor American. In zazen we are neither rich nor poor, neither Buddhist nor Christian. The terms "Japanese," "American," "Buddhist," "Christian," "man," and "woman" are only relevant when we compare ourselves with others. When I compare myself with Americans, I am Japanese, but before I knew of people who weren't Japanese I didn't know that I was Japanese. When we just sit facing the wall in zazen, we are neither deluded living beings nor enlightened buddhas; we are neither alive nor dead; we are just as we are. That's it. In zazen we take off all of our clothing and become the naked self.

We have many different experiences during the course of our lives, and in the process of experiencing these billions of things we create a self-image. We come to consider ourselves as capable or incapable, superior or inferior, rich or poor, honest or dishonest. We define ourselves in this way and hold on to ideas of who we are; we create the karmic self. But when we sit in zazen, we let go of all of these self-images. When we open the hand of thought, these concepts drop off and the body and mind are released from karmic bindings. This is what *datsuraku* means. As Rujing said, we are then released from the five desires and the six coverings. In zazen we are not pulled around by the objects of our thinking or emotions, so we are released from the three poisonous minds that bind us to samsara. This just sitting in zazen is itself the practice of nirvana.

I am a Buddhist priest and I am also my wife's husband and my children's father. When I am with my family, I am a father, so I play the role of a father. When I give a lecture, I am a teacher so I do my best to talk about Dōgen Zenji's teachings in an understandable way, though I don't know if I succeed. These roles are like clothing I put on in different situations, and I define who I am according to the role I am doing my best to fulfill at the time. But when I sit facing the wall,

I am neither a father nor a Buddhist priest. At that time I am nothing. I am empty. I am just who I am. This is liberation from my karmic life. This does not mean that my zazen practice is necessarily easy or painless, of course.

So Dōgen's statement "To be verified by all things is to let the body and mind of the self and the body and mind of others drop off" simply means that in zazen the separation between self and others falls away, is dropped off. Zazen reveals the total reality of interdependent origination. When we let go of thought, we settle our whole being into interpenetrating reality. This is how we are verified by all beings.

There is a trace of realization that cannot be grasped.

The original expression Dōgen Zenji uses for "cannot be grasped" is *kyukatsu*. *Kyu* means to be at rest, not working, not in action. *Katsu* means to stop. "Trace of realization" and *kyukatsu* are in contradiction to each other. *Kyukatsu* means to be traceless, so all trace of enlightenment is at rest and has stopped existing. "There is a trace of realization that cannot be grasped" means that there is a "traceless trace" of realization. Here Dōgen is saying both that "there is" and "there is not" a trace of realization. In other words, as soon as we grasp this realization, we miss it. Instead we must just keep practicing without grasping any trace of realization. If one thinks, "Now I am verified by all things," one has already missed realization. Just practice, then the trace is there and yet it isn't there. This trace of realization is like the trace of birds flying and fish swimming. It is there but we cannot see or grasp it. If we try to grasp it we miss it, but when we open the hand of thought, it is there.

Dōgen also wrote about this traceless trace in Shōbōgenzō Yuibutsu-yobutsu (Only Buddha Together with Buddha):

> Again, when a bird flies in the sky, beasts do not even dream of finding or following its trace. Since they do not know that there is such a thing, they cannot even imagine

this. However, a bird can see traces of hundreds and thousands of small birds having passed in flocks, or traces of so many lines of large birds having flown south or north. Those traces may be even more evident than the carriage tracks left on a road or the hoofprints of a horse seen in the grass. In this way, a bird sees birds' traces.

Buddhas are like this. You may wonder how many lifetimes buddhas have been practicing. Buddhas, large or small, although they are countless, all know their own traces; you never know a buddha's trace when you are not a buddha.

You may wonder why you do not know. The reason is that while buddhas see these traces with a buddha's eye, those who are not buddhas do not have a buddha's eye, and they just notice the Buddha's attributes.

All who do not know should search out the trace of the Buddha's path. If you find footprints, you should investigate whether they are the Buddha's. Upon being investigated, the Buddha's trace is known, and whether it is long or short, shallow or deep, is also known. To illuminate your trace is accomplished by studying the Buddha's trace. Accomplishing this is Buddha Dharma.[16]

And Zen Master Linji (Jap.: Rinzai) said:

If bodhisattvas, even those who have completed the ten stages of mind practice, were all to seek for the traces of such a follower of the Way, they could never find them. Therefore the heavenly beings rejoice, the gods of the earth stand guard with their legs, and the buddhas of the ten directions sing his praise. Why? Because this man of the Way who is now listening to the Dharma acts in a manner that leaves no traces.[17]

In Zen teachings such as this quote from Linji, "traces" refers to attachment to one's own actions, and "leaving no traces" is generally regarded as a positive thing. But Dōgen Zenji's usage of "trace" differs from the usage commonly found in Zen teachings. He did say, as Linji did, that one should simply keep practicing without self-attachment, leaving no visible traces. But according to Dōgen, the trace of practice that leaves no visible trace can be seen by other bodhisattvas who share our aspiration, just as the path of passing birds can later be seen by other birds of the same kind.

We endlessly express this ungraspable trace of realization.

In zazen and in all the activities of our daily lives, our practice is to try to express this traceless trace of realization and the reality of interdependent origination. This is the point of Dōgen Zenji's teaching in Genjōkōan. When we practice in order to express reality, we can see that practice and realization are one. Without practice there is no such thing as enlightenment, although we usually think practice is one thing and enlightenment is another. We usually approach practice as the means and enlightenment as the reward, but realization is only manifested within the process of practice, moment by moment.

# WHEN WE SEEK WE ARE FAR AWAY

P ERHAPS A BRIEF review of some of the sections we have already discussed will be helpful at this point. As you will recall, each of the first three sections of Genjōkōan presents an understanding of reality from a different view. In the first two, Dōgen Zenji discusses the Dharma from two different perspectives. When reality is viewed from the first perspective, there is practice, delusion and realization, life and death, buddhas and living beings. When viewed from a different Dharma perspective, within reality there are no delusion and no realization, no buddhas and no living beings, no birth and no death.

In section 3 Dōgen discusses the Buddha Way, the concrete life experience of practice. Within this concrete experience of life, there is a time of arising (birth) and a time of perishing (death), but these are not distinctly separate from each other. When there is arising, for example, there is just arising, and this arising is not in opposition to perishing. When we are alive, we are totally alive regardless of the condition of our lives. No matter how seriously sick one may be, for example, one's life is still 100 percent life. Life and death do exist, but there is no dichotomy between life and death in our actual experience. Since birth, we are each of us living 100 percent, but in a sense we are simultaneously dying as well; each moment we live we also are approaching the event we call death. Life is opposed to death only in the world of thought. In reality, life and death completely interpenetrate each other, although they never meet in our conceptual experiences. Within our thinking minds, life is desirable whereas death is undesirable, and a buddha is enlightened whereas deluded beings wander in samsara, continually being reborn through the six realms. Yet in truth, sentient beings existing as sentient beings is simply reality; sentient beings do not exist in opposition to buddhas, and delusion does not exist in opposition to enlightenment. So within the reality of the Buddha Way, buddhas are simply buddhas, sentient beings are simply sentient beings, birth is simply birth, and death is simply death. Dōgen continues this discussion of enlightenment and delusion, buddhas and sentient beings, in sections 4 through 7. In section 8, which we will discuss in the next chapter, he discusses arising and perishing, birth and death.

In section 4 Dōgen says,

> Conveying oneself toward all things to carry out practice-enlightenment is delusion. All things coming and carrying out practice-enlightenment through the self is realization.

This is Dōgen's definition of delusion and enlightenment. The section continues:

> Those who greatly realize delusion are buddhas. Those who are greatly deluded in realization are living beings.

This is Dōgen's definition of sentient beings and buddhas. For him, delusion and enlightenment exist only in the relationship between the self and all dharmas (i.e., all sentient and insentient beings). In other words, when we actively try to move toward things, measuring, evaluating, and relating with them based upon our limited ideas, we act in delusion. True enlightenment, in contrast to mere ideas about enlightenment, is manifest as all things carrying out practice-enlightenment through the self.

> (7) When one first seeks the Dharma, one strays far from the boundary of the Dharma. When the Dharma is correctly transmitted to the self, one is immediately an original person.
>
> If one riding in a boat watches the coast, one mistakenly perceives the coast as moving. If one watches the boat [in relation to the surface of the water], then one notices that the boat is moving. Similarly, when we perceive the body and mind in a confused way and grasp all things with a discriminating mind, we mistakenly think that the self-nature of the mind is permanent. When we intimately practice and return right here, it is clear that all things have no [fixed] self.

Here in section 7 Dōgen discusses delusion and enlightenment in relation to the search for truth within our practice.

> When one first seeks the Dharma, one strays far from the boundary of the Dharma.

In this first sentence he refers to our motivation in beginning practice. The search for truth, for the Dharma, or for a spiritual path almost always begins as the desire to solve some problem or answer some life question. We may feel a sense of lack in our lives. Some personal crisis may prompt us to question our way of life. Aging, sickness, the death of others, personal conflicts, loss of wealth or status, or poor judgment can cause us much suffering. One may come to feel that one's lifestyle is unhealthy, and the wish to abandon a materialistic approach to life may prompt a search for some spiritual path. I think most of us begin to practice in an attempt to fill an empty place in our lives or to recover from an unhealthy way of living. In Buddhism this aspiration to awaken is called *bodhicitta* (Jap.: *bodai-shin*), a term often translated into English as "bodhi-mind," "awakening mind," or "way-seeking mind."

But isn't this aspiration another kind of desire? Indeed it is. The object of desire differs from our usual ones, but it is still an object of desire. When a person tires of seeking material fulfillment, she may turn the focus of her life to seeking spiritual peace or relief. In Buddhism we call this the search for liberation, enlightenment, or nirvana. Without this desire to change our lives, there is no motivation for us to begin a spiritual search. Yet according to Dōgen, when we first seek the Dharma, we move far from the boundary of the Dharma. This is because our aspiration still involves a kind of hunting mind; we feel our lives are lacking something so we pursue what we think we are missing. The target is different, but the process happening in the mind is the same process that happens when we are hungry and searching for food, or when we are poor and searching for money. It is this attitude that Dōgen refers to in section 4 when he writes, "Conveying oneself toward all things to carry out practice-enlightenment is delusion." In other words, the more a person practices with an agenda or goal, the more she moves away from the boundary of the Dharma.

In the early part of their zazen practice, people often have some sort of special experience that makes them feel fantastic. When the good feelings wear off, they practice hard to re-create the special experience, but usually to no avail. Soon frustration and disappointment set in, and eventually fatigue and boredom may even cause the person to quit practicing. This is "conveying oneself toward all things," practice in which one tries to catch enlightenment with a hunting mind. According to Dōgen, this is delusion, far away from the boundary of Dharma.

What can we do in this situation? Because of our desire to attain enlightenment, liberation, or awakening, we practice. Without such desire it is very difficult to find the motivation to realize the truth; it is like trying to practice zazen after removing the very cushion upon which we sit. Often this problem becomes apparent after many years of diligent practice. When we discover that our very aspiration to attain enlightenment is itself an obstacle to realizing the Buddha Dharma, it seems we must fight to free ourselves from our own way-seeking minds. Can we really practice without the desire to practice? When we finally tire of fighting ourselves, all we can really do is just sit.

Sitting zazen without desire is shikantaza, or just sitting, the practice that Dōgen Zenji described as "all things coming and carrying out practice-enlightenment through the self." The subject of this sitting is no longer "I," because in shikantaza we let go of all thoughts, including concepts of "me" and the desire for enlightenment; we really just sit. As Dōgen wrote in Fukanzazengi (Universal Recommendations for Zazen), we even let go of the intention to become a buddha. In Shōbōgenzō Zuimonki, Dōgen writes of this attitude toward zazen:

> Sitting is the practice of the Buddha. Sitting itself is non-doing. It is nothing but the true form of the Self. Apart from sitting, there is nothing to seek as the Buddha Dharma.

And later in that text, he writes:

> Do not think that you learn the Buddha Dharma for the sake of some reward for practicing the Buddha Way. Just practice the Buddha Dharma for the sake of the Buddha Dharma. Even if you study a thousand sutras and ten thousand commentaries on them, or even if you have sat zazen until your cushion is worn out, it is impossible to attain the Way of the buddhas and ancestors if this attitude is lacking. Just cast your body and mind into the Buddha Dharma, practice alongside others without holding on to previous views, and you will be in accordance with the Way immediately.

When we just sit, when we let go of the desire for enlightenment and all other thoughts and emotions, all dharmas carry out practice through the body and mind. This zazen is not "my" personal attempt to attain something; rather, as Dōgen said, this sitting is actually the Buddha's practice (*Butsu-gyō*).

> When the Dharma is correctly transmitted to the self, the person is immediately an original person.

"Original person" is a translation of *honbun nin*, a reference to the self living in the network of interdependent origination. *Hon* can be literally translated as *original, true, root,* or *source, bun* means *part* or *portion,* and *nin* is *person.* So this word, which has the same meaning as "original face," refers to a person who is one with the original source that exists before karmic conditioning. This original person is actualized when we sit zazen and let go of thinking. When we open the hand of thought, in a sense we negate everything within our karmic consciousness, even the aspiration to become a Buddha. Thoughts well up even when we let go, but we just keep releasing them without grasping. We are also in a sense accepting anything that springs up from our consciousness; in zazen we neither negate nor affirm anything. We don't control the mind; we just sit. We really do nothing. We just keep sitting upright and waking up, breathing naturally, deeply, and quietly from the abdomen as we let go of thoughts. This is why Dōgen says, "zazen is non-doing"; *I* do nothing. Sitting is no longer *my* action anymore. The entire universe is sitting, using this body and mind; that's all. In so doing, we put our entire being on the ground of interdependent origination, on the ground of impermanence and lack of independent existence that is the original source. This zazen is itself dropping off body and mind.

> If one riding in a boat watches the coast, one mistakenly perceives the coast as moving. If one watches the boat [in relation to the surface of the water], then one notices that

the boat is moving. Similarly, when we perceive the body and mind in a confused way and grasp all things with a discriminating mind, we mistakenly think that the self-nature of the mind is permanent. When we intimately practice and return right here, it is clear that all things have no [fixed] self.

Here Dōgen uses the analogy of a person's perception of movement while riding in a boat with the shore in sight. To this person it may look as if the shore is moving when in fact it is the boat that moves. In the same way, it usually seems that things around us are changing and moving while we stay the same, and we try to find the underlying principle of this change so that we can control things. This has been the basic motivation for the development of human civilization. Modern society uses its accumulation of knowledge to develop technologies that manipulate the environment for the gratification of human beings. This view of technological development is a typical example of what Dōgen defined as delusion. When we think of scientific development without taking into consideration our own continually changing existence, our interconnectedness, and our mortality, our views are necessarily limited and inaccurate.

In the quest to make life more comfortable and luxurious, human beings have invented many things. We have killed many living beings, and we have destroyed a large part of the earth under the banner of the pursuit of happiness, prosperity, and progress. When we harm the earth and kill living beings, we are in fact harming and killing ourselves. This destruction results from an approach to life based on delusion. Yet when we intimately practice and return to "right here," we see that we are impermanent, lack independent existence, and are connected to all things. "Right here" is the reality of interdependent origination, the reality in which everything, including human beings, exists within the vast network of causes and conditions. When we become one with this reality, we see that we share the same life with all things, and we learn to relate to the earth and all living beings with care and compassion. Zazen is the practice in which we become intimate with this reality.

Dōgen Zenji used the analogy of riding in a boat in two other chapters of Shōbōgenzō: Zenki (Total Dynamic Function) and Tsuki (The Moon). These chapters, consecutive in the seventy-five-chapter version Shōbōgenzō, were written within a month of each other and are closely related. The Chinese characters for "moon" (in *manyōgana*, a phonetic method that used Chinese characters to show Japanese pronunciation) also mean "entire function." In Zenki, Dōgen writes:

> Life is, for example, similar to a person riding in a boat. In this boat, "I" use the sails, "I" am at the helm, and "I" pole the boat. Although "I" operate the boat, the boat is carrying "me" and there is no "I" other than the boat. "I" am on the boat and "I" make the boat into the boat. We should inquire and study this very moment. At this very moment, there is nothing other than the "world" of the boat. The sky, the water, and the coast, all become the "time" of the boat. This is not the same as the time of not riding in the boat. Therefore, "I" give birth to "life." "Life" makes "me" into "me." When we are riding in a boat, our body and mind, self and environment, are all "essential parts" of the boat. The whole great earth and the whole of empty space are essential parts of the boat. "I" as "life" and "life" as "I" are thus.

This passage explains the preceding paragraph of Genjōkōan. The self, the boat, the coast, the entire ocean, and the whole universe are all moving and functioning together. Dōgen Zenji says that there is no fixed self that does not move; all things are moving, and this entire world which is always moving is "me." In Tsuki, Dōgen quotes Engakukyō (The Sutra of Complete Enlightenment, a sutra used by many Zen masters but thought to have originated in China), in which the Buddha says:

Just as, for example, moving eyes are able to stir calm waters and still eyes are able to make fire seem to swirl, so too it is that [when] a cloud flies the moon moves, and [when] a boat sails the shore drifts.

Dōgen's comment on this quote reads:

The words now spoken by the Tathagata that "[when] a cloud flies the moon moves and [when] a boat sails the shore drifts" means that at the time of the cloud's flight, the moon is moving, and at the time of the boat's sailing, the shore is drifting. The point is that the moving together of the cloud and the moon, in the same step, at the same time, in the same way, is beyond beginning and ending and is beyond before and after. The moving together of the boat and the shore, in the same step, at the same time, in the same way, is beyond starting and stopping and is not a cycle. Similarly, when we learn human action, a person's action is beyond starting and stopping, and the action of stopping and starting is beyond the person. Do not think of human action in the relative terms of starting and stopping. The flying of a cloud, the moving of the moon, the sailing of a boat, and the drifting of a shore are all like this. Do not mistakenly think limited thoughts according to your small view. Do not forget the principle that the flying of a cloud is beyond east, west, north, and south, and the moving of the moon is ceaseless day and night, past and present. The sailing of a boat and the drifting of a shore, both being beyond the three times, are able to utilize the three times. For this reason, "Having arrived directly at the present, we are filled up and not hungry."[18]

Later in the text Dōgen writes:

Still, foolish people have understood that the unmoving moon appears to move because of the flying of a cloud, and that the motionless shore seems to drift because of the sailing of a boat. If it were as foolish people say, how could it be the teaching of the Tathagata? The fundamental principle of the Buddha Dharma is never the small thoughts of human beings and gods: although it is unthinkable, it is that there is only practice at every opportunity. Who could fail to sift through the boat and the shore over and over again? Who could fail to put on their eyes at once and look at the cloud and the moon?[19]

In a talk entitled "Living with Dōgen"[20] given at the Dōgen Zenji Conference at Stanford University a number of years ago, Professor Bielefeldt said that Dōgen is "not an easy person to live with." I really agree with him because it can seem very difficult to live according to Dōgen's principles; he is as strict, precise, and unwavering in his admonitions to us as he is critical of our mistakes, yet he sometimes seems to contradict himself in his teachings! For example, Dōgen uses analogies such as a boat and the coast, the moon and clouds, or the moon and a dewdrop, throughout Shōbōgenzō. If we study the "boat and coast analogy" only in Genjōkōan, we may think that perceiving the shore (others) as moving is delusion and seeing the boat (self) as moving is correct. But Dōgen says in Tsuki that thinking that the coast is stationary while only the boat is moving is also a mistaken view. In other words, he says that if we take only the view that he presents in Genjōkōan, we are mistaken. Did Dōgen present a mistaken view in Genjōkōan and then later criticize it in Tsuki? If so, why didn't he rewrite Genjōkōan? Why, in the year before he died, did Dōgen place Genjōkōan as the first chapter of Shōbōgenzō without correcting his "foolish" view? Did Dōgen use one analogy to say two different things in these writings because both views are correct?

There are many such contradictory statements in Dōgen's writings, and there is still much scholarly discussion of the true or final meaning of Dōgen's teachings. When we encounter a contradiction, should we simply choose one side or the other? Or is it possible to accept both views and try to find some common ground on which both make sense?

Because I am a practitioner rather than a scholar, I believe we should study the contradictions in Dōgen's teachings in relation to our own experience of contradictions we encounter in practice. I have not had the experience of riding in a boat on the ocean, as Dōgen did on his trip to China, but when I lived in Minneapolis I drove a car across some of the vast spaces of the Midwest. Based on that experience, I believe we sometimes think that mountains, rivers, buildings, and the vast earth are all moving around us. At other times, often during the course of the same trip, we look at a map and create concepts of mountains, rivers, buildings, and the vast earth. We conceptualize to measure how far we have driven and how far we need to travel to reach our destination. Then when we see the actual mountains and rivers and towns during our trip, we think they are stationary points on the map that we pass as we travel along the unmoving earth. In a sense both of these views are reality and both are illusion. The shapes of the mountains, for example, change before us as we drive, and if we believe the mountains are moving, we are deceived by our senses. If we believe we are moving and the mountains are stationary, we are deceived by our thoughts.

Dōgen also writes in Shōbōgenzō Shinjin-gakudō (Studying the Way with Body and Mind),

> Going-and-coming, with the whole Universe in the ten directions as two wings or three wings, it goes flying away and comes flying back, and with the whole Universe in the ten directions as three or five feet, it steps forward and it steps backward.[21]

Here Dōgen says that within life and death, within coming and going, we move using the entire universe as our wings and our feet;

the movement of everything in the universe is part of our flight. But what is actually moving? Is the coast moving or is the boat moving? Am I a part of the movement of the entire universe? Is the entire universe a part of my movement? Which view is right? Which is wrong? This movement of "two or three wings" and "three or five feet" is truly beyond the grasp or our intellect and imagination.

In Shōbōgenzō Maka Hannya Haramitsu, Dōgen presents a poem about a windbell that was written by his teacher, Tiantong Rujing.

> The whole body is like a mouth hanging in empty space.
> Not questioning the winds from east, west, south, or north,
> Equally with all of them, speaking of prajna:
> Ding-dong-a-ling ding-dong.

Is it the wind or is it the bell that makes the *ding-dong-a-ling ding-dong*? This is similar to asking whether it is the boat that is moving or the coast that is moving when we sail the ocean. These examples are reminiscent of the classic story by Huineng (the Sixth Ancestor of Zen) about two monks discussing a banner blowing in the wind. Is the wind moving or is the banner moving? Huineng said it was neither; it is the mind that is moving. Yet, returning to the windbell, Dōgen, in a talk recorded in the Eihei Kōroku (Dōgen's Extensive Record), a collection of his formal discourses and the second of his two major works, says:

> The sounding of the mind must be simply the sounding of emptiness. What we call the sounding of mind is actually the sounding of a bell. If the windbell does not sound, the mind does not sound. How can we call this the mind's sounds?

This is Dōgen's question for Huineng. Does the bell make the sound or does the wind make the sound? Does our mind make the sound? Is it the sound of emptiness? Does everything in the universe participate in making the sound? What is the sound? Who is the hearer? Does the sound exist even when no one hears it? Is the sound made by the vibration of the bell or by the vibration in the hearer's ear? Or is the sound something that happens in the brain? If a person's mind is occupied, he might not hear the sound of the windbell. Does this sound still exist? Such questions arise for us when we intellectually analyze the reality of interdependent origination.

In Shōbōgenzō Tsuki, Dōgen says that in reality both the mountains and the person move. When I move, the mountains also move, so we are moving simultaneously. Both self and mountains have no permanent, independent nature because they are moving and changing and are therefore empty. Everything in the universe is moving and changing, and this *total dynamic function* (including the seacoast, the boat, the mountains, the car, the wind, the windbell, and the hearer) is the reality of our lives. Our movement within this reality is expressed when we arouse bodhi-mind and continue to practice as we meet every situation in our lives. When we cling to certain views, theories, or concepts of reality, we become caught up in mere thinking and lose sight of true reality. Dōgen believed that we should not cling to any fixed view, so he wrote, "When one first seeks the Dharma, one strays far away from the boundary of the Dharma." In such statements he tries to show us the reality of life before it is processed by our thoughts. He always urges us to escape from the cave of thinking and to meet and live out reality as it comes to us.

Another point we have to understand is that Dōgen uses language to negate language and to go beyond its ordinary limits. For Dōgen, language and thinking can function as tools to help us to awaken to the reality beyond language and thinking. This is what Dōgen calls *dōtoku* (being able to speak). When we truly see reality, we can say that the mountain is moving, the boat is moving, or both are moving simultaneously; all of these are expressions of reality. We can say the wind makes the sound, the bell makes the sound, the mind makes the sound, or the entire universe makes the sound, and all of these can be expressions of reality as well. This is what Dōgen meant when he wrote, "When the Dharma is correctly transmitted to the self, the person is immediately an original person." In other words, an "original person" meets reality as it comes, without clinging to any particular fixed concept of reality.

In Dōgen's Fukanzazengi we read,

> Think of not thinking. How do you think of not-thinking?
> Beyond thinking. This is the essential art of zazen.

Here Dōgen is writing about zazen practice, and he is also using language in a manner that is itself beyond thinking. He uses his own thinking to "think of not-thinking" and writes: "think[ing] of not-thinking" is thinking of "how" (thusness). Dōgen is saying, in other words, that we must think of the reality that is unthinkable to release ourselves from the prison built by our karmic experiences and habitual ways of thinking. And this "think[ing] of not-thinking" is itself a function of the reality of life that is "beyond thinking."

> Similarly, when we perceive the body and mind in a confused way and grasp all things with a discriminating mind, we mistakenly think that the self-nature of the mind is permanent. When we intimately practice and return right here, it is clear that all things have no [fixed] self.

To think that the "self-nature of the mind is permanent" is to think there is some fixed, permanent entity that leaves the body at death to enter a new body. Dōgen compared this kind of thought to the "non-Buddhist" view of Senika in Bendōwa (Talk on the Wholehearted Practice of the Way) and Shōbōgenzō Sokushin Zebutsu (The Mind Is Itself Buddha). This theory, which Dōgen considered fallacious, states that there is some unchanging essence within the mind that is the permanent owner/operator of the body and mind. Here in section 7 Dōgen says that this is a confused view born of the discriminating mind, a view that distinguishes between the body (form) as impermanent and the mind (nature) as permanent. When we take a close look at ourselves, we see that we cannot make such distinctions between body and mind because all their elements (the five skandhas) are moving and changing, coming and going. This is true not only of ourselves but also of everything "outside" the self, such as mountains, rivers, and oceans; all things and beings are moving and changing, having no independent existence and no fixed self.

We have seen that in this section 7 Dōgen discusses the centrality of the relationship between self and all things in the search for the way, presenting this relationship first in terms of space. As we will see in the next chapter, he then discusses this relationship in terms of time.

(8) Firewood becomes ash. Ash cannot become firewood again. However, we should not view ash as after and firewood as before. We should know that firewood dwells in the dharma position of firewood and has its own before and after. Although before and after exist, past and future are cut off. Ash stays in the position of ash, with its own before and after. As firewood never becomes firewood again after it has burned to ash, there is no return to living after a person dies. However, in Buddha Dharma it is an unchanged tradition not to say that life becomes death. Therefore we call it no-arising. It is the established way of buddhas' turning the Dharma wheel not to say that death becomes life. Therefore, we call it no-perishing. Life is a position in time; death is also a position in time. This is like winter and spring. We don't think that winter becomes spring, and we don't say that spring becomes summer.

## LIFE AND DEATH AND "SELF"

IN THE PASSAGE above, Dōgen again discusses the "no fixed self" that he presents at the end of section 7—"When we intimately practice and return right here, it is clear that all things have no [fixed] self"—but now he considers it in terms of time. This "no fixed self" is the reality of life that includes arising and perishing, life and death, impermanence and lack of independent existence. In order to discuss this reality of "no fixed self" and arising and perishing, we must consider how things change within time. We usually think of ourselves as being born, living, and dying within a stream of time that flows from past to present to future. But Dōgen says that this is not the only way to view time. We will examine his views of time closely later, but first I would like to speak about the term "life and death" as it is used in this section.

"Life and death" is an English translation of the Japanese expression *shōji* (生死). As a verb, the Japanese word (生) means "to live" (*ikiru*) or "to be born" (*umareru*), and the second word (死) means "to die" or "to be dead." This expression can be translated into English as "birth and death" or "life and death." *Shōji* is the process of life in which we are born, live, and die. As a Buddhist term, the Japanese word *shōji* is used as the equivalent of the Sanskrit words *jatimarana* and *samsara*. *Jatimarana* refers both to the process of being born, living, and dying, and also to the four kinds of suffering, or *duhkha* (birth, aging, sickness, and death).

In Buddhist philosophy, the process of birth and death is separated into two types. One type is the birth, life, and death of ordinary living beings that transmigrate within the six realms in the three worlds of desire, form, and formlessness. These beings live being pulled by karma, and their kind of life and death is called *bundan-shōji* in Japanese, or "separating life and death." Another type of life and death refers to the practice of bodhisattvas that have been released from the karma produced by the three poisonous minds. Though they have been freed from transmigration, they keep returning to the three worlds in order to save beings from suffering. Life after life they work diligently, eventually passing through each of the fifty-two bodhisattva stages that culminate in buddhahood. Rather than karma, this process of life and death is moved by the bodhisattva vow and is referred to as *henyaku-shōji*, which means "transforming life and death."

*Ichigo-shōji* and *setsuna-shōji* are two other Buddhist terms that also refer to the process of being born, living, and dying. *Ichigo-shōji* can be translated as "life and death as one period," and this refers to the period of living between birth and death as we usually understand it. *Setsuna-shōji* means "moment by moment life and death." *Setsuna* is a very brief increment of time (the merest fraction of a second), and *setsuna-shōji* refers to the process of the body and mind arising (being born) and perishing (dying) over and over again, moment by moment.

*Shōji* is also used as a translation of the Sanskrit word *samsara*. Samsara, you will recall, refers to the cycle of suffering in which beings transmigrate through the six realms of hell, hungry ghosts, animals, asuras, human beings, and heavenly beings. It is important to remember that the common Buddhist usage of "life and death" refers to the cycle of samsara, the opposite of nirvana. When Dōgen says in Shōbōgenzō Shōji (Life and Death) that "life and death is Buddha's Life," he means our life in samsara is nothing other than nirvana. Unless we understand this point, we cannot fully appreciate the power of Dōgen's words.

The two above meanings of *shōji* are often used interchangeably, since the process of birth, living, and dying is actually a part of the process of transmigration within samsara. But in this section of Genjōkōan, Dōgen specifically uses the expression *shōji* in referring to the process of arising, dwelling, and perishing that applies to all sentient and insentient beings.

As part of this process, each person is born at a certain time in the past. In my case, I was born on June 22, 1948. At that time my body was tiny, but since then my body and mind have been constantly changing. The baby Shohaku became a boy, the boy became a teenager, the teenager became a young adult, and the young adult became the middle-aged person that I am now. If I am lucky, the middle-aged person will become an old person, but if that is so, that old person will eventually die and disappear.

From birth until death we are constantly changing and experiencing variations in our conditions. Yet in our common way of thinking, we say that over sixty years ago Shohaku was that little baby, and years from now this middle-aged person will still be the same Shohaku. Over thirty years ago I was a young, newly ordained monk with lots of energy and many problems, but now my energy is decreasing and my problems are very different. When I was twenty, I never imagined that one day I would live in the United States and speak English. Since coming to the United States, I have been much influenced by American culture, so I think differently than before I came. But we commonly understand that I was the same person when I was a baby, when I was a teenager, and when I was in my twenties, thirties, forties, and fifties. Most of us believe this, but is it really true?

## BUDDHA'S TEACHING OF NO-SELF

If we imagine it is somehow true that one remains the same person throughout time, then we must posit something within us that remains unchanged through the process of change. This entity, which is not the baby, teenager, young man, middle-aged man, or older man, changes only in outer appearance with the flow of time. According to this view, only the appearance of the body and mind change, like articles of clothing we wear on different occasions; although a person's appearance changes, she keeps essentially the same body and mind from birth until death. This is an idea that people in India believed at the time of the Buddha. The unchanging inner entity was called *atman*, and it was believed to transmigrate through many different conditions, being pulled by good and bad karma. They believed that although *atman* is pure, it is imprisoned in a body that is impure and is therefore the source of delusive desires.

According to atman theory, the changing body and mind are like a car, and atman is like the owner and operator of the car. *Abhidharma-kosa*, written by the famous Indian Buddhist philosopher Vasuban-dhu, contains the most clear and precise definition of atman I have found. In the process of refuting the existence of atman, Vasubandhu defines it as a single, permanent owner/operator of what we call the body and mind, the union of the five aggregates. This owner (atman) of the car (the five aggregates) keeps and drives the car as long as it keeps running, but when the car wears out, the owner gives it up and buys a new one. According to this theory, when the body and mind die, the owner (atman) leaves and is born into a new body and mind. This is the basic idea of the transmigration of the atman, a process that happens over and over, life after life. In the Buddha's day, conventional Indian ideology taught that a person is reborn into one of the six realms of samsara, depending upon whether the individual generates good or bad karma during his or her lifetime. If the person accumulates good karma through good actions, the person will be born with the body and mind of a heavenly being, living in favorable circumstances. If the person accumulates bad karma through bad actions, the person is born into difficult circumstances, with an inferior body and mind, for example. This theory of karma was widely believed in Indian society at the time of the Buddha, and the atman theory existed as one interpretation of the more general belief in karmic transmigration.

The Buddha's teaching on this subject was called *an*atman, or no-atman ("no soul," "no essential existence," or "no self"). He opposed the basic idea of atman as a permanent entity that transmigrates in samsara. The Buddha taught that the world is comprised solely of five aggregates (form/materiality, sensations, perception, mental formations, and consciousness) that are themselves neither substantial nor permanent. He taught that these aggregates are the sole constituents of the human body and mind, and that there is no separate, permanent owner/operator that is the essence of a human being. The Buddha said that only the five aggregates exist—nothing else.

The Buddha negated the theory of atman, but he did not negate the belief in transmigration since it was the basis of Indian social morality during his time. But if nothing but the five aggregates exists, what is it that transmigrates? This is a very natural question. The Buddha emphasized the principle of causality, the teaching of cause and result. This teaching says that a person's negative actions cause painful effects, while positive actions create pleasurable effects. But if there is no atman, who is it that performs the action and who is it that receives the result? The Buddha said that the self must receive the result of its own karmic actions. We might be moved to ask, then, what is this self if it is not atman? Indeed, this is a common question asked about the Buddha's teachings, and though many Buddhist philosophers have tried to answer this question logically, no one has been able to provide an adequate answer. Yet to this day almost all Buddhist traditions teach both the theory of anatman and the belief in transmigration.

## DŌGEN AND NO-SELF

In Bendōwa (Talk on the Wholehearted Practice of the Way) and also in chapters of Shōbōgenzō such as Sokushin Zebutsu (Mind Is Itself Buddha) and Busshō (Buddha nature), Dōgen clearly negates the theory of atman. In his response to question 10 in Bendōwa, for example, Dōgen writes:

> The idea you have just mentioned is not Buddha Dharma at all, but the fallacious view of Senika.[22]
> This fallacy says that there is a spiritual intelligence in one's body which discriminates love and hatred or right and wrong as soon as it encounters phenomena, and has the capacity to distinguish all such things as pain and

itching or suffering and pleasure. Furthermore, when this body perishes, the spirit-nature escapes and is born elsewhere. Therefore, although it seems to expire here, since [the spirit-nature] is born elsewhere, it is said to be permanent, never perishing. Such is this fallacious doctrine.

However, to learn this theory and suppose it is Buddha Dharma is more stupid than grasping a tile or a pebble and thinking it is a golden treasure. Nothing can compare to the shamefulness of this idiocy. National Teacher Echū (Huizhong) of Tang China strictly admonished [against this mistake]. So, now isn't it ridiculous to consider that the erroneous view of mind being permanent and material form being impermanent is the same as the Wondrous Dharma of the buddhas, and to think that you become free from life and death when actually you are arousing the fundamental cause of life and death? This indeed is most pitiful. Just realize that this is a mistaken view. You should give no ear to it.[23]

Some people living in Dōgen's time thought the mind was permanent and the body impermanent. The mind was considered to be like the pure, permanent atman, and the body was considered to be impure and the source of delusive desire. These people called the mind *shinshō*, or mind-nature, and they called the body *shinsō*, or bodily form. This mind-nature was often used as a synonym for Buddha nature, and this misunderstanding of the Buddha's teaching prompted Dōgen's negation of the idea of *kenshō*, or "seeing the nature."

*Kenshō* is a term often used in the Rinzai Zen tradition, where it refers to an enlightenment experience that usually happens as a result of kōan practice. Zen masters began using this expression in China's Tang dynasty. The term appears many times, for example, in the Platform Sutra of the Sixth Ancestor, Huineng. Dōgen, however, did not like this word. In Shōbōgenzō Shizenbiku (The Bhikshu in the Fourth Dhyana) he writes:

The essence of the Buddha Dharma is never seeing the nature [*kenshō*]. Which of the twenty-eight ancestors of India and the seven buddhas [in the past] said that the Buddha Dharma is simply seeing the nature? Although the term seeing the nature [*kenshō*] appears in the Platform Sutra of the Sixth Ancestor, that text is a forgery. It is not the writing of a person who received the transmission of the Dharma treasury. It is not Caoxi's[24] words. Any descendants of the buddhas and ancestors never trust and use the text at all.

And yet I am quite sure, based on my studies, that Dōgen did believe in the *henyaku-shōji* (transforming life and death) of the bodhisattva. In Shōbōgenzō Sanjigō (Karma in the Three Times) and Jinshin-inga (Deeply Believing in Cause and Result), for example, Dōgen emphasized having faith in the principle of cause and result beyond the present lifetime. And in Shōbōgenzō Dōshin (Way Mind), Dōgen encourages us to chant "I take refuge in the Buddha" life after life until reaching buddhahood. He also instructs us in Dōshin to ceaselessly chant "I take refuge in the Buddha, the Dharma, and the Sangha" during *chūu* (*antara-bhava*), the usually forty-nine-day intermediate period that according to classical Buddhist teaching exists between the end of one life and rebirth into the next.

As you can see, Dōgen's teaching of no-self and his view of rebirth seem to contradict each other. If there is no permanent self, or atman, and our bodies and minds are transitory, what entity is it that can chant "I take refuge in Buddha" after death? In any case, if this is a contradiction, Buddhism has always held it.

People often ask me, "What is the Sōtō Zen view of rebirth?" This is a difficult question because Dōgen Zenji, I believe, advocates "not knowing" in this case. Rather than offering us a consistent view on rebirth, he teaches that we should let go of our limiting concepts and beliefs and simply practice right here, right now. When we do so, we naturally and responsibly care for the future as our practice in the present. I also believe this is the reason Shakyamuni Buddha did not deny transmigration, although he refuted the existence of the atman. His teaching of anatman shows us that the truth of emptiness applies even to our own bodies and minds, allowing us freedom from the reification of ourselves and our views, while cause and effect as the underlying principle for transmigration illustrates that we must nonetheless take responsibility for our activities of body, speech, and mind. That the Buddha offered both of these seemingly contradictory teachings indicates, I think, that we must embrace the principles supporting both while attaching to neither.

Personally, I don't believe in literal rebirth, yet I don't deny its existence either. I have no basis for either believing in or denying literal rebirth; the only thing I can say about it with surety is "I don't know." For me, the important point is to practice in this lifetime as the Buddha taught in *Dhammapada*:

> Refrain from anything bad and practice everything good. Purify your mind. This is the teaching of the seven Buddhas.

If rebirth exists, that is all right: I will simply try to continue practicing everything good and refrain from everything bad through my next life. If there is no rebirth, I will have nothing to do after my death and I will have no need to consider my practice. This was my view of rebirth for most of my life as a Buddhist.

When I turned fifty, however, I began to think about rebirth differently, and I wish to speak about that briefly because I believe it may illustrate a key reason for the development of the bodhisattva's *henyaku-shōji* (transforming life and death) as a principle of Mahayana Buddhism. As I enter the latter period of my life, I now find that I do hope I will live another life after this one, since this life has been too short to do all I need to in practicing the Buddha Way. For example, for many years I have been working on the translation of Zen Buddhist texts from Japanese to English. Yet I know that my life will be too short to even fully understand the true, deep meaning of the teachings of Shakyamuni Buddha, Dōgen, and other great teachers, let alone translate them into English. So I actually do hope to be reborn as a Buddhist so I can continue the work I am now doing. I think this wish has arisen because the aging process has shown me my limitations, and I suspect that the Mahayana belief in the bodhisattva's *henyaku-shōji* originated in this type of awakening to the limitations of individual life.

## LIFE, DEATH, AND "TIME"

This section of Genjōkōan is one of the source writings that explain Dōgen's idea that time and being are identified with each other. This is stated very clearly in one of his later writings, Shōbōgenzō Uji (Being Time): "The essential point is: every being in the entire world is each time an [independent] time, even as it makes a continuous series. Inasmuch as they are being-time, they are my being-time."[25]

> Firewood becomes ash. Ash cannot become firewood again. However, we should not view ash as after and firewood as before. We should know that firewood dwells in the dharma position of firewood and has its own before and after. Although before and after exist, past and future are cut off. Ash stays in the position of ash, with its own before and after.

Here Dōgen compares life and death to firewood and ash. Seen from our usual view, an acorn sprouts and grows gradually over a long period of time until it becomes a big tree. When firewood is needed, the tree is cut down, split into pieces, and the pieces are stacked. When the pieces are dry, we call them firewood, and when we burn the firewood, it becomes ash. We think of human life and death in the same way: "I was a baby, I grew up for about twenty years, and then I stopped growing. I will live as an adult for some time and then continue to get older and older until I finally die."

Commonly, we think of time as a stream that flows like a river from the beginningless past to the endless future. We believe that individuals are born and appear in the stream and later die and disappear from the stream. We think, "The stream of time has been flowing before my birth and it will continue to flow after my death." This is the way usually we think about time, history, and our own lives. Yet this is not the true nature of life and death.

The true nature and actual experience of time, life, and death is the subject of Dōgen's analysis of firewood and ash. With this discussion he says that time is being and being is time. According to Dōgen, a tree, firewood, ash, and all things in existence have their own time, or dharma position (*hōi*), and at each dharma position the being has its own past and future. For example, when a tree is at the dharma position of a tree, it has its own past as a former seed and its own future as firewood. When firewood is at the dharma position of firewood, it has its own past as a tree and its own future as ash. When ash is at the dharma position of ash, it has its own past as firewood and its own future as something else. If the ash is scattered on a mountain, for example, it will become part of the mountain and help other beings grow.

The dharma positions of tree, firewood, and ash are all independent of one another, and when we use this as an analogy for birth, living, and dying, each dharma position seems to have a length of time. But in reality, each stage or dharma position of living and dying can only be experienced in the present moment, and the present moment does not have any length. If the present moment did have a length, no matter how short it were, we could divide it into a half that was already in the past and a half still in the future. When I say the word "now," as I pronounce "*n-*," the "*-ow*" is still in the future, and as I pronounce "*-ow*," "n-" is already in the past. So the present moment has no length, a length of zero. This is to say, the present moment is *empty*. Whenever we think of any "period of time," including the immediate present, it is only the past and the future that actually exist in any moment. The present moment is actually just a "geometrical line" without any width that separates past and future. Isn't this strange? Indeed it is.

The present moment is the only reality we experience because the past is already gone and the future has not yet come. Yet there is nothing, no actual unit of time, we can say constitutes the present moment; the present moment does not exist and therefore *time itself* does not really exist. Still, from this present moment which is empty and does not exist, the entire past and the entire future are reflected. This present moment, which has no length, is the only true reality of life as we experience it. And since everything is always changing, at each present moment everything arises and perishes over and over again; each moment everything is new and fresh.

This present moment is the only true reality because the past has already gone and the future has not yet come. We can only encounter the past in this present moment as sweet, bitter, or neutral memories, or through referring to historical accounts and other records. The future exists for us in this moment as our plans, desires, projections, and hopes. But these experiences of past and future exist simply as products of the mind within this present moment; the actual past no longer exists and the actual future has not yet come. Reality unfolds only within this present moment, and yet our mind cannot grasp this present moment. This is so because even to think a very simple thought we need some length of time, yet the present moment has no length; the present moment is the only actual moment, the only actual immediate experience, and it cannot be grasped by the mind. Yet we each think of the present moment as having some length of time, and we place it in the midst of our own story, a story in which we are the hero or heroine.

There is always some gap between the actual experience of the present moment and our thoughts about the present moment and how we define it; the present moment is ungraspable even though it is the only actual moment of experience. Yet when we open the hand of thought in zazen, we let go of our story and sit right here, right now, in the present moment.

A seed is in the dharma position of a seed and has its own past and future. Since a seed has the potential for life, it has the power to negate[26] its current dharma position when it encounters appropriate conditions for growth such as moisture, correct temperature, sunlight, and so on. When it sprouts it becomes something other than a seed. In other words, when a seed fully functions as a seed according to its own life force, it negates itself by becoming something else. The nature of a seed is that it is not bound to being a seed. Human life is the same as this. When a baby fully expresses its life force, for example, it negates babyhood and become a boy or a girl; that is the functional expression of the life force as a baby. Everything has this life force which negates itself and changes into something else. This is the meaning of the statement that everything is empty of a permanent self-nature.

The baby Shohaku negated itself and became the boy Shohaku, and the boy Shohaku negated itself, becoming the teenage Shohaku. Shohaku the teenager negated itself and became the adult Shohaku. Throughout this process of negation there is some quality of continuation, but the baby Shohaku was not the boy Shohaku and the boy Shohaku was not the teenage Shohaku. Is there something that does not change within this constant change? According to the Buddha's teachings, there is not. All things are simply collections of the five aggregates in a position of time. Yet the baby Shohaku did not become a bird, a dog, or some other person besides Shohaku; therefore there is a quality of continuity within change. Still, there is no Shohaku that exists as a fixed self. This is very strange, isn't it? This reality is very difficult for us to grasp. This is why we refer to reality as the "wondrous dharma" (*myōhō*), as in the full title of the Lotus Sutra (The Sutra of the Wondrous Dharma Like a Lotus Flower).

When we see this reality, we see that our lives are always new and fresh, even though we continue to have karma, or influences from immediate or more distant past experiences (such as those we had when we were babies or children). For example, a Japanese Sōtō Zen priest named Reverend Dōyū Ozawa lost both of his legs when he was a young soldier in World War II. When he returned from the war, he went through many difficulties in dealing with the loss of his legs. After much struggle, he decided to view himself in each moment as having just been born as he was at that time, without legs. In that way he could accept the reality of his life without legs in each present moment. After this change in view he was always smiling and he was able to live a rich, positive life. In fact, with Uchiyama Rōshi's encouragement, Rev. Ozawa wrote a book about his experiences that became a bestseller the year it was published.

This present moment is the only true reality. We all have karma from the past that influences us through memories, habits, and experiences, but the past has already gone. We hold the future as the container of our hopes, wishes, vows, ambitions, and goals, but the future has not yet come. Then how can we live fully in this moment? If we are caught up in the past, we are afraid to change. If we put too much emphasis on what will come, this moment becomes merely a means to reach the future and our lives become meaningless if we do not reach our goals.

Dōgen's teachings about time help us see the importance of living fully in the present, right now and right here. He says that we can accept our present condition and work to change conditions for the future as a practice in the present moment. This is the meaning of "Although there is before and after, past and future are cut off," which echoes the message of the first three sentences of Genjōkōan. In those lines, we saw earlier, Dōgen says that there is life and death, enlightenment and delusion, buddhas and living beings, and yet from another perspective, none of these things exist. Then he tells us how we should practice in each moment with life and death, living beings and buddhas, delusion and enlightenment, within the reality that both perspectives are the truth of our lives.

When we see practice from the perspective of the first sentence of Genjōkōan, we see ourselves in the dharma position of deluded human beings, and we see the dharma position of an enlightened buddha as being in the future. We practice as if we are beginning at some point and walking toward a goal, creating a story that our path contains different steps we must attain on the way to our destination. On this path we try to measure how far we have walked and how much farther we need to travel. Yet in the second sentence of Genjō-kōan, Dōgen says that since there are no such dichotomies as delusion and enlightenment, living beings and buddhas, and life and death, the process of attaining goals does not exist; we cannot separate reality or practice into the categories of deluded beings or enlightened bud-dhas because only this ungraspable, moment-by-moment experience is true reality. And since we are always within this reality that can-not be grasped, since we cannot be somewhere other than this present moment, Dōgen Zenji tells us in the third sentence of Genjōkōan that we can only truly practice in the present. He says our practice is to be fully present, right now and right here, whether we are at the dharma position of deluded beings or at the dharma position of enlightened buddhas.

> However, in Buddha Dharma it is an unchanged tradition not to say that life becomes death. Therefore we call it no-arising. It is the established way of buddhas' turning the Dharma wheel not to say that death becomes life. There-fore, we call it no-perishing. Life is a position in time; death is also a position in time. This is like winter and spring. We don't think that winter becomes spring, and we don't say that spring becomes summer.

In Shōbōgenzō Shōji (Life and Death), Dōgen says exactly the same thing as this part of Genjōkōan:

> It is a mistake to think that life turns into death. Life is a position at one time with its own before and after.

Consequently, in the Buddha Dharma it is said that life is itself no-arising. Death is a position at one time with its own before and after. Consequently, it is said that death is itself no-perishing. In life there is nothing other than life. In death, there is nothing other than death. Therefore, when life comes, just live. And when death comes, just die. Neither avoid them nor desire them.

Yet so often we find this advice difficult to put into practice. We usually feel we must pursue things we desire such as life, enlightenment, or Buddha, and we feel we must avoid things we don't like such as death, delusion, or being a regular living being. The primary motivations of our lives are usually greed and hatred, desire and aversion. Sometimes we are successful in satisfying our preferences, and we feel like heavenly beings; sometimes we fail, and we feel as miserable as hell dwellers. This is the cycle of samsara manifesting in our present lives.

In Shōbōgenzō Zenki (Total Dynamic Function), Dōgen says:

> The life of this present moment is within this functioning; this functioning is within the life of this present moment. Life is not coming, life is not going, life is not appearing, life is not becoming. And yet, life is the manifestation of the total function, and death is the manifestation of the total function. We should know that among the numberless dharmas in the self, there is life and there is death.

In 1975 Uchiyama Rōshi retired from Antaiji when he was sixty-three years old. He retired at that young age because physically he was very weak. He said that after retirement his practice was facing his own life and death. When he was around seventy years old, he published a collection of poems about life and death. Here are a few of those poems:

## LIFE AND DEATH

Water isn't formed by being ladled into a bucket
Simply the water of the whole Universe has been ladled
    into a bucket
The water does not disappear because it has been scattered
    over the ground
It is only that the water of the whole Universe has been
    emptied into the whole Universe
Life is not born because a person is born
The life of the whole Universe has been ladled into the
    hardened "idea" called "I"
Life does not disappear because a person dies
Simply, the life of the whole Universe has been poured out
    of this hardened "idea" of "I" back into the Universe


## JUST LIVE, JUST DIE

The Reality prior to the division into two
Thinking it to be so, or not thinking it to be so
Believing it to be so, or not believing it to be so
Existence-nonexistence, life-death
Truth-falsehood, delusion-enlightenment
Self-others, happiness-unhappiness
We live and die within the profundity of Reality
Whatever we encounter is buddha-life
This present Reality is buddha-life
Just living, just dying—within no life or death


## SAMADHI OF THE TREASURY OF THE RADIANT LIGHT

Though poor, never poor
Though sick, never sick

Though aging, never aging
Though dying, never dying
Reality prior to division—
Herein lies unlimited depth

I think these poems are additional clear expressions of the same reality that Dōgen called "life and death within no life and death."

(9) When a person attains realization, it is like the moon's reflection in water. The moon never becomes wet; the water is never disturbed. Although the moon is a vast and great light, it is reflected in a drop of water. The whole moon and even the whole sky are reflected in a drop of dew on a blade of grass. Realization does not destroy the person, as the moon does not make a hole in the water. The person does not obstruct realization, as a drop of dew does not obstruct the moon in the sky. The depth is the same as the height. [To investigate the significance of] the length and brevity of time, we should consider whether the water is great or small, and understand the size of the moon in the sky.

IN THIS SECTION Dōgen Zenji discusses realization. We cannot be sure of the exact meaning of the word translated here as "realization" because it appears phonetically as the Japanese word *satori*: there are three Chinese words, each possessing differing subtleties in meaning, that are pronounced *satori* in Japanese, and each would have a different set of Chinese characters. Dōgen, however, does not use a Chinese character for this word but a *hiragana* character instead. *Hiragana* and *katakana* are the two systems used in the Japanese phonetic alphabet.

The three Chinese characters read as *satori* in Japanese are: *kaku* (覚), *go* (悟), and *shō* (証). One may see any one of these words translated as "enlightenment," but the words "awakening" and "realization," among others, are also used by English translators. The meaning of these words are sometimes confused because any one of them may appear simply as "satori" in Japanese syllabic writing.

The literal meaning of *kaku* (覚) is "awakening" or "to wake up." The opposite of *kaku* is *mu* (夢), "dream," "dreaming," or "sleeping." The connotation here is that when we are asleep and dreaming we don't see reality clearly, but when we wake up we begin to see reality as it is. This is the meaning of *kaku*, and I usually translate this word as "awakening."

*Go* (悟) indicates that we clearly know our destination and how to reach it. The left part of the kanji means "mind" and the right part (吾) means "self," indicating that we are mindful, truly in tune with what is before us. *Mei* (迷), the opposite of *go*, indicates that one is lost, not knowing which way to turn. Part of the word *mei* resembles an intersection (米), perhaps a place where one is lost and hesitating, unsure of which road to take. In contrast, *go* means that we can act without hesitation, that we see our destination clearly and know what must be done to get to it. Due to the more intellectual nature of *go*, I translate it as "realization": one realizes where one needs to go.

The literal meaning of *shō* (証) is "proof," "evidence," or as I usually translate it, "verification." In terms of Buddhist practice, *shō* is usually thought of as the result of practice. The compound word *shushō* (修証), for example, is an abbreviation of *mon shi shu shō* (聞思修証). *Mon* (聞) is "to hear," *shi* (思) is "to think," *shu* (修) is "practice," and *shō* (証) is "verification." When we listen to a Dharma talk, we may think about its contents and try to understand them, for instance. If we consider the teachings meaningful, we adopt them as part of our practice, and as a result of our experience we may come to know directly that the teachings are true. So *shō*, the result of *shu* (practice), is proof or evidence acquired from direct experience that something is true.

As noted, it is not clear which of these Chinese characters Dōgen intended in section 9. Perhaps he used hiragana in this case in order to allow *satori* to be interpreted with any or all three of the above meanings.

## THE MOON IN WATER AS EMPTINESS, AND AS THE BODY

> When a person attains realization, it is like the moon's reflection in water. The moon never becomes wet; the water is never disturbed.

The image of the moon reflected in water has been used as a symbol of emptiness in many Buddhist scriptures since Buddhism began in India. Here is an example from the Vimalakirti Sutra in which the layman Vimalakirti is speaking to Upali, one of the Buddha's disciples:

> Reverend Upali, all things are without production, destruction, and duration, like magical illusions, clouds, and lightning; all things are evanescent, not remaining even for an instant; all things are like dreams, hallucinations, and unreal vision; all things are like the reflection of the moon in water and like a mirror image; they are born of mental construction.[27]

Here Vimalakirti speaks of the moon in water as a simile representing the emptiness of all things. He is saying that all things lack independent existence, are ungraspable and transitory, and neither arise nor perish.

The image of the moon in water can also evoke the body. An example of an ancient Chinese Zen master using that image in this way is found in *Lengga-shizi-ji* (Jap.: *Ryōga-shijiki*; The Record of Teachers and Disciples of the Ryoga Tradition), a history of the northern school of Chinese Zen written in the early eighth century. In this account the Zen master Daoxin (Jap.: Dōshin, 580–651, the Fourth Ancestor of Chinese Zen), after giving instructions for the practice of zazen, says:

> Day and night, whether walking, standing still, sitting, or lying down, if you continuously contemplate things in this way you will know that your own body is like the moon in water, a reflection in a mirror, heat waves on a hot day, or an echo in an empty valley. You cannot say it has being (*u*) because even if you try to catch it you cannot see its substance. You also cannot say [it has no being] (*mu*) because it is clearly in front of your eyes.

In Mahayana Buddhism and in the Chinese Zen tradition, all dharmas (all things) and the human body are said to be like the moon in water. In these traditions, the human body is often compared to the moon in water, as in the above example from *Lengga-shizi-ji*. Teachers presented such illustrations to show that the self is empty of both being and nonbeing. It is clear that Dōgen Zenji presents the symbolism of the moon in water in the same tradition, using it as a simile for emptiness and prajna paramita.

Dōgen Zenji devoted an entire chapter of Shōbōgenzō, Tsuki (Moon), to discussing the symbolic image of the moon as it is used in Buddhist teachings. Instead of using the usual Chinese character, 月, for "moon," he uses the *manyōgana* characters, 都機.[28] Although Dōgen used the Chinese characters for "moon" (都機) in Tsuki to indicate the phonetic pronunciation of the word in Japanese, these characters also have the meaning "total function" in Chinese, the same meaning as the expression *zenki* (全機). Dōgen is obviously using word-play here. He uses the well-known image of the moon in water found in traditional scriptures such as the Vimalakirti Sutra and the *Lengga-shizi-ji*, but he uses the image as more than just a metaphor for emptiness. In choosing the characters he did, Dōgen uses the image of the moon as a symbol of the dynamic movement of the network of interdependent origination. This is *zenki*, the "total function" that includes the self and all dharmas.

In Shōbōgenzō Tsuki, Dōgen Zenji presents several selections from Chinese Zen ancestors and Buddhist sutras that use the image of the moon in water. In the very beginning of Tsuki, for example, he quotes Konkōmyōkyō (Sutra of Golden Radiance):

> Shakyamuni Buddha says,
> "The true Dharma Body of the Buddha
> Is like empty space.
> Responding to things, it manifests its form.
> It is like the moon in water."

Dōgen's comment on this saying is as follows:

> The thusness of "like the moon in water" is water-moon.
> It is water-thus, moon-thus, thus-within, within-thus.
> "Thus" does not mean "to be like." Thusness is thisness.[29]

In this commentary, Dōgen uses a word from the text in an unconventional yet deeply meaningful way. The common meaning of the Chinese word *nyo* (如) is "to be like," "such as," "as if," or "to be equal to." In Chinese, the final sentence from the quote above (如水中月) can be read as "It is like the moon in water." This is an accurate translation, but Dōgen reads the *nyo* (如) in this sentence as the *nyo* in *shinnyo* (真如). *Shinnyo* is a Chinese translation of the Sanskrit word *tathata* which is translated into English as "thusness," "suchness," "as-it-is-ness," or simply "true reality." "Thisness" (是, *ze*) means "concrete," "definite," or "each and every thing."

## THE MOON IN WATER AS THE MIDDLE WAY

Dōgen also uses the Chinese word *chū* (中) in the above sentences in a way that has deep significance. *Chu*, meaning "within," can also mean "middle," as in Middle Way, a very important term in the philosophy of Nagarjuna, the great Mahayana Buddhist teacher and philosopher. The Tendai teachings that the young Dōgen studied at Mt. Hiei in Japan are founded upon Nagarjuna's philosophy of the Middle Way. So it is important to understand something about Nagarjuna's philosophy when studying Dōgen's teachings, and this especially applies to the above section of Tsuki.

In his Mulamadhyamakakarika, Nagarjuna discusses the two truths, absolute truth and conventional truth, as the basis of his philosophy. Here is an excerpt:

> The teaching of the Dharma by the various Buddhas is based on the two truths, namely, the relative (worldly) truth and the absolute (supreme) truth.
>
> Those who do not know the distinction between the two truths cannot understand the profound nature of the Buddha's teaching.
>
> Without relying on everyday common practices [i.e., relative truths], the absolute truth cannot be expressed. Without approaching the absolute truth, nirvana cannot be attained. . . .
>
> We declare that whatever is relational origination is sunyata. It is a provisional name (i.e., thought construction) for the mutuality (of being) and, indeed, it is the middle path.[30]

There are several terms used within this piece that are important to an understanding of Nagarjuna's philosophy. "Relational origination" is a translation of the Sanskrit word *pratitya-samutpada* (Pali: *paticca-samuppada*). This word is often translated as "interdependent origination," and it refers to the reality of our lives within the vast network of all beings. *Sunyata*, often translated as "emptiness," is another word for this reality of our lives that is beyond any wording, conceptualization, or categorization. It is a "provisional name" for absolute truth.

"Conventional truth" refers to words, concepts, and categories that we use in order to try to grasp this ungraspable reality. Seeing reality from both sides, without clinging to either, is the middle path.

Tiantai Zhiyi (Jap.: Tendai Chigi, 538–97) the great master of the Chinese Tendai school, used Nagarjuna's philosophy of the Middle Way to formulate his teaching of the three truths, one of the essential teachings of that school. The three truths consist of the Truth of Emptiness (空諦), the Truth of the Expedient (仮諦), and the Truth of the Middle (中諦). The teachings of these three truths are based on the Buddha's teachings of interdependent origination.

The Truth of Emptiness refers to seeing the reality of interdependent origination as insubstantiality or lack of independent existence (*anatman*), as we explored in chapter 3 of this book.

The Truth of the Expedient refers to seeing the reality of interdependent origination as a temporal collection of causes and conditions. From this view we see that each and every thing for which we have a name is simply a conceptual expedient, since everything exists only in relation to other things. Therefore we also see that when things in relation to a being change, the being must also change. Yet from the view of the Truth of the Expedient, we do not deny that things do exist as collections of causes and conditions, as temporal and expedient beings.

The Truth of the Middle refers to seeing the reality of each and every being from both the side of emptiness ("there is not") and from the side of temporal being ("there is"). For example, Shohaku has no substance since he is just a collection of causes and conditions that give form to his body. His body and mind have no separate "owner and operator" and are always changing according to conditions within and outside of them. Yet Shohaku *is here* as an empty collection of causes and conditions that comprise his body and mind. He is Japanese, he is a Buddhist, and he is a priest. He is teaching Buddhism because that is the responsibility of a Buddhist priest. Shohaku is here but he does not really exist as a fixed entity because neither his body nor his mind contain the totality of Shohaku. He is simply a collection of different elements, just as a car is made up of different parts. Although no single part of a car is a complete car, a car consists of nothing other than a collection of its parts, and although Shohaku is here, he is nothing but a collection of parts or elements. This Shohaku is discussing Dōgen, but he learned what he is talking about from studying many Buddhist texts in the past. What he is doing now is simply a result of what he did in the past; it is simply a collection of the results of his past experiences and circumstances, or karma. His knowledge and words are gifts from the society in which he was raised and educated. This explanation of the nature of Shohaku is an example of the Truth of the Middle, or *chū*.

Returning for a moment to the first three sentences of Genjōkōan, each sentence corresponds to one of these three truths. The first sentence corresponds to the Truth of the Expedient, the second sentence to the Truth of Emptiness, and the third sentence to the Truth of the Middle, the actual practice of the Buddha Way as the reality of our lives. This practice is based on the teachings of the first two truths and yet it goes beyond viewing reality from either of their perspectives. Practicing in this way transcends both "abundance [expedient being] and deficiency [emptiness]."

In choosing this character (中) for discussing the "moon"reflected on the water, in the section from Shōbōgenzō Tsuki above, Dōgen is saying that the image of the moon in water is more than simply a symbol of the emptiness of all dharmas or a metaphor for the Buddha's Dharma Body. He is telling us that the moon in water refers to reality as the Truth of the Middle, or *chū*. I think Dōgen wants to show us that we must live, practice, and perform all of our activities in accordance with the first two truths, using the transitory body and mind that each of us has. He is saying that when we practice in this way, we live in accordance with the Truth of the Middle.

In this section of Genjōkōan Dōgen is not lecturing on the basic philosophy of Mahayana Buddhism. Dōgen was a Zen master, not a philosopher. Using some theories of Mahayana Buddhism as tools, he helps us to see the actual reality of our lives. Dōgen would probably laugh at me if he heard me speaking about his teachings in this philosophical way, just as the Zen master Daowu (Jap.: Dōgo; 769–835) laughed at a lecture by Jishan (Jap.: Kassan; 805–81) in the following story:

> (Later,) Daowu went to Jinkou where he happened to see Jishan Shanhui give a lecture. A monk attending the talk asked Jishan, "What is the dharmakaya?"
> Jishan said. "The dharmakaya is formless."
> The monk asked, "What is the Dharma eye?"
> Jishan said, "The Dharma eye is without defect."
> When he heard this, Daowu laughed loudly in spite of himself.[ ... ][31]

Daowu laughed because Jishan gave the monk only intellectual answers, and now I, too, am discussing the Dharma from a philosophical perspective. Yet because we are conditioned to process what we learn intellectually, it is important for modern people like us to understand what Dōgen is saying on a philosophical basis. Once we have this philosophical understanding, we are free to let go of it. When we encounter *chū* in Dōgen's writings, it is important to be able to refer to its meaning in Mahayana philosophy, yet we should not cling to any logical or philosophical concept when we study Dōgen. His teachings are meant to reveal to us the reality of life immediately *"within"* (中, *chū*) our ordinary day-to-day lives.

In the above verse from Konkōmyōkyō, the moon in water is a simile for the manifestation of the formless Dharma Body of the Buddha. Like empty space, the Buddha's Dharma Body has no form, but this formless Dharma Body manifests itself within the phenomenal world as each and every phenomenal thing, just as the moon is reflected in water. So the verse is saying that formlessness, or *thusness* (如), should be expressed as form, or *thisness* (是), in our day-to-day activities using our bodies and minds.

## THE MOON AS THE SELF

Let's now turn our attention to a second quote in Shōbōgenzō Tsuki, a poem by the Chinese Zen master Panshan Baoji (Jap.: Banzan Hoshaku; 720–814), a disciple of Mazu Daoyi (Jap.: Baso Doitsu; 709–88):

> The perfect circle of the mind-moon is alone.
> Its light swallows ten-thousand things.
> The light does not illuminate objects.
> Neither do objects exist.
> The light and objects both cease to exist.
> What is this?

In his comment on this poem, Dōgen writes:

> The ancient buddha said, "One mind is all dharmas and all dharmas are one-mind."[32] Therefore, the mind is all things. All things are one mind. Because the mind is the moon, the moon is the moon. Because all things that are the mind are without exception the moon, the entire universe is the entire moon. The whole body is the whole moon. Within the "before and after three and three" in the ten-thousand years of a moment, which one is not the moon? The sun-face buddha and moon-face buddha that are our body, mind, and environs are all within the moon. Coming and going within [the cycle of] birth and death are both within the moon. The ten-direction world is the up and down, the left and right of the moon. The present activities of our daily lives are the bright hundred grasses within the moon and the bright ancestral-teacher's mind within the moon.

I think this part of Shōbōgenzō Tsuki can serve as an explanation of section 9 of Genjōkōan, the section we are examining. Although in Panshan's poem the moon represents the self illuminating all phenomenal beings, the topic of both the poem and this section of Genjōkōan is the interconnectedness and total function of the self and all beings.

The mind that Dōgen speaks of when he says "One mind is all dharmas" is not the psychological mind. My teacher Kōshō Uchiyama Rōshi called this mind "the reality of our lives." That we are connected with all beings is this reality of our lives. We can also speak of this reality as the reality that exists before we separate it into self (subject) and other (objects). We separate reality into self and other with our discriminating thinking, yet when we open the hand of thought and let go of discrimination we become one with the network of inter-dependent origination and manifest our connection with everything. Uchiyama Rōshi called this unity of self and all things "original self" or "universal self," the reality that is manifested in our zazen practice. In Shōbōgenzō Tsuki Dōgen Zenji calls this reality the moon. The moonlight swallows all things, and all things disappear and become part of the self. Expressed another way, when all things become the contents of the self, there are no longer any objects to illuminate. In zazen the entire universe becomes moonlight, and the entire body of the self is the entire moon. All things are the entire moon, and we are born, live, and die within the moon. When we live in accordance with reality, our ordinary daily activities become the moon. This is the reality that Dōgen Zenji said manifests "when a person attains realization."

## THE RABBIT IN THE MOON

For me, the image of "the moon in water" has another significance. Whenever I read this part of Genjōkōan, I think of a story I have known since I was a child, the tale of the rabbit in the moon. In Japan all children know this story, which originated from the Jataka, a col-lection of Indian tales about the Buddha's previous lives. In Japanese literature this story was introduced in Konjaku-monogatari-shū

(Stories of the Ancient and the Present), a collection of many tales from India, China, and Japan compiled in the eleventh century. Here is the story:

> Long ago a rabbit, a fox, and a monkey were living together as friends in the forest. Indra, the king of the gods, having heard of the trio, decided to appear on Earth as an old man to see for himself if the strange alliance truly existed. Finding the three together in the forest, he called to them saying, "I hear you three are the best of friends, although of different species. If this is true, please save this feeble old man by bringing him nourishment!"
>
> Thinking this an easy task, each of the trio went to work searching for food for the old man. Soon the monkey returned with nuts he had gathered from a nearby thicket, and the fox appeared with a fish he had caught in nearby a stream. However, although the poor rabbit searched and searched, to his dismay he could find nothing to offer the hungry old man, and he became increasingly vexed with sorrow and shame as his friends scorned him.
>
> Then in a burst of insight the rabbit called to his friends, "Monkey! Please gather some firewood! Fox! Please build a fire with the wood!" When they had done as he asked, the rabbit jumped into the fire, making his own body an offering to the unknown old man.
>
> Seeing this, Indra said, "Each of you has done your best, but what the rabbit did touches me most!" Then in honor of the selfless offering, Indra restored the rabbit's body and placed it to rest in the palace of the moon, where to this day it can be seen.

Dōgen does not refer to this story in Genjōkōan, but when I read Dōgen's writings about the moonlight, I naturally associate them with this story. I think this story is important because it adds even more depth to the symbolism of the vast and boundless moonlight. It shows us that the moonlight is also a symbol of the Buddha's compassion as expressed through the bodhisattva's vow to save all beings.

The story of the rabbit in the moon is also important to me personally. I was ordained when I was a twenty-two-year-old university student studying Buddhism at Komazawa University. I have been practicing zazen since then, so I have not acquired any skill that allows me to have a regular job. Although I have been relatively poor in monetary terms, I have led a rich life filled with wonderful teachers and many Dharma friends. I am very grateful for being able to live such a life. Like the rabbit in the story, often I felt I had nothing to give except to offer up my body and mind in zazen. I often recalled that an important teaching of Kōdō Sawaki Rōshi was "gaining is delusion; losing is enlightenment," but the problem for me was I had nothing to lose!

When I lived on money from *takuhatsu* (traditional Buddhist begging rounds), I felt guilty because I received offerings from many people without giving anything in return. Especially at this time, the story of the rabbit and the moon held great significance for me. I, of course, did not burn my body as the rabbit did, but I tried to practice zazen as though it were an offering of my body and mind to all buddhas. Yet I still sometimes felt I might be using my zazen practice as an excuse not to help others in need. I saw that it can be very difficult to care for this fragile practice while simultaneously keeping our vows and maintaining a healthy psychological condition.

When I thought of Dōgen Zenji's image of the vast moonlight reflecting on a tiny drop of water, I was inspired to keep on practicing. I felt that even though I had only a small, fragile, impermanent body and a deluded, self-centered mind to practice with, I could continue to practice since the Buddha's boundless compassion is reflected in that practice. I saw that when I let go of my ego-centered thoughts and desires through practice, the Buddha's compassion was there. Without this illuminating moonlight of the Buddha's vow and compassion, to this day I do not think I could continue to practice.

So, returning to Dōgen:

> The moon never becomes wet; the water is never disturbed. Although the moon is a vast and great light, it is reflected in a drop of water. The whole moon and even the whole sky are reflected in a drop of dew on a blade of grass. Realization does not destroy the person, as the moon does not make a hole in the water. The person does not obstruct realization, as a drop of dew does not obstruct the moon in the sky.

In this passage, the drop of water represents the self and the moon represents the ten-thousand dharmas (all things, the myriad things). As we read this, we should keep in mind that the self Dōgen speaks of is a knot in the network of interdependent origination. There is no self that is without relationship to this network of the myriad things, and in fact, the self's relationship to the network *is* the self. As Zen master Panshan said, "The self swallows the myriad things and the myriad things swallow the self." What is it that is swallowed by both the self and the myriad things? Dōgen speaks of it by saying that the moon is reflected in each and every drop of water, no matter how small it is.

Dōgen wrote about this relationship in a *waka* poem (a Japanese traditional poetic form using a fixed number of syllables) titled "Impermanence":

| | |
|---|---|
| What is this world like? | 世の中は |
| As a waterfowl shakes its bill, | 何にたとへん、水鳥の、 |
| On each drop of water, | はしふる露に |
| The moon is reflected. | やどる月影 |

A waterfowl dives deep into a pond, surfaces, and shakes its bill. Tiny drops of water from the bird's bill scatter in the air and return to the surface of the pond. The moon is reflected in each and every drop, even though each drop exists for less than a second. Our lives are like this, like moonlight reflected on a drop of dew. When we think about ourselves in relation to absolute reality, we see that we are as tiny and transitory as a dewdrop, yet the vast, boundless, eternal moonlight reflects on each and every "drop" of life. This is a beautiful expression of our lives. It embodies the intersections of impermanence and eternity, individuality and universality. Within this short poem, I think the essential point of Mahayana Buddhist teachings is vividly expressed.

In Genjōkōan, Dōgen tells us we must see that our lives are limited and brief, yet we must awaken to the vast and eternal moonlight of the Buddha's wisdom and compassion reflecting in them. This is what Dōgen means when he says in section 4:

> Conveying oneself toward all things to carry out practice-enlightenment is delusion. All things coming and carrying out practice-enlightenment through the self is realization.

If our practice is genuine, we cannot view ourselves as subjects who practice to attain some desirable object such as satori. When Dōgen uses the word *satori*, he is not speaking of a particular psychological experience that we need only experience once. He is rather referring to our acceptance of a very ordinary reality: that we are self-centered, limited, temporary beings, and we live within the vast, boundless network of interdependent origination that is beyond discrimination. To awaken to reality therefore means that we see that reality awakens to reality and reality actualizes reality. We see that even though the vast moonlight is reflected in our practice, we remain tiny drops of dew as individual persons. The vastness of the moon does not overwhelm the dewdrop of our lives, and the limits of our lives do not prevent the moonlight from reflecting in our practice.

> The depth is the same as the height. [To investigate the significance of] the length and brevity of time, we should

consider whether the water is great or small, and understand the size of the moon in the sky.

As bodhisattvas, we must see how limited and deluded we are, and
how short our lives. We must recognize that the path we walk is a long
one, and in our practice we must investigate the height and vastness
of the moon. Yet when we deeply question or search this length and
shortness, greatness and smallness, we discover that all these aspects
of our lives perfectly penetrate one another. Eternity is reflected in
impermanence, and the vast moonlight penetrates the tiny drop of
water. Though we are tiny, impermanent, and ego-centered as individuals, our lives are immeasurably deep and boundless. The depth of
our life is the same as the height of the moon. In our practice we must
investigate how high and vast the moon is, and how deep and subtle
the reality of our lives. We must endlessly go ever higher and deeper
in our practice so we can express the height and depth of the moon in
all our activities.

# Something Is Still Lacking

(10) When the Dharma has not yet fully penetrated body and mind, one thinks one is already filled with it. When the Dharma fills body and mind, one thinks something is [still] lacking. For example, when we sail a boat into the ocean beyond sight of land and our eyes scan [the horizon in] the four directions, it simply looks like a circle. No other shape appears. This great ocean, however, is neither round nor square. It has inexhaustible characteristics. [To a fish] it looks like a palace; [to a heavenly being] a jeweled necklace. [To us] as far as our eyes can see, it looks like a circle. All the myriad things are like this. Within the dusty world and beyond, there are innumerable aspects and characteristics; we only see or grasp as far as the power of our eye of study and practice can see. When we listen to the reality of myriad things, we must know that there are inexhaustible characteristics in both ocean and mountains, and there are many other worlds in the four directions. This is true not only in the external world, but also right under our feet or within a single drop of water.

## SEEING THE OCEAN AS ONE CIRCLE

As YOU MAY recall, Dōgen says in section 7 that when we first seek the Dharma, we stray far from the boundary of the Dharma, and when the Dharma is correctly transmitted to us, we are *immediately* original persons. In other words, practice allows us to live as an original person in this moment rather than become an original person sometime in the future. To illustrate that practicing as an original person is beyond any fixed view of practice and enlightenment, or of self and object, Dōgen compares the self to a boat sailing on the ocean with the coast in view. He says that just as it is a mistake to think that the coast is moving rather than the boat, it is also a mistake to think of the self as a fixed, unchanging subject around which shifting objects revolve.

In section 10 Dōgen again compares the self to a person riding in a boat on the ocean. In this comparison, however, the coast is no longer in sight and the ocean appears as a circle at the horizon. Here Dōgen is discussing the matter of living as an original person based on the clear insight that all things are empty, lacking independent existence.

My guess is that these images of a boat on the ocean derive from the twenty-three-year-old Dōgen's trip to China in 1223. Dōgen and his first Zen teacher, Butsuju Myōzen (1183–1225), made an ocean voyage to discover the genuine Buddha Dharma in China.

In Shōbōgenzō Zuimonki, Dōgen spoke to his own students about Myozen's decision to travel to China. When Myōzen's original teacher, a Tendai monk named Myōyū, was on his deathbed, he asked Myōzen to postpone his trip to China. Myōyū asked Myōzen to take care of him and to conduct his funeral service after he died. After discussing this matter during a meeting with his dharma brothers and disciples, Myōzen said:

> Even if I put off my trip for the time being, one who is certain to die will die. My remaining here won't help to

prolong his life. Even if I stay to nurse him, his pain will not cease. Also, it would not be possible to escape from life and death because I took care of him before his death. It would just be following his request and comforting his feelings for a while. It is entirely useless for gaining emancipation and attaining the Way. To mistakenly allow him to hinder my aspiration to seek the Dharma would be a cause of evil deeds. However, if I carry out my aspiration to go to China to seek the Dharma, and gain a bit of enlightenment, although it goes against one person's deluded feelings, it would become a cause for attaining the Way for many people. Since this merit is greater, it will help return the debt of gratitude to my teacher. Even if I were to die while crossing the ocean and failed to accomplish my aspiration, since I would have died with the aspiration to seek the Dharma, my vow would not cease in any future life. We should ponder Genjō Sanzō's (Tripitaka master Xuanzang) journey to India. Vainly spending time easily lost for the sake of one person would not be in accordance with the Buddha's will. Therefore, I have firmly resolved to go to China now.[33]

In Dōgen's day, a trip to China was a serious undertaking. Today traveling to China from Japan takes only a few hours by airplane, and since there are many daily flights available on different airlines, it seems a relatively small matter to postpone such a trip. But in thirteenth-century Japan sailing to China was dangerous, and many who embarked did not return. Such voyages were also rare then, so those who missed a trip never knew when another opportunity would arise. The next trip made by Japanese Buddhist monks after Dōgen and Myōzen, for example, did not occur until ten years later, in 1233. And as it turned out, Myōzen's resolution to make the trip at the risk of his life was not an exaggeration. He died at Tiantong monastery in China when he was forty-two years old (Dōgen returned to Japan with Myōzen's ashes in 1227).

With two other attendant monks, Dōgen and Myōzen left Kenninji temple in Kyōto during February of 1223. After having most likely reached Hakata, Kyūshū, by boat, they boarded a vessel destined for China. As they sailed the Inland Sea between Ōsaka and Kyūshū, they must have been able to see the coast of Honshū, Shikoku, and other numerous smaller islands. After departing from Hakata at the end of March, however, they could see nothing but the circular horizon until they arrived at the port of Ninbo in April.

The voyage to China must have been a very impressive and important experience for Dōgen. I think his voyage, his quest for the true Dharma, and his search for a true teacher were intertwined in Dōgen's mind.

### IS SEEING A SINGLE CIRCLE ENLIGHTENMENT?

When sailing an inland sea, mountains, trees, villages, and people can be seen along the coast. At times during the voyage it may feel as if the coast is moving and at other times it may feel as if the boat, and we along with it, are moving. Sometimes it seems that boat and coast move together.

After sailing out to the vast ocean, one can only see the ocean, its circular horizon, and the vast sky. Only the oneness (or not-twoness) of all things can be seen. This is a surprising experience, but is it enlightenment? Is it the goal of practice? Dōgen answers this question with a resounding no. He says that "the Dharma has not yet fully penetrated into body and mind" when we think seeing the unity of things is enlightenment.

True realization, Dōgen wrote, goes beyond seeing the unity of things. The sentence "When the Dharma fills body and mind, one thinks something is [still] lacking" means that when truly filled by Dharma, we see the incompleteness of our practice and perceive that the characteristics of all things are subtle, complex, and innumerable. We then understand that we must inquire endlessly into the nature of all things, and as bodhisattvas, we must perpetually explore the proper way to sincerely practice with all beings. We see that the moon has infinite height and that our lives as individuals have infinite depth. Yet we also realize that as individuals, what we can see is limited. No matter how deep, how high, or how broadly we focus our vision, our view will always be limited. To see this limit is wisdom.

Since we are finite, limited human beings, we cannot see the entirety of reality as it truly is. We are born, live, and die within this reality so we can only see it from the inside. Because we must take a position in reality, we cannot see the parts of it that are hidden by our own individual existence. Because the range of our eyesight, for example, is less than 180 degrees, when we are looking forward, we cannot see what is behind us. And when we turn to see what is behind us, we cannot see what lies ahead, just as we cannot see our own backs without a mirror.

Yet we do have the ability to remember things we have seen before and integrate them with what we are seeing now. In this way we can create a mental picture representing a visual range of 360 degrees, and in a similar way we are capable of creating a mental image of what we think is total reality. We must understand, however, that these images are simply mental representations of the world that we create within our minds; they are only constructs. Even the circular horizon of the ocean is a mental construct and is therefore a limited view of the conditioned self. When we see that our views of oneness, as well as our discriminating views, are simply mental constructs, we begin to see true reality. Seeing that we are deluded is the wisdom of seeing the true reality of our lives.

Kōdō Sawaki Rōshi said:

> Everyone reads the sections of the newspaper in a different order. One person reads the stock market page first,

another turns first to the sports page, a serial novel, or the political columns. We are all different because we see things through our own individual discriminating consciousness. Grasping things with human thought, we each behave differently. We can't know the actual world, the world common to everyone, until we stop discriminating.[34]

Because we each have different karma, each of us sees the world differently. And yet one often thinks, "My opinion is absolutely right, and all other views are wrong." To open the hand of thought, or to stop discriminating, is to stop judging things solely on the basis of one's own limited views. Because any view is the product of a particular set of conditioned circumstances and experiences, we must give up seeing our own views as absolutely true.

Nondiscrimination is sometimes represented as a circle, just as Dōgen expressed it as the circular horizon of the ocean. Yet when we conceptualize anything as a true description of reality, as an *absolutely* true description, we are already outside reality. To "stop discriminating" occurs only when we let go of thought in the sitting practice of zazen.

Sawaki Rōshi also said, "People often say, 'In my opinion . . .' Anyhow, 'my opinion' is no good—so keep your mouth shut!"[35] Keeping our mouths shut does not mean we stop thinking or even stop talking. It means we try to see true reality more and more clearly and deeply as we strive to broaden our perspectives, rather than simply using words or thoughts to justify our own limited views. It also means that we see not only that things around us are changing but that we are moving and changing as well. Because of changes in the "external" conditions of my life, as well as changes in my "inner" values and perspectives, for example, things that were very attractive to me in my twenties are not at all attractive to me now that I am in my sixties. When we can see that our world changes as a result of change within and without, it is easier for us to appreciate our connection to all things and to let go of a self-centered approach to life.

## A Palace for Fish, Water for Human Beings

Let's turn our attention to the next lines of this passage:

> This great ocean, however, is neither round nor square. It has inexhaustible characteristics. [To a fish] it looks like a palace; [to a heavenly being] a jeweled necklace. [To us] as far as our eyes can see, it looks like a circle.

This description of how different kinds of beings see water in different ways originally appeared in a commentary on Shōdaijōron (Skt.: Mahayanasamgraha; Compendium of Mahayana). Shōdaijōron was written by Asanga (310–90?), an important master of the Yogacara school, one of the two Mahayana schools originating in India (the other was the Madhyamika school). According to the commentary on Shōdaijōron, human beings see water as water, fish see water as a palace, heavenly beings see water as a jewel, and hungry ghosts see water as pus and blood. This description, which is used in Yogacara philosophy, symbolically illustrates how each of us views reality differently, using concepts and images that depend on our karma.

Dōgen elaborates on this theme in Shōbōgenzō Sansuikyō (Mountains and Waters Sutra) and the following excerpt can help us understand this section of Genjōkōan:

> The ways of viewing mountains and waters are different for different kinds of beings. Some beings view water as a jewel. However, this does not mean that these beings view [what is seen as] a jewel [by human beings] as water. How do we see what they view as water? What they see as a jewel is what we see as water. Some beings see water as wondrous flowers. But they do not see [what human beings see as] flowers as water. Hungry ghosts view water as raging fire or pus and blood. Dragons and fish view it as a palace or a lofty building. [Some beings] see it as the seven treasures or

the mani jewel.[36] [Others] see it as either a forest, walls, the Dharma nature of immaculate liberation, the true human body, or as the body as form and the mind as [true] nature. Human beings view it as water. And these [different ways of viewing] are the conditions under which [water] is killed or given life.

Thus the views of different beings are diverse depending upon their karmic conditions. We should question this now. Should we think that each being views one and the same object in different ways? Or do all kinds of beings make a mistake because they see one and the same object as various different forms? We should inquire beyond our efforts of inquiry. Therefore our practice-realization of engaging the Way should not be limited to one way or two ways. The ultimate realm has one thousand or ten thousand ways.

Here Dōgen questions the fixed, independent existence—or self-nature—of even the water that the different kinds of beings see; this is the most important point of Sansuikyō. The common interpretation of this analogy (that different beings view water in different ways) is that each type of being sees the one true reality of water according to one of four different, incomplete views. Yet Dōgen says that we cannot be certain that there is an objective "true reality of water" that exists outside of the relationship between beings that are viewing and the "water" that is being viewed. This is what Dōgen meant when he said, "Therefore, flowers fall down even though we love them; weeds grow even though we dislike them." We feel sad when we see that a flower we love is fading, and we dislike weeds if we have to pull them up from a garden. We don't mind weeds if we don't have to pull them. In fact, when they grow on a mountain or meadow, it is likely that we will enjoy them as part of the scenery; weeds are only weeds when we label them so.

We can further study Dōgen's use of this analogy by comparing it to the Yogacara interpretation. Yogacara teachers say the analogy shows that only consciousness exists, and each being sees its own version of water according to its own conditioned consciousness. For Yogacara teachers, nothing exists outside consciousness. Dōgen, however, uses the same analogy to say that the self and the world are working together within a relationship of interdependent origination. The world and all its contents appear within this relationship between the self and the myriad dharmas. In a sense, the relationship between beings and water creates the beings' views of water. The important point for Dōgen is how one acts, or practices, in this relationship with the myriad dharmas. His concern is not with the existence or nonexistence of the self and the myriad dharmas. In fact, he questions all philosophical views we might hold concerning our relationship to the myriad dharmas and deconstructs any concepts we might cling to.

## ENDLESS INQUIRY

All the myriad things are like this. Within the dusty world and beyond, there are innumerable aspects and characteristics; we only see or grasp as far as the power of our eye of study and practice can see. When we listen to the reality of myriad things, we must know that there are inexhaustible characteristics in both ocean and mountains, and there are many other worlds in the four directions. This is true not only in the external world, but also right under our feet or within a single drop of water.

"The dusty world" refers to the ordinary secular world, and "the world beyond" refers to the world of Dharma, the world that is beyond the standards of the ordinary world. Viewing and judging with the discriminating mind, as we do in the secular world, is *laukika* in Sanskrit, and "the world beyond" is *loka-uttara*. These two terms correspond to conventional truth and ultimate truth in Nagarjuna's philosophy. When Bodhidharma, for example, told Emperor Wu that the emperor's contribution to the Buddhist sangha had "no merit," he was speaking from the *loka-uttara* point of view, saying that merit gained from the perspective of *laukika* is not really merit at all. Dōgen, however, suggests in this section that we must see reality from both views. *Loka-uttara* is not necessarily superior to *laukika* because bodhisattvas should not try to escape the world; our bodhisattva practice takes place within the world of desire, walking with all beings.

In Shōbōgenzō Ikka-no-myōju (One Bright Jewel) Dōgen introduces a story about the Chinese Zen master Xuansha Shibei (Jap.: Gensha Shibi, 835–908) before he became a master. Once when Xuansha was leaving his teacher's monastery to visit other masters, he stubbed his toe on a stone. As his toe bled and he experienced terrible pain, Xuansha suddenly had a deep insight and said, "This body is nonexistent. Where does this pain come from?"

In studying Mahayana Buddhism we learn that the body is empty, merely a collection of five skandhas that does not really exist; and yet, when a part of the body as small as a toe is injured, we experience terrible pain. If the body is empty, where does the pain come from? For Xuansha, this was not a question he needed to answer but rather an expression of reality. To see the emptiness of all beings, or to see that the body and mind are just a collection of the five skandhas, is exactly the same as seeing the ocean as one circle.

Although we are not individual, independent, fixed entities, we still have to experience pain. This pain is real, so fresh, and so immediate that it must be taken care of in some way. All pain originates from emptiness, but each individual pain has its particular causes and conditions. We must find the cause of each particular pain and decide how to take care of it. Simply seeing the emptiness or oneness of all beings does not relieve pain. As Xuansha eventually said after becoming a master, seeing the ocean as one circle is perceiving that the entire ten-direction world is one bright jewel. Yet he also said that within this one bright jewel there are many different kinds of pain that create suffering for many people. Each pain has a different cause and needs its own cure; we must therefore study each pain individually.

As Dōgen sailed the great single circle of the ocean on his way to China, he experienced not only beautiful, peaceful days, but tumultuous, stormy days as well. In Shōbōgenzō Zuimonki Dōgen spoke of the voyage saying,

> On my way to China, I suffered from diarrhea on the ship, yet when a storm came up and people on the ship made a great fuss, I forgot about the sickness and it went away.[37]

Sometimes things like this happen in our lives; we have a certain problem, but when some larger, more serious problem arises, we forget about the less important one and it somehow disappears. Many of us may have had this experience, but it does not always happen when we suffer. More often, we create a story around our problems and situations, a story that includes us as the main subjects. In our daily lives, we find ourselves in many different situations, and we interpret each situation and experience according to our individual karmic conditions. This is part of the reality of the universal emptiness of all beings and things; pain, sickness, and other problems are always happening within the perfect circle of the great ocean. We therefore cannot say that to see only the one circle of ultimate reality is the goal of our practice. As bodhisattvas, we must continue to see and address our own suffering and the suffering of others.

It is precisely when we are in the middle of a self-created story that we need to keep our eyes open. When these stories arise, it is crucial that we examine ourselves and our relationship to the myriad dharmas very closely; this is an important way to study the reality of interdependent origination. We should always try to see reality with fresh eyes and avoid grasping fixed ideas or any system of values we have created from our previous experiences.

As Dōgen said, we see or grasp only as far as the power of our eye of study and practice can see. I have been practicing zazen and studying Dōgen Zenji's teachings for over forty years, since I was nineteen years old. In each stage of my life, throughout my twenties, thirties, forties, fifties, and now my sixties, the power of my eye of study and practice has been changing. On the one hand, since the scope of my vision and understanding has been broadening, I feel that the longer I practice and study, the more clearly and deeply I see myself and things around me. On the other hand, I also feel that as I age I am losing the energy it takes to change myself and my circumstances.

I don't think it is appropriate to say that I am improving and growing, nor is it appropriate to say that I am losing energy and backsliding; both of these statements are true and both are untrue. Though my understanding was not deep when I was nineteen, I think I was much more sincere in my practice. When I was young, I was just young. Now that I am in my sixties, I am just in my sixties. I am getting older, and my internal and external conditions will continue to change. At each stage of the rest of my life, I will try to be honest and to keep practicing and studying endlessly; there will be no time that I will graduate from this practice.

In this way I hope to follow the example of my teacher, Kōshō Uchiyama Rōshi. The day he died, he wrote a poem in his diary. He noted that this poem finally and fully expressed what he had wished to say during his life of practice. Throughout his life he kept studying and practicing, and every day he tried to express his dharma slightly better than the day before. He kept this practice until the day he died, when he was eighty-six. Here is Uchiyama Rōshi's last poem:

JUST BOW

Putting my right and left hands together as one, I just bow.
Just bow to become one with Buddha and God.
Just bow to become one with everything I encounter.
Just bow to become one with all the myriad things.
Just bow as life becomes life.[38]

## The Single Circle as the Logo of Zen

Calligraphy of the single circle is very common. For example, some years ago there was an exhibit of Zen art at the San Francisco Asian Art Museum, and the poster for the exhibition included calligraphy of the single circle. Also, a recently published book, *Enso: Zen Circles of Enlightenment*,[39] contains a collection of the *ensō* (circle) calligraphy of many Zen masters. The single-circle is so widely associated with Zen that we could almost say that it has become a Zen logo. There was at least one Zen master, however, who did not like the single circle: Dōgen Zenji (he makes no appearance in the *Zen Circle* book).

In Shōbōgenzō Busshō (Buddha nature) Dōgen wrote about an experience he had at a Chinese Zen monastery. On a wall of a walkway he saw the painting of a single circle and asked his guide what the circle represented. The monk said that it was a painting of Nagarjuna manifesting the form of a round moon. This painting represented a story about Nagarjuna's zazen; it is said that people only saw the form of the round moon when Nagarjuna sat zazen (I believe this story was the origin of the symbolism of the single circle). Dōgen criticized the painting in the Chinese monastery, saying that if the artist wanted to paint Nagarjuna's form manifesting a round moon, he should have just painted Nagarjuna sitting in zazen with his usual human form. For Dōgen, the way to manifest the round moon is to sit zazen with this whole body and mind, to practice using the five aggregates themselves. From this story we can see that Dōgen was a unique Zen master. He was a Zen master, in fact, who was not concerned with being a Zen master.

Dōgen Zenji did not strive to be famous or promote a particular philosophy of Zen; he simply wanted to show us how to manifest enlightenment in every aspect of our lives.

# A Fish Swims, a Bird Flies

(11) When a fish swims, no matter how far it swims, it doesn't reach the end of the water. When a bird flies, no matter how high it flies, it cannot reach the end of the sky. Therefore, since ancient times, no fish has ever left the water and no bird has ever left the sky. When the bird's need or the fish's need is great, the range is large. When the need is small, the range is small. In this way, each fish and each bird uses the whole of space and vigorously acts in every place. However, if a bird departs from the sky, or a fish leaves the water, it immediately dies. We should know that [for a fish] water is life, [for a bird] sky is life. A bird is life; a fish is life. Life is a bird; life is a fish. And we should go beyond this. There is practice-enlightenment[40]—this is the way of living beings.

## Fish and Birds in Zazen

IN THIS SECTION Dōgen introduces another image from the natural world, an analogy that makes his discussion more concrete. Since observing the activity of fish and birds is a more common experience than sailing a boat on the ocean, the image used in this section is more direct and lively than the imagery used in section 10. Dōgen did, however, return to the boat/ocean imagery later when he wrote Shōbōgenzō Zenki (Total Dynamic Function) in 1243.

In Shōbōgenzō Zazenshin (The Acupuncture Needle of Zazen), written nine years after Genjōkōan, Dōgen discusses the poem "Zazenshin" by Hongzhi Zhengjue (Jap.: Wanshi Shōgaku, 1091– 1157). Hongzhi Zhengjue was a famous Chinese Sōtō (Ch.: Caodong) Zen master who served as the abbot of Tiantong monastery from 1129 until his death in 1157, a tenure of almost thirty years. It is said that the temple buildings, which accommodated twelve hundred monks, were completed during his abbacy. Hongzhi, who was well known for his excellent poetry, also composed verses to accompany one hundred kōans. Wansong Xingxiu (Jap.: Banshō Gyōshū, 1166–1246) later wrote commentaries on these verses and created the Congronglu (Jap.: Shōyōroku; Book of Serenity), a classic text that is still studied by Zen students today.

Dōgen, who decades after Hongzhi's death practiced at Tiantong under Rujing, respected Hongzhi immensely, calling him Wanshi *Kobutsu* (Ancient Buddha Wanshi). As one can clearly see in the Eihei Kōroku (Dōgen's Extensive Record), many of Dōgen's formal teachings contain Hongzhi's verse or quote from his formal discourses. Hongzhi's poem "Zuochanzhen" (Jap.: "Zazenshin") is obviously the source of the fish and birds imagery found in Genjōkōan. My translation of that poem is as follows:

## ZAZENSHIN

The essential-function of each buddha and the functioning-
    essence of each ancestor.
Knowing without touching things,
Illuminating without facing objects,
Knowing without touching things—the wisdom is by
    nature inconspicuous.

Illuminating without facing objects, the illumination is
    by nature subtle.
The wisdom, by nature inconspicuous, never has
    discriminative thoughts.
The illumination, by nature subtle, never has the slightest
    separation.
The wisdom that never has discriminative thoughts has
    no dichotomy but sees oneness.
The illumination that never has the slightest separation
    has no attachment, but is evident.
The water is clear to the bottom; a fish is swimming slowly,
    slowly.
The sky is infinitely vast; a bird is flying far, far away.

Even though Dōgen does not use the word "zazen" at all in
Genjōkōan, it is clear that the analogy of fish and birds is about our
zazen practice. According to this analogy, our zazen practice and the
day-to-day activities based on it are connected to the entire universe.
In this section of Genjōkōan, Dōgen discusses the nature of our zazen
and how it forms the foundation of our attitude toward our entire
lives. The water and sky in these images do not represent an environment outside the self; they are, in fact, inseparable from the beings
that inhabit them.

## WHAT IS THE WATER?

In Shōbōgenzō Zazenshin Dōgen comments on the significance of
water as it appears in Hongzhi's verse:

As to the meaning of "the water is clear," water suspended
in space is not thoroughly clear to the bottom. [This
water in Wanshi's verse] is not the clean water that is
deep and clear in the external world. [The water] that has

no boundary, no bank or shore, is thoroughly clear to the bottom.

According to Dōgen, the water in Hongzhi's poem is symbolic of something more than the ocean or river environment in which a fish swims. This water is not separate from us and does not belong to an "external" world. The water Hongzhi speaks of is boundless, having neither bank nor shore:

> When a fish goes through this water, we cannot say that there is no movement. Although [the fish] migrates more than ten thousand miles, [its movement] cannot be measured and is unlimited. There is no bank from which to survey it, there is no air into which [the fish] might break the surface, and there is no bottom to which it might sink. Therefore, there is no one who can measure it. If we want to discuss its measurements, [we say] only that the water is thoroughly clear to the bottom. The virtue of zazen is like the fish swimming. [Even though we may progress in our sitting] a thousand or ten thousand miles, who can estimate it? The process of going that thoroughly penetrates to the bottom is that the whole body is "not flying the way of the birds."[41]

Here Dōgen says that the water in Hongzhi's verse is boundless and unlimited. This water has no bank or shore that could be used to objectively measure its vastness or smallness. This is, of course, the water of emptiness. Within this water there is no separation between the fish, the water, the earth, and the air. This image is another expression of the reality Dōgen referred to in section 4 of Genjōkōan:

> Conveying oneself toward all things to carry out practice-

enlightenment is delusion. All things coming and carrying out practice-enlightenment through the self is realization.

Dōgen's treatment of Hongzhi's verse does not emphasize objectivity but rather points to the reality that is manifested when we practice with the attitude that "all things carry out practice-enlightenment through the self." In Bendōwa (Wholehearted Practice of the Way) Dōgen wrote of this reality:

> When one displays the Buddha mudra with one's whole body and mind, sitting upright in this samadhi even for a short time, everything in the entire dharma world becomes buddha mudra, and all space in the universe completely becomes enlightenment.

> Even if only one person sits for a short time, because this zazen is one with all existence and completely permeates all time, it performs everlasting buddha guidance within the inexhaustible dharma world in the past, present, and future.[42]

Here Dōgen makes it clear that the key to practice-enlightenment is our practice of zazen.

## WHAT IS THE SKY?

In the next part of Shōbōgenzō Zazenshin, Dōgen comments on the image of the sky in Hongzhi's verse:

> The "infinitely vast" sky is not what is suspended in the firmament. The sky suspended in the firmament is not the infinitely vast sky. Moreover, the space that permeates here and there is not the infinitely vast sky. [The sky] that

is never concealed nor revealed and that has neither outside nor inside is the infinitely vast sky.

Like the water in Hongzhi's verse, the sky is not a space outside of
us. The sky and the bird are one without separation, and we are completely part of this sky that is also inside of us.

When a bird flies through this sky, flying in the sky is the
undivided dharma. Its activity of flying in the sky cannot be measured. Flying in the sky is the entire universe,
because the entire universe is flying in the sky. Although
we do not know the distance of this flying, in expressing it
with words beyond distinction, we say "far, far away," and
"Go straightforwardly, there should be no string under the
feet."[43] When the sky is flying away, the birds also are flying
away; and when the birds are flying away, the sky also is
flying away. In studying and penetrating the "flying away,"
we say "simply being here." This is the acupuncture needle
for immovable sitting. In traveling ten thousand miles by
"simply being here," we express it [zazen] in this way.

When a bird is flying, the sky is also flying. The bird is part of the
sky and the sky is part of the bird. The entire sky is the wings of the
bird. This is true not just in our zazen practice, for as we live our lives
the entire universe is living with us. When a fish is swimming, the
whole body of water is swimming; when a bird is flying, the entire sky
is flying. At this time, fish and water, bird and sky, all living beings and
the universe, are one. When we sit in zazen and let go of our discriminative thoughts, we are completely one with the universe.

When we rise from our cushions and leave the zendo, however, we
again begin to think and make distinctions, evaluations, and judgments. When we do this, according to Dōgen, sometimes we think
"the shore" is moving, sometimes we think we are moving, and at
other times we think that both "the shore" and our individual selves

are moving simultaneously. Sometimes we think all things in the world are totally separate entities that move independently. We naturally make choices and take action based on these different ways of viewing reality, but no matter what we think, we remain united with all beings. Reality remains reality regardless of what we think of it, because thinking is just thinking; thinking cannot change reality.

Take, for example, how European people thought that the sun, the moon, and the stars all moved around the earth until the discoveries of Galileo proved otherwise. From a certain perspective, Galileo's discoveries were indeed a great accomplishment, yet in reality, the earth has been orbiting the sun since its birth forty-six billion years ago, regardless of what Galileo or anyone else has ever said or thought; human thought has existed only a fraction as long as the earth and sun. Although we usually place great importance on what we think, our thinking cannot change the vast reality of all beings.

We may think that we are the most important elements of this life, but in reality we are all just tiny parts of the universe. Each one of us is a collection of causes and conditions, products of the coevolution of life and the earth. I, for example, am made up of things that are not me. The foods I eat are "not me," the air I breathe is "not me," and the water I drink is "not me," yet I cannot exist without all of these things that are "not me." In fact, all of these things that sustain our lives, and even life itself, are gifts we receive from the universe.

When we think even briefly about the life of a human being, it is easy to see that even the most basic elements of our lives are given to us. For example, because humans are developmentally very immature when born, young human beings must be supported by others for a long time in order to stay alive. Human infants cannot even stand up until they are over a year old, so they are really helpless, and children must be fed and cared for without earning their own living for a long time, at least until they become teenagers. To become truly independent members of our society, human beings must study for perhaps twenty years or more. Until we can take care of ourselves, we are basically supported and cared for by society.

Even language, the essential tool we use in thinking, is a gift from our society, and we are taught how to think and behave through the education that society gives us. Because I was born and raised in Japan, I think in Japanese, and I mostly act according to Japanese values. The Japanese language and Japanese system of values arose from a culture created by all the Japanese people who throughout history have lived in the lands of Japan, so my manner of speaking, thinking, and behaving are products of all those people's lives.

Each of us is connected to all past, present, and future beings in the entire universe. This is not a mysterious truth that can only be attained through some special spiritual intuition, trance, or other extraordinary mental condition. This is a very simple, plain reality we can understand rationally, yet we lose sight of it because we cling to words and concepts, separating ourselves from reality with discriminating thoughts.

## Dōgen's Poem "Zazenshin"

Let us now look at Dōgen's own poem that he also entitled "Zazenshin," which appears at the end of the Shōbōgenzō chapter of the same name.

### Zazenshin

The essential-function of each buddha and the functioning-
    essence of each ancestor—
Being actualized within not-thinking,
Being manifested within non-interacting.
Being actualized within not-thinking, the actualization
    is by nature intimate.
Being manifested within non-interacting, the manifestation
    is itself verification.
The actualization, by nature intimate, never has defilement.

The manifestation, by nature verification, never has
distinction between absolute and relative.
The intimacy without defilement is dropping off without
relying on anything.
The verification beyond distinction between absolute and
relative is making effort without aiming at it.
The water is clear to the earth; a fish is swimming like a fish.
The sky is vast, extending to the heavens; a bird is flying
like a bird.

A valuable exercise might be to explore a comparison of Dōgen's expression and Hongzhi's—but for our purposes in this volume, we will confine our exploration to Dōgen's verse. Dōgen is saying in his poem that fish and birds do not exist as entities that are separate and independent from the water or the sky, yet there is still something like a fish or a bird that is swimming or flying. The verse is his expression of the reality of our lives—that our lives function together with all beings of the past, present, and future. The verse points to the total reality in which each and every thing, each fish and each bird, exists within the vast network of all beings, yet Dōgen simultaneously indicates that we must not forget that we are still living as individuals within this total reality. When we carry out our individual practice in harmony with this network of all beings, we swim the water that is "clear to the earth" and we fly the sky that is "extending to the heavens"; letting go of our self-centered views in practice we are freed from the three poisonous minds, supporting the entire network of interdependent origination as it supports us.

In my case, for instance, Shohaku does not exist as a fixed entity, but Shohaku is nevertheless living as Shohaku, and Shohaku needs to take responsibility for what Shohaku does. When it was my job to cook for the monks at Antaiji, for example, my practice was to carefully plan the meals, obtain the food, and cook the food. Even though my practice could manifest only in interconnection with all beings, and my cooking was actually only a tiny part of the process of bringing food to the community, I had to take full responsibility for my job; if I behaved carelessly I could ruin the meal I was preparing. Although my cooking practice was the practice of the community and the practice of all beings, it was also *my* practice and I had to carry it out with care and responsibility. This integration of totality and individuality is the way we actually live and the reason we must practice. Although the boundless moonlight is reflected in each drop of water, we must still care for the drop.

Our sitting practice is another example of this integration. When we sit zazen during sesshin, each of us sits facing the wall by ourselves. No matter how many other people are sitting in the same zendo, when I sit sesshin no one can sit for me; my determination supports my sitting. But if those other people were not sitting with me as a sangha, I could not sit so many fifty-minute periods of zazen for five or seven days at a time. We cannot practice zazen for many years without the support of the sangha and the support of society in general. As our individual practice, we must sit alone, yet we cannot sit alone without the support of others. Even beyond needing the support of co-practitioners in the zendo, we need the tenzo who cooks for us and those who work to produce the vegetables, spices, teas, coffee, and other materials the tenzo uses. We also depend on those who process the water, electricity, gas, oil, and many other things we consume during sesshin. In a sense, all of these people are part of our zazen. We must appreciate that we can practice as a result of such interconnectedness. Dōgen Zenji offers us this very important teaching of integrated practice throughout Genjōkōan.

## RANGE OF LIFE

> When a fish swims, no matter how far it swims, it doesn't reach the end of the water. When a bird flies, no matter how high it flies, it cannot reach the end of the sky. When the bird's need or the fish's need is great, the range is large.

When the need is small, the range is small. In this way, each fish and each bird uses the whole of space and vigorously acts in every place.

From 1976 to 1981, when I was living at Pioneer Valley Zendo, my range was very small. Valley Zendo is located on about five acres of land, but at that time the land was mostly covered with trees. We cut trees and dug out stumps from an area of approximately one acre, and there we built the zendo and planted a garden. That single acre of land was the entire range of my life for five years. I did not leave the zendo very often and I rarely traveled anywhere beyond western Massachusetts. Since I had neither TV nor radio and did not read newspapers, I knew almost nothing about what was going on in the world beyond my immediate vicinity. The range of my life was tiny. I just practiced zazen with two other Japanese priests and a few American practitioners. During this time I knew very little about the world and almost no one knew me.

In contrast, since I began to work for the Soto Zen Education Center in 1997, I have traveled extensively from California to New England and from Alaska to Florida. I have met and practiced with many people, and I find myself on an airplane almost every month. Today I am able to stay informed of world events by means of several types of news media, and I also give many lectures. My range seems much bigger than at Valley Zendo. Yet now as then, I have simply been sitting and facing the wall with body and mind, and talking about my understanding of zazen; that's all. In whatever condition I find myself, I simply live my own life, a life that is connected with all things in the universe.

No matter how large our range of life, we can never reach the end of the universe, and yet no matter how small our range of life, we are living in connection with the entire universe. Our bodies and minds are much larger than we usually think, and our lives have a much more intimate connection with all things than we can imagine. We share, for example, the same DNA structure with all living beings on the earth. In Shōbōgenzō Shinjin-gakudō (Studying the Way with Body and Mind) Dōgen speaks of the mind:

> Mountains, rivers, and the great earth; the sun, the moon, and stars are nothing other than the mind.

And of the body he says:

> The entire ten-direction world is nothing other than the true human body. Coming and going within life and death is the true human body. Turning this body, we depart from the ten unwholesome deeds, keep the eight precepts, take refuge in the Three Treasures, give up our home and become a home-leaver; this is studying the Way in its true meaning.

## THE SOURCE OF FISH AND BIRD IMAGERY

It is certain that the source of Dōgen's imagery in Genjōkōan is Hongzhi's Zazenshin. I am not 100 percent certain, but my guess is that the source of Hongzhi's images of fish and birds is the writing of Zhuangzi (also transliterated as Chuang Tzu; fourth c. to third c. BCE). The very beginning of the first chapter of Zhuangzi's "Free and Easy Wandering" gives an account of a huge fish that was transformed into an enormous bird and flew to heaven:

> In the northern darkness there is a fish and his name is K'un. The K'un is so huge I don't know how many thousand li he measures. He changes and becomes a bird whose name is P'eng. The back of the P'eng measures I don't know how many thousand li across and, when he rises up and flies off, his wings are like clouds all over the sky. When the sea begins to move, this bird sets off for the southern darkness, which is the Lake of Heaven.[44]

According to one Japanese commentary on this text, one li is about 405 meters (¼ mile), so the size of the fish/bird is beyond imagination.

There is, however, an important difference between Zhuangzi's use of the image and Dōgen's. In Zhuangzi's writing, small creatures such as cicadas, doves, and quail laugh at the large bird:

> Where does he think he's going? I give a great leap and fly up, but I never get more than ten or twelve yards before I come down fluttering among the weeds and brambles. And that's the best kind of flying anyway! Where does he think he's going?[45]

Zhuangzi then goes on to say, "Such is the difference between big and little." It is clear from this passage that Zhuangzi regarded the smaller creatures in his story as inferior to the large bird. He concluded that people in the mundane world who are caught up in conventional concepts and systems of value are like the small creatures in his story, and his ideal person is like the large bird. He writes about people who hold worldly values as follows:

> Therefore a man who has wisdom enough to fill one office effectively, good conduct enough to impress one community, virtue enough to please one ruler, or talent enough to be called into service in one state, has the same kind of self-pride as these creatures.[46]

Zhuangzi compares people who are adept in worldly affairs to the cicadas, doves, and quail that laughed at the big bird in the story. He says that although such people may have good reputations and be seen as assets to society, they may at any time lose their status as a result of changing conditions in their political, social, or economic environments. Of those who are, according to Zhuangzi, truly superior people, he says:

> Therefore I say, the Perfect Man has no self; the Holy Man
> has no merit; the Sage has no fame.[47]

In contrast, Dōgen says that even a small bird such as a quail flies together with the entire sky, and even a cicada that lives for only a few days in the summer is at one with the entire past, present, and future. Dōgen felt that we are all like the small living beings in the story, and he considered it important for a bodhisattva to be aware of how small he or she is. Yet he also said that no matter how tiny we are as individuals, we are flying throughout the entire sky and the entire sky is flying with us. I think Taoism and Buddhism differ in their teachings on this point.

## LIFE IS A BIRD; LIFE IS A FISH

> However, if a bird departs from the sky, or a fish leaves
> the water, it immediately dies. We should know that [for a
> fish] water is life, [for a bird] sky is life. A bird is life; a fish
> is life. Life is a bird; life is a fish. And we should go beyond
> this. There is practice-enlightenment—this is the way of
> living beings.

We cannot live separately from the world. For us, this world is our life. Since we are one with the world and supported by all things as a part of the network of interdependent origination, we must take care of this world that includes both self and others. Yet we must ask ourselves, how can we live our lives with this magnanimous view of the self, others, and the world?

Life, or the natural universal life force, must be expressed as a bird, a fish, or another individual being in order to manifest. Otherwise, life is just an abstract concept. Without the particular body, mind, and activity of a living being, no matter how tiny, weak, deluded, or self-centered it may be, there is no way for life to manifest itself.

The Buddha encouraged us to study and awaken to the reality of all beings (which is to say, the Dharma) so that we can live our lives harmoniously within this reality. Human beings usually don't see that the world we live in is actually our own life, and this lack of insight is one of our primary sources of suffering. We commonly think our lives begin with the birth of an individual body and end with its death, viewing ourselves as the center of life and all other people and things as objects we can use to satisfy our desires. This deluded view of reality causes suffering for ourselves and others.

## THE NECESSITY OF FINDING ONE'S OWN PLACE AND PATH

(12) Therefore, if there are fish that would swim or birds that would fly only after investigating the entire ocean or sky, they would find neither path nor place. When we make this very place our own, our practice becomes the actualization of reality (*genjōkōan*). When we make this path our own, our activity naturally becomes actualized reality (*genjōkōan*). This path, this place, is neither big nor small, neither self nor others. It has not existed before this moment nor has it come into existence now. Therefore [the reality of all things] is thus. In the same way, when a person engages in practice-enlightenment in the Buddha Way, as the person realizes one dharma, the person permeates that dharma; as the person encounters one practice, the person [fully] practices that practice. [For this] there is a place and a path. The boundary of the known is not clear; this is because the known [which appears limited] is born and practiced simultaneously with the complete penetration of the Buddha Dharma. We should not think that what we have attained is conceived by ourselves and known by our discriminating mind. Although complete enlightenment is immediately actualized, its intimacy is

such that it does not necessarily form as a view. [In fact] viewing is not something fixed.

This section is the conclusion of Dōgen's discussion of how one lives according to the Buddha Dharma. Let's begin by looking at the first portion of this passage:

> Therefore, if there are fish that would swim or birds that would fly only after investigating the entire ocean or sky, they would find neither path nor place.

When I was a high school student, I was exactly like the hesitating fish or birds in this passage. I wanted to find the purpose and meaning of life before starting to do anything. I was very childish but extremely serious, and I thought that if life is meaningless, I should not continue to live. I tried to find the answer to my questions in books, reading widely about religion, philosophy, and science. From reading these books I concluded that there is no meaning that supports our lives. I found that things can have meaning or value only in relation to other things, and in order to judge the ultimate value of something, we have to be separate from it. I therefore cannot judge the meaning of my own life because I cannot remove myself from my own life; I cannot see it objectively. In the same way, human beings cannot measure the value of human life because they cannot be outside human life, and anyone in the universe cannot evaluate the universe because they cannot be outside it. In order to make ultimate judgments about such things as the meaning of life and the value of human beings, we would need something like an absolute Other, such as God.

I thought, for example, of a shell that lies unseen by any human on an island beach for many years. This shell would have no meaning or value for anyone. If a girl walking along the beach finds the shell and treasures it for its beauty, the shell becomes meaningful and valuable to her. But does the fact that she loves the shell have any meaning or value beyond her? The girl's love of the shell has no wider meaning or value until someone else evaluates that love. If a poet, for instance, sees the girl with her shell and is moved to write a poem about them, then the girl's love for the shell is meaningful and valuable to the poet. But the poet's poem has no meaning or value beyond the poet until someone else reads and likes the poem. In other words, for something to become meaningful or valuable beyond one's own perception or opinion, someone else must see and evaluate it. There have been many different systems of value established within human society, and different people evaluate things in different ways. But there can be no ultimate evaluation of the meaning of these systems of value unless some observer exists beyond human experience. Only such a being could evaluate human experience, and we could call such a being "God." Unless such a being exists, there is no way that the totality of human civilization can have any ultimate meaning or value.

As a teenager I could not believe that there is a God who judges human activity, so I became nihilistic and completely lost. I felt that I could not do anything, not even commit suicide. To commit suicide, I would need a reason to do so, but if life has no meaning, to kill myself would also be meaningless. I felt I could not live and I could not die; I faced a dead end. As you can imagine, my high school life was not a joyful one.

I think that if I had not had the opportunity to read a book by my teacher, Uchiyama Rōshi, this nihilistic period would have lasted much longer for me. As it turned out, I made a friend who had the same kinds of questions about life that I did. Because he knew someone who had gone to Antaiji to practice zazen with Sawaki Kōdō Rōshi, my friend visited Antaiji and stayed there during a summer vacation. This was around the same time Uchiyama Rōshi published his first book, *Jiko* (Self), and my friend lent me the book after he returned from Antaiji.

In *Jiko* Uchiyama Rōshi wrote about his own search for the meaning of life. From reading the book, I learned that Uchiyama Rōshi had the same question about life as I did and that he had spent his life searching for the answer to that question. When he found the answer, he practiced what he had learned and taught it to others. Since I knew nothing about Buddhism or Zen, I did not understand what Uchiyama Rōshi's answer actually was, but I knew I wanted to live as he lived. It was primarily for that reason that I began to study Buddhism and became Uchiyama Rōshi's disciple. Although I had read about many spiritual teachers who claimed to teach the truth, Uchiyama Rōshi was the first person I met who actually lived according to the truth.

After practicing with my teacher for some time, I found that meaning is created in our lives when we find our own place and path and begin to do something. Until that moment, there is no "ready-made" meaning or purpose to our lives. When I found my place as a student in the lineage of Uchiyama Rōshi and Sawaki Rōshi, life became meaningful and precious to me. I was very grateful to receive their teachings based on the teachings of Dōgen Zenji and Shakyamuni Buddha. When I decided that my path would be to continue my teacher's vow to transmit the tradition to the next generation, I found that many different kinds of support for my practice opened up.

When I first read Genjōkōan, this point of creating meaning in life made a great impression on me. Even though I did not understand the rest of Genjōkōan or Dōgen's other writings, I decided to become a follower of his teachings simply because of this one point. Before I reached this point in my life, I was like a bird that refuses to fly until it investigates the entire sky. Dōgen Zenji and Uchiyama Rōshi saved me from my nihilism and despair.

> When we make this very place our own, our practice becomes the actualization of reality (*genjōkōan*). When we make this path our own, our activity naturally becomes actualized reality (*genjōkōan*). This path, this place, is neither big nor small, neither self nor others. It has not existed before this moment nor has it come into existence now. Therefore [the reality of all things] is thus.

When I decided to become Uchiyama Rōshi's disciple and actually began to practice zazen, I finally found my own place and path. When I chose one thing and actually did it, I had a path on which I could proceed. The actualization of reality (*genjōkōan*) is not a concept or philosophical idea, it is actual practice using one's body and mind, a body and mind that are connected with the entire world. This broad, flexible, and endless path of zazen practice has led me to a wondrous and unbelievable way of life. I have been walking this path for over forty years, but I am still a beginner. Although having no beginning or end, and permeating all time and space, this path exists only at this very moment, right now and right here. Before I began walking this path, absolutely no path existed for me, and yet, this path did not simply come into being when I began to walk it. Whether I walk it or not, bodhisattvas have been walking the bodhisattva path since ancient times. As Dōgen says in Shōbōgenzō Yuibutsu-yobutsu (Only Buddha Together with Buddha),[48] the birds' path is very evident and clear to birds of the same species, even though other beings cannot see their path.

## ONE THING AT A TIME

> In the same way, when a person engages in practice-enlightenment in the Buddha Way, as the person realizes one dharma, the person permeates that dharma; as the person encounters one practice, the person [fully] practices that practice. [For this] there is a place and a path.

I found my place as a zazen practitioner under the guidance of Uchiyama Rōshi, and I made a commitment to practice. I have tried in each moment, each day, and through each stage of my life, to see the many people, things, and situations I encounter as my own life and practice. Whatever I encounter, I try to do my best to practice with a sincere attitude.

Using the act of cooking as an illustration, in Tenzo-Kyōkun

(Instructions for the Cook), Dōgen Zenji explains how to work with each and every thing we encounter with a sincere heart:

> Next, get ready the following morning's breakfast. Select the rice and prepare the vegetables by yourself with your own hands, watching closely with sincere diligence. You should not attend to some things and neglect or be slack with others for even one moment. Do not give a single drop from within the ocean of virtues; you must not fail to add a single speck on top of the mountain of good deeds.[49]

When we give all of our attention and energy to the task or practice before us, we can truly penetrate it. We work on the practice, study it, experiment with it, and care for it. We do this over and over again with whatever we encounter, one thing at a time, each time. This is how we study the characteristics of all things, one thing at a time. When we practice whatever role we are in sincerely, we penetrate that role. When we make a mistake, we penetrate that mistake and learn from it. Then our mistakes become great teachers for us. Nothing is meaningless when we have our own place and path. In reality our place and our path are not something outside us. Our place and path are nothing other than ourselves.

## THE WAY IS ENDLESS

> The boundary of the known is not clear; this is because the known [which appears limited] is born and practiced simultaneously with the complete penetration of the Buddha Dharma. We should not think that what we have attained is conceived by ourselves and known by our discriminating mind. Although complete enlightenment is immediately actualized, its intimacy is such that it does not necessarily form as a view. [In fact] viewing is not something fixed.

Even though we walk on the path, we cannot measure how far we have come and how much farther we have to go to reach our goal. As Buddhist practitioners, we often think our goal is clear—to become a buddha. According to Mahayana Buddhist teachings, a bodhisattva must pass through fifty-two stages in order to reach buddhahood, and this takes three great kalpas, almost an eternity. Yet becoming a buddha is not the end of the story, it is simply the starting point of life as a buddha. A buddha practices a buddha's practice, which is helping all living beings to become buddhas and to make the entire world into a buddha land. This is also a practice that takes almost an eternity.

Within this process of the Buddha Way that is endless, it is nonsense to measure how much we have achieved, which stage we are now at, and what we must do to go further. In Buddhist teachings of many different traditions there are various stages of spiritual achievement, such as the four stages achieved in becoming an arhat and the fifty-two stages of the bodhisattva. Yet these stages are all examples of expedient means.

Dōgen Zenji does not use such expedients. He simply says the Buddha Way is endless and there is no way to measure our current stage of practice. This is the meaning of "the boundary of the known is not clear." No matter how long and how hard we have been practicing, when considering the infinite length of the Buddha Way, the distance we have traveled is essentially zero.

When faced with this truth, we realize that what matters in our practice is to try to be mindful in each moment and to practice one thing wholeheartedly in a way that allows us to penetrate that one thing. This is what Dōgen means when he says: "When buddhas are truly buddhas they don't need to perceive they are buddhas; however, they are enlightened buddhas and they continue actualizing buddha."

This is a lesson we can apply to many parts of our lives. For example, if we consider peace a condition in which there is no war among countries, no fighting or conflict among people, and no pain, anxiety, or struggle in our minds, there will probably never be a time when such a condition can be completely achieved. Does this make peace a meaningless dream? Not at all. According to Dōgen, our efforts to achieve peace are themselves a source of peace in each moment of each step we take toward peace. This is true of our efforts to realize nirvana or buddhahood as well.

> . . . the known [which appears limited] is born and practiced simultaneously with the complete penetration of the Buddha Dharma.

Our practice is to just practice one thing at a time wholeheartedly and manifest our own life force moment by moment without evaluation. That is all. This is what *shikan* (just) in Dōgen's expression *shikantaza* (just sitting) means, and this is also what Dōgen means when he says that practice and enlightenment are one.

As I wrote earlier, a baby just being 100 percent a baby has the energy to negate babyhood and become a boy or girl. Similarly, when we do something wholeheartedly with full attentiveness, that focused practice provides the energy that enables us to grow. In this sense, a baby is not simply a baby; within the complete babyhood of being a baby, the baby negates babyhood itself. Therefore, the way we view a baby must not be limited to a fixed concept.

> Although complete enlightenment is immediately actualized, its intimacy is such that it does not necessarily form as a view. [In fact] viewing is not something fixed.

And although the baby is doing such a complicated thing as negating babyhood, the baby does not conceive this; the baby is just wholeheartedly being a baby. Our practice of zazen is the same as this.

When we sit upright in the zazen posture, keeping the eyes open, breathing through the nose, and letting go of thoughts, we in a sense negate our individual, limited, karmic selves and become one with the unlimited, vast network of interdependent origination. Dropping our conceptual views of who we are, we actualize reality and settle into the true self that is one with the universe. Yet in our zazen we are just completely who we are, we just wholeheartedly sit, letting go of all judgments of our practice and comparisons of any kind.

When we sit in this way we cannot say "Now I am one with the universe, actualizing the true self beyond space and time." Of course if we think this, we are just thinking about zazen rather than actualizing it. So our sitting is really nothing special; rather than thinking that we are actualizing enlightenment, we just sit wholeheartedly moment by moment. And yet in this simple sitting practice we go beyond our limited individuality as the Buddha Dharma is realized.

# We Wave a Fan Because Wind Nature Is Everywhere

(13) Zen master Baoche of Mt. Magu was waving a fan. A monk approached him and asked, "The nature of wind is ever present and permeates everywhere. Why are you waving a fan?"

The master said, "You know only that wind's nature is ever present—you don't know that it permeates everywhere."

The monk said, "How does wind permeate everywhere?"

The master just continued waving the fan.

The monk bowed deeply.

The genuine experience of Buddha Dharma and the vital path that has been correctly transmitted are like this. To say we should not wave a fan because the nature of wind is ever present, and that we should feel the wind even when we don't wave a fan, is to know neither ever-presence nor the wind's nature. Since the wind's nature is ever present, the wind of the Buddha's family enables us to realize the gold of the great Earth and to transform the [water of] the long river into cream.

## ZEN MASTER MAGU BAOCHE

MAGU BAOCHE (Jap.: Mayoku Hōtetsu) was a Chinese Zen master who trained with Mazu Daoyi (Jap.: Baso Doitsu, 709–88) and became his Dharma heir. As was the custom in China at the time, Magu took his name from the mountain where he lived as a Zen teacher. Before I discuss this final section of Genjōkōan, I would like to talk about who Magu was, because I believe Dōgen Zenji considered his identity to be an important point in the message of Genjōkōan.

In his collection of three hundred kōans titled Mana-Shōbōgenzō, Dōgen included three stories about Magu. One of these kōans (no. 123) is the one presented here in Genjōkōan. Another kōan of Mana-Shōbōgenzō (no. 244), the story of Magu's visit to master Linji Yixuan (Jap.: Rinzai Gigen), also appears in the Linji-lu (Rinzai-roku; The Record of Zen Master Rinzai). Here is the story as it appears in the Linji-lu:

> Magu once asked Linji, "[The Bodhisattva of] the Great Compassion (Avalokiteshvara) has one thousand hands and eyes. Which one is the true eye?"
>
> Linji said, "[The Bodhisattva of] the Great Compassion has one thousand hands and eyes. Which one is the true eye? Say quickly! Say quickly!"
>
> Magu grabbed Linji's hand and dragged him down from his seat and Magu sat on the seat.
>
> Linji finally stood up and said, "How are you?"
>
> Magu tried to say something. Linji shouted and grabbed Magu's hand and dragged him down from his seat and he sat in it. Magu walked out of the hall.[50]

Here is another similar story about the two masters from the Linji-lu:

Magu visited. He spread his sitting cloth and asked, "Avalokiteshvara has twelve faces. Which one is the true face?"

The master came down from the corded chair. He folded the sitting cloth and hung it in one hand and with the other hand he held Magu and said, "Where has the twelve-faced Avalokiteshvara gone?"

Magu turned his body and tried to sit on Linji's corded chair.

The master held his monk's staff and hit him.

Magu grabbed the staff. Both held on one end of it and went off to the master's room.[51]

It is not certain that the Magu who appears in these stories with Linji is indeed Magu Baoche, Mazu's disciple. Because "Magu" is the name of a mountain, it is possible that these stories refer to someone else who lived on that mountain. As I mentioned above, Magu Baoche (Mayoku Hōtetsu) was a disciple of Mazu Daoyi (Baso Doitsu), but Linji was a member of the third generation of Mazu's lineage (Mazu → Baizhang [Hyakujō] → Huangbo [Ōbaku] → Linji). Did Magu live long enough to see Linji joining his assembly? We are not sure because Magu's birth and death dates are unknown.

There also is a lack of consistent information concerning Magu's background in traditional Zen source texts. For example, a note in the Linji section of Jingde Chuandeng Lu (Jap.: Keitoku Dentoroku; Transmission of the Dharma Lamp) says that the Magu in the story of the twelve-faced Avalokiteshvara was the second abbot of Mt. Magu. However, Magu Baoche's own biography, written after his death by his only disciple Liangsui, contains no mention of this fact. In the Mana-Shōbōgenzō, Dōgen Zenji writes that Magu was the Dharma heir of Mazu, and although it is possible that Dōgen's information was mistaken, I think the Master Magu who Linji praises so highly in the Linji-lu (Rinzai-roku) is indeed Magu Baoche (Mayoku Hotetsu), Mazu's disciple.

The important point for us in our study of Genjōkōan is that for Dōgen, Magu represented a master who was a vehicle of the authentic Buddhist teachings before the Zen tradition separated into the Five Schools. Dōgen wanted simply to transmit Buddha Dharma, not the teachings of any particular school or philosophy of Zen.

In any case, the two preceding stories of Magu and Linji are much alike, and both may have evolved from one original tale. In the stories, both Magu and Linji (Rinzai) take the role of the face and eyes of Avalokiteshvara. This symbolism suggests that both masters had the true eyes and face of the Bodhisattva of Great Compassion, and we can see from these stories that Master Linji held Magu in great respect. And although Huangbo Xiyun (Ōbaku Kiun, d. 850) was his primary teacher, Linji spoke of four other masters who had a great influence on him in the Linji-lu: "Followers of the way, this mountain monk's Buddha Dharma has been transmitted to me in a very clear line, from Master Magu, Master Danxia (Tanka), Master Daoyi (Doitsu), the Master Lu-shan (Rosan), and Master Shi-kung (Sekkyo). This single road permeates the entire world. But no one trusts this, and everyone slanders it."[52]

Linji then proceeds to comment on each of these masters' styles. Of Magu he writes, "Magu's way of doing things was as bitter as the bark of the Chinese cork tree; no one could get near him." The word Linji used for "Chinese cork tree" is *obaku*, the name of Rinzai's own master. I think this suggests that Magu was as important to Linji as his own master, Huangbo (Obaku), and it indicates that Linji considered the two masters' teaching styles to be very similar. The fact that the great Linji respected Magu so deeply undoubtedly influenced Dōgen Zenji's choice to include in Genjōkōan the story of the master waving a fan.

The third "Magu story" (no. 121) in Mana-Shōbōgenzō involves Magu and Shouchou Liangsui (Jap.: Jushu Ryosui), who would eventually become Magu's Dharma successor. Before visiting Magu, Liangsui was a Buddhist lecturer. Here is the story:

Liangsui first visited Magu. Upon seeing Liangsui coming, Magu took a hoe and went to hoeing up weeds. Although Liangsui went to where Magu was working, Magu paid no attention to him, but rather immediately went back to the abbot's room and shut the gate.

The next day, Liangsui visited again and Magu shut the gate again. Liangsui then knocked on the gate. Magu asked, "Who is this?" (Who are you?)

He said, "Liangsui."

Upon calling out his own name, Liangsui suddenly attained realization. He said, "Master, do not impose upon Liangsui. If I had not come to see you, I would be deceived by the sutras and commentaries my whole life."

When Liangsui went back, he gave a speech to his assembly, "All that you know, Liangsui knows. What Liangsui knows, you don't know."

Then he quit giving lectures and dispersed his assembly.[53]

From the story we learn that although Liangsui was a lecturer who was well versed in Buddhist philosophy, he felt his understanding lacked some important elements. This feeling of lack prompted Liangsui to visit Magu, but Magu completely ignored him when Liangsui arrived at the Magu's monastery. When Magu finally asked him, "Who are you?" Liangsui understood that the Buddha's teaching is not a philosophical system but rather a mirror that reveals one's essential self. After he saw this essential self, Liangsui's feeling of inadequacy was finally alleviated, and he knew that it had been his clinging to the sutras and commentaries that had deceived him.

One of Dōgen's informal talks about this story is recorded in Shōbōgenzō Zuimonki as follows:

Essentially beginners in the Way should just practice [the Way] following the other members of the sangha. Do not

be in a hurry to study and understand the essential points
and ancient examples. It is good to understand such things
without misinterpretation when you enter the mountains
or seclude yourselves in a city. If you practice following
the other practitioners, you will surely attain the Way. It
is like making a voyage; even though you don't know how
to steer the ship, if you leave everything to the skill of the
sailors, whether you understand or not, you will reach the
other shore. Only if you follow a good teacher and practice
with fellow practitioners without harboring personal views
will you naturally become a person of the Way. Students
of the Way, even if you have attained enlightenment, do
not stop practicing. Do not think that you have reached
the pinnacle. The Way is endless. Even if you have attained
realization, continue to practice the Way. Remember the
story of Liangsui who visited Zen master Magu.⁵⁴

It seems clear from this talk that Dōgen regarded Magu as a venerable master. Dōgen is saying that to truly practice we must continually
inquire into the Dharma; the Way is endless. This is the same point,
you will recall, he makes in section 10 of Genjōkōan using the analogy of sailing on the ocean. Here he urges us to use our "eye of study
and practice" to investigate the ocean's inexhaustible characteristics:

This great ocean, however, is neither round nor square. It
has inexhaustible characteristics. [To a fish] it looks like a
palace; [to a heavenly being] a jeweled necklace. [To us] as
far as our eyes can see, it looks like a circle. All the myriad
things are like this. Within the dusty world and beyond,
there are innumerable aspects and characteristics; we only
see or grasp as far as the power of our eye of study and practice can see. When we listen to the reality of myriad things,
we must know that there are inexhaustible characteristics
in both oceans and mountains and there are many other

worlds in the four directions. This is true not only in the external world, but also right under our feet or within a single drop of water.

Since Dōgen associates Magu with endless inquiry in Zuimonki, we can infer that the kōan he presents about wind nature is addressing the same theme: endless practice and inquiry into the nature of reality.

## WIND AND FAN

> Zen Master Baoche of Mt. Magu was waving a fan. A monk approached him and asked, "The nature of wind is ever present and permeates everywhere. Why are you waving a fan?"
>
> The master said, "You know only that wind's nature is ever present—you don't know that it permeates everywhere."
>
> The monk said, "How does wind permeate everywhere?"
>
> The master just continued waving the fan.
>
> The monk bowed deeply.

The story of Magu fanning himself in Mana-Shōbōgenzō differs in a few details from the version in Genjōkōan. Here is a literal translation of the story from Mana-Shōbōgenzō:

> Zen master Baoche of Mt. Magu was Mazu (Baso)'s heir. One day he was waving a fan. A monk asked him, "The Wind Nature abides permanently and there is no place it does not permeate. Why do you wave a fan?"
>
> The master said, "You know only that wind's nature abides permanently—you don't know that there is no place it does not permeate."

The monk said, "What is the principle of there is no place Wind Nature does not permeate?"

The master waved the fan all the more.

The monk made a prostration.

The master said, "Even if I have a thousand monks, what is the merit of those monks if they don't have the actual function?"

One of the eminent Sōtō scholar monks in the Edo period, Shigetsu Ein (1689–1764), wrote a short commentary on each of the three hundred kōans of Mana-Shōbōgenzō in a work titled Nentei Sanbyakusoku Funōgo (Holding and Commenting on the Three Hundred Cases: the Ineffable). Shigetsu's commentary on the story of Magu reads: "This story certainly causes the wind even today. Magu waved the fan and the monk made a prostration. What is this?" Here "what is this" is not a question but a statement. Shigetsu is saying that the reality beyond words and concepts is manifested in both Magu's use of the fan and the monk's prostration.

I have introduced a few stories about Zen Master Magu to show that he was an important Chinese master to both Linji and Dōgen. In these stories we see that rather than intellectual understanding, Magu emphasized practice and function (i.e., work or actions functioning as expressions of Dharma). Dōgen later introduced many other stories in his Chiji-shingi (Pure Standards for the Temple Administrators) with the same theme. Here at the end of Genjōkōan, he cites the story of Magu and wind nature to illustrate the teaching he has presented throughout the text.

"Wind nature" in this story is a reference to Buddha nature. The monk questioning Baoche thought that Buddha nature was, like wind nature, ever present in time and all pervading in space. In studying the history of Mahayana Buddhist philosophy, we find that this is a very different understanding of Buddha nature from its original conception.

In India the word *tathagata-garbha* was more commonly used than *buddhata* (buddha nature). *Garbha* means "womb" or "embryo" in Sanskrit, so *tathagata-garbha* can be translated as "the womb or the embryo of a tathagata," or buddha. In other words, *tathagata-garbha* refers to the teaching that each living being is a womb containing the embryo of a tathagata, of a buddha. If this embryo is well cared for, it will be born and grow to be a mature tathagata in the future.

*Buddha nature*, a synonym for *tathagata-garba*, was first used in the Mahayana Mahaparinirvana Sutra (Mahayana Sutra Concerning the Great Entering of Nirvana). The most famous statement regarding Buddha nature in the sutra is "All living beings without exception have Buddha nature"—a sentiment which has become very familiar to us. In China the term *Buddha nature* (Ch.: *fo-xing*) became much more popular than the term *tathagata-garbha*.

In any case, Buddha nature was originally defined as the hidden, dormant potential to become a tathagata; it is inherent in all living beings. A famous analogy uses the image of a diamond covered with rock and dirt. The diamond represents the Buddha nature that exists in all of us; it is always with us but is hidden beneath the rock and dirt of delusion. One must therefore first discover the diamond and then remove the dirt and rock and polish the diamond with Buddhist practice. Only when a person becomes an enlightened buddha is the true beauty of the diamond revealed.

This theory of Tathagata-garbha, or Buddha nature, which was originally developed to explain how it is possible for ordinary sentient beings to become Buddhas, has been problematic throughout the history of Buddhist philosophy. This is because of its apparent similarity to the ancient Hindu theory of the atman, a teaching Shakyamuni Buddha clearly negated. According to this theory, the atman is a pure, changeless spiritual nature confined within the body. The imprisonment of the atman was seen as the source of delusion and defilement, and it was thought that a person would continue to create karma and transmigrate within samsara as long as the atman was trapped. Ancient Hindus therefore thought that the purpose of religious practice was to release the atman from the prison of the physical body.

Tathagata-garba or Buddha nature theory became the basis for the teachings of many Chinese Buddhist schools through the influence of a work titled Awakening the Faith in the Mahayana (Jap.: *Daijō-kishin-ron*). The text says that the One Mind or "life of living beings" (Jap.: *shujō-shin*; literally, "the mind/heart of living beings") has two aspects. One is the aspect of mind in terms of the absolute, or *tathata* (suchness). The other aspect is the aspect of mind in terms of phenomena, or samsara (the cycle of birth and death). According to the text, these two aspects are mutually inclusive. The absolute tathata is like water, and beings living in samsara are like waves of water created by the "wind" of ignorance. This wind both disturbs the calmness of the water and separates it into the individual waves. In terms of absolute tathata, all living beings (waves) are fundamentally tathata (water), being enlightened from the beginning. This aspect of reality is called "original enlightenment" (*hongaku*), or "ultimate reality" (*li*). Living beings, however, are influenced by the wind of ignorance and therefore create karma that causes them to transmigrate within samsara. The basic idea of this teaching is that we must practice to become free of ignorance and return to original enlightenment. This aspect of reality is called "the process of actualization of enlightenment" (*shikaku*) or "concrete reality" (*ji*).

In sum, this teaching from Awakening the Faith in the Mahayana says that, in ultimate reality (*li*), all living beings are enlightened buddhas from the beginning, but in phenomenal reality (*ji*), we are deluded beings and therefore we need to study and practice to restore our original enlightenment and become buddhas.

## BUDDHA NATURE IN ZEN

The famous debate between the southern and northern schools of Chinese Zen concerning sudden versus gradual enlightenment turned on the teaching of One Mind. Traditionally the southern school is considered to have emphasized original enlightenment (*hongaku*), while the northern school emphasized the process of actualization of enlightenment (*shikaku*). This debate is clearly expressed in the story of the Fifth Ancestor's Dharma transmission to the Sixth Ancestor, found in the biography of Dajian Huineng (Jap.: Daikan Enō, 638–713).

In that story, Yuquan Shenxiu (Jap.: Gyokusen Jinshū, 605–706), the senior monk in his assembly, presented a poem:

> The body is the *bodhi* tree.
> The mind is like a bright mirror's stand.
> At all times we must strive to polish it
> And must not let dust collect.[55]

Huineng, who at the time was a lay worker at the monastery, composed a poem in response:

> Bodhi originally has no tree.
> The bright mirror also has no stand.
> Fundamentally there is not a single thing.
> Where could dust arise?[56]

This pair of poems is considered to contrast the sudden and gradual approaches to enlightenment. Shenxiu's poem says that original enlightenment must be restored by "polishing" away the "dust" of delusion through practice, while Huineng's poem, illustrative of the sudden teaching, says that awakening to fundamental reality is realizing nothingness (there is no mirror, there is no dust). Today's scholars think this is a fictitious story created generations after Huineng by those who wished to raise his status, which at the time was that of a relatively unknown teacher, to that of the Sixth Ancestor. The story was considered to be a historical event in the history of Zen Buddhism, however, from the time of the Song dynasty in China (tenth to thirteenth c.) up to the mid-twentieth century.

Many Zen scholars believe Mazu Daoyi (Jap.: Baso Doitsu; 709–88) was responsible for Zen's emphasis on immediate, concrete reality. Subsequent Zen masters taught that our actions are nothing other than manifestations of tathata, or suchness itself. The two famous sayings of Mazu and his students are "The mind is itself Buddha" (*Sokushin zebutsu*) and "Ordinary mind is the Way" (*Heijo-shin ze-do*). Seeing ultimate reality (*li*) within concrete phenomena (*ji*) was the basis of their teachings. In other words, they taught that Buddha nature is not something hidden in living beings. They said, rather, that all concrete phenomena and all beings are themselves manifestations of tathata, or ultimate reality.

When the monk in this final story of Genjōkōan says, "Wind Nature is ever present and all pervading," he is referring to the traditional Zen teaching that Buddha nature is always manifesting and never hidden. Yet this idea creates another problem: If this teaching is true, why did Magu have to wave a fan in order to reveal the wind (Buddha nature)? If everything is the manifestation of ultimate reality (*tathata*) and we are enlightened from the beginning, why do we have to study and practice? This is a very natural question. In fact, traditionally it is said that the search for an answer to this question was the motivation for Dōgen Zenji's trip to China.

In the story, however, Magu did not answer this question with a theoretical explanation; instead he simply continued waving the fan. Here Dōgen is indicating that practice is not a philosophical debate. We can argue endlessly with our teacher or anyone else, but Dōgen suggests that we simply stop arguing and make a prostration to the person who knows how to wave a fan—that is, to a person who knows how to practice. Perhaps this admonition should prompt us to sincerely ask ourselves, "Have I ever met a person who is actually waving a fan? Am I able to make a sincere prostration to such a person?" and "What is the value of the activity of waving a fan, and what does it say about our practice?"

## DŌGEN AND ORIGINAL ENLIGHTENMENT

As I mentioned above, the question of the value of practice was an issue for Dōgen himself at a certain point in his life. When Dōgen was ordained as a Tendai monk, the movement known as Tendai Hongaku Hōmon (The Dharma Gate of Original Enlightenment) was very popular. The theory emphasized concrete phenomena (*ji*) as absolute, ultimate reality. In other words, it said that deluded living beings are actually enlightened buddhas.

According to his biography, Dōgen Zenji had a question regarding this theory when he was a teenager. He asked, "If all beings are the Dharma nature from the beginning, why do all buddhas have to arouse bodhi-mind, engage in difficult practices, attain awakening, and enter nirvana?" Upon close examination, it becomes clear that Dōgen's question about the theory of original enlightenment and the monk's question to Magu Baoche are the same. Both questions are asking, "If all phenomena are themselves ultimate reality and all living beings are themselves Buddha nature, why do we have to study and practice? Why do we have to make such an effort to improve ourselves and our world?"

Dōgen eventually posed this question to his teacher Tiantong Rujing and recorded their subsequent dialogues about it in *Hōkyōki* (Record in the Hōkyō Era). One of the dialogues reads as follows:

> Teachers in the past and present have said that self-awareness is like a fish that knows whether water is cold or warm when it drinks; this Wisdom is awakening and the realization of enlightenment. I (Dōgen) criticized this understanding. If self-awareness is the true awakening, then all living beings have such awareness. Because all living being know themselves (to be cold or warm, itchy or in pain), are they all tathagatas with true awakening? Some people answered, "Yes, all living beings are the original tathagata from the beginningless beginning." Others said,

"All living beings are not necessarily tathagatas." Why is this so? If they know that self-awareness and natural wisdom are (supreme awakening), they are tathagatas, and if they do not know this, they are not (tathagatas). Are these opinions the Buddha Dharma or not?

Tiantong Rujing answered Dōgen's question in this way:

If people say that all living beings are from the beginning buddhas, they are the same as the non-Buddhists of naturalness. Comparing the self and the attributes of the self to buddhas is nothing other than considering those who have not yet attained to be as those who have attained and those who are not enlightened to be as those who are enlightened.

Here Rujing says that understanding self-awareness to be true awakening is not in accordance with the Buddha's teachings. He says that this understanding is the same as that of non-Buddhists who say that things in their natural states are equal to enlightenment. These people, according to Rujing, say that all man-made things, including practice, originate from delusion and are therefore unnecessary or even evil. But Rujing taught that we cannot see reality and practice from only the absolute perspective. Saying there is no need to practice because everything is already part of enlightenment is to deny the relative reality of cause and effect. Since human beings have the ability to express both delusion and enlightenment, we must practice in order to manifest true awakening, or Buddha nature. This reply from Rujing, which contains the foundational teaching that practice and enlightenment are one, became the basis of Dōgen's own teachings when he returned to Japan.

Before we return to our exploration of Genjōkōan, let's briefly take a look at the texts Dōgen wrote just before he wrote Genjōkōan. Soon after returning to Japan, Dōgen wrote an instructional essay on zazen practice titled Fukanzazengi (Universal Recommendations for Zazen). The essay begins as follows:

> Originally, the Way is complete and universal. How can we distinguish practice from enlightenment? The Vehicle of Reality is in the self. Why should we waste our efforts trying to attain it? Still more, the whole body is free from the world's dust. Why should we believe in a means to sweep it away? The Way is never separated from where we are now. Why should we wander here and there to practice? Yet, if there is the slightest deviation, you will be as far from the Way as heaven is from earth. If adverse or favorable conditions arise to even a small degree, you will lose your mind in confusion—moreover, consider Shakyamuni Buddha who was enlightened from birth; to this day you can see the traces of his sitting in the upright posture for six years. And Bodhidharma who transmitted the mind-seal—even now you can hear of the fame of his facing the wall for nine years. These ancient sages practiced in this way. How can you people of today refrain from practice?

Here Dōgen clearly states that even though the Way is perfect and universal, we must still practice as Shakyamuni Buddha and Bodhidharma did. Why does he say this? Dōgen does not offer an in-depth explanation; he simply says that we should practice because this is what these great sages did. In my opinion Dōgen Zenji is not promoting blind emulation of the actions of those who practiced before us. He is, rather, saying that we must awaken to the same reality that the great sages realized, but we must do this in our own practice. We can only emulate Shakyamuni Buddha and Bodhidharma after entering the truth of practice that they realized; just as a fish must swim rather than fly, and a bird must fly rather than swim, we must practice within our own culture and time with our own bodies and minds. No one can practice for us, even though our expression of enlightenment through practice is the same enlightenment manifested by Shakya-muni Buddha and Bodhidharma.

Bendōwa (Wholehearted Practice of the Way) is Dōgen's second essay and was written in 1231, four years after he returned from China. Here he describes zazen practice as *jijuyu-zanmai* (self-receiving and self-employing samadhi), saying, "When we sit in an upright posture, the entire universe becomes enlightenment." For Dōgen, zazen is the pivotal point of practice.

In the latter section of Bendōwa, which consists of a series of questions and answers, Dōgen discusses various views regarding practice and enlightenment. By studying this section we can see some examples of the views that Dōgen encountered in his search for the Buddha Dharma. Questions 10 and 16, for example, address a certain view of Buddha nature. According to this idea, all beings from their beginning are Buddha, since they all have Buddha nature. From this perspective, to know that one is Buddha is enough, and it is therefore not necessary to practice.

Question 7 deals with the belief that although it is necessary to practice to attain enlightenment, once enlightenment is achieved, practice is no longer needed. This was a common understanding in Rinzai Zen, but Dōgen disagreed. As I discussed earlier, this view emphasizes the "process of actualization of enlightenment" (*shikaku*). According to this view, within ultimate reality we are all enlightened from the beginning, but in actuality we are deluded. We must therefore practice until we rediscover Buddha nature. We make this rediscovery with a *kensho* experience, but after having attained this, further zazen practice is not needed.

These questions give us examples of two opposite extremes Dōgen encountered in his search for the answer to the question "Why practice?"

Genjōkōan is Dōgen's fourth text, written after Fukanzazengi, Bedōwa, and Maka Hannya Haramitsu, and was composed in the fall of 1233, the year he founded his own monastery, Kōshōji. Dōgen gave the manuscript to his lay student Yōkōshū and later placed it at the very beginning of Shōbōgenzō. Maka Hannya Haramitsu, the writing that Dōgen placed as the second chapter of Shōbōgenzō, was actually written before Genjōkōan, in the summer of 1233. Since I think these two writings are closely connected, I would like to compare them once again as we approach the end of our discussion of Genjōkōan.

Recall that in the beginning of Maka Hannya Haramitsu, Dōgen Zenji paraphrases the Heart Sutra:

> The time of Avalokiteshvara Bodhisattva practicing profound prajna paramita is the whole body clearly seeing the emptiness of all five aggregates. The five aggregates are forms, sensations, perceptions, mental formations, and consciousness; this is the fivefold prajna. Clear seeing is itself prajna.
>
> To unfold and manifest this essential truth, [the Heart Sutra] states that "form is emptiness; emptiness is form." Form is nothing but form; emptiness is nothing but emptiness—one hundred blades of grass, ten thousand things.
>
> The twelve sense fields are twelve instances of prajna paramita. Also, there are eighteen instances of prajna: eye, ear, nose, tongue, body, mind; sight, sound, smell, taste, touch, objects of mind; as well as the consciousnesses of eye, ear, nose, tongue, body, and mind. Also, there are four instances of prajna: suffering, its cause, its cessation, and the path [to cessation]. Also, there are six instances of prajna: generosity, pure precepts, calm patience, diligence, quiet meditation, and wisdom. There is also a single instance of prajna manifesting itself right now—unsurpassable complete, perfect awakening. Also, there are three instances of prajna: past, present, and future. Also, there are six instances of prajna: earth, water, fire, wind, space, and consciousness. Also, four instances of prajna are going on daily: walking, standing, sitting, and lying down.

Thus, to reiterate some of what we looked at earlier, here Dōgen tells us that prajna (wisdom) is a practice we perform with our whole body and mind. The whole body and mind clearly sees the emptiness of the five aggregates, and that perception is nothing other than the whole body and mind revealed. The five aggregates themselves (represented by Avalokiteshvara Bodhisattva) see the emptiness of the five aggregates. So this prajna cannot be a particular way in which a subject views objects; in other words, it cannot be just another viewpoint. In the beginning of Genjōkōan Dōgen discusses this point in great detail, and in the latter part he shows us how to practice based on its understanding.

According to Dōgen Zenji, attaining a one-time enlightenment experience in which we recover our Buddha nature is not the goal of practice. Practice for Dōgen is an ongoing activity in which we continue to deepen and broaden our understanding, day by day, moment after moment. For him, enlightenment is a vital life activity that we must nurture, just as we must nurture our bodies. To stay alive, we must digest the food we have eaten every day and breathe moment by moment. In the same way, to manifest awakening we must continually return to awakening day after day, moment by moment; whenever we find that we have strayed from awakening, we must return to it in practice.

Our zazen practice is bodhisattva practice, and it is therefore the foundation of the four bodhisattva vows. The bodhisattva vows are the basis for our practice outside the zendo:

> Beings are numberless, I vow to free them.
> Delusions are inexhaustible, I vow to end them.
> Dharma gates are boundless, I vow to enter them.
> Buddha's Way is unsurpassable, I vow to realize it.

When we begin to practice with the four bodhisattva vows, sooner or later we will see the incompleteness of our practice or notice that we have deviated from the bodhisattva path. Just as we return to our posture in zazen, we practice repentance by returning to the path of the bodhisattva vows. Whether in the zendo or going about our daily routine, moment by moment we simply return to awakening in genuine practice. We must do this over and over again; our practice is endless.

## EXPRESSING THE VITAL FUNCTION

One of the key reasons Dōgen presents the story of Magu waving a fan in Genjokōan is to emphasize the importance of this moment-by-moment practice. His comments here near the conclusion of the text express a central principle of his teachings:

> The genuine experience of Buddha Dharma and the vital path that has been correctly transmitted are like this. To say we should not wave a fan because the nature of wind is ever present, and that we should feel the wind even when we don't wave a fan, is to know neither ever-presence nor the wind's nature.

In the story presented in this final section of Genjōkōan, Magu says that though the monk knows about the ever-presence of wind nature, he does not understand the way it permeates every place. The act of waving a fan represents our moment-by-moment practice, and according to Magu it is through such practice that Wind Nature is able to permeate all existence. Dōgen, however, was even more strict than Magu on this point. He says that the monk understands neither the ever-presence of wind nor its permeating everywhere.

In the original version of this story, the one Dōgen cites in Mana-Shōbōgenzō, Magu makes another statement after the monk's prostration. He says, "Even if I have a thousand monks, what is the merit of monks if they don't have the vital function?" So in the original story it is not clear if Magu acknowledged the monk's prostration or not; it is possible that he thought that the monk's prostration still failed to demonstrate vital function. I think Dōgen omitted Magu's final statement to demonstrate that the monk's final activity can be seen as an instance of waving a fan to produce wind. Or we could say that because the monk was enveloped by the wind of Magu's fanning, he understood the point of practice and demonstrated his understanding with the practice of making a prostration. In either case, he used the activity of practice rather than speech to express the vital function.

Incidentally, in Kazuaki Tanahashi and John Daido Loori's translation of Mana-Shōbōgenzō, *The True Dharma Eye: Dōgen's Three Hundred Kōans*, the final statement of Magu is omitted. This is probably because the translators wanted to make the story consistent with Dōgen's interpretation of it in Genjōkōan.

## THE WIND OF THE BUDDHA'S FAMILY

> Since the wind's nature is ever present, the wind of the Buddha's family enables us to realize the gold of the great Earth and to transform the [water of] the long river into cream.

Like the water for fish and the sky for birds, "the great Earth" symbolizes the world we live in, and "the water of the long river" symbolizes the stream of our lives. "The wind of the Buddha's family" is the product of our ceaseless practice of vow and repentance, which is firmly rooted in shikantaza, or just sitting. This ceaseless practice makes our world as precious as gold and our lives as rich as cream. Here again Dōgen reveals the self and the world of the self (the ten thousand things) as they really are, totally interdependent.

Humans usually think of themselves as individuals separate from other beings and the world, and we moderns even seem to believe that we are the center of the world and owners of all it contains. We think we are entitled to use our environment as a resource to fulfill our desires and make ourselves happy. We fabricate a wall between ourselves and the rest of the world, considering everything inside that wall "my territory" or "my possession," and we continually calculate how many incomings and outgoings we have. If we reckon the inflows are greater than the outflows, we judge our lives successful. Sometimes we manipulate people around us and exploit the natural environment to create this greater income. But no matter how much wealth we accumulate within our fabricated walls, a self-centered attitude toward the world and our own lives does not make the world into gold and transform our lives into nourishing cream. Our zazen practice enables us to reverse this fundamentally upside-down view of the self and the world, and our bodhisattva vows then become the guidelines for a life lived together with all beings. When we become aware that our practice is incomplete and we have strayed from the bodhisattva path, we practice repentance and return to our vows. This is the way our bodhisattva practice enriches our lives endlessly.

*Like a fish in the water*
*Like a bird in the sky.*
*A fish is swimming like a fish.*
*A bird is flying like a bird.*

—Shohaku Okumura

AVALOKITESHVARA BODHISATTVA, when deeply practicing prajna paramita, clearly saw that all five aggregates are empty and thus relieved all suffering. Shariputra, form does not differ from emptiness, emptiness does not differ from form. Form itself is emptiness, emptiness itself form. Sensations, perceptions, mental formations, and consciousness are also like this. Shariputra, all dharmas are marked by emptiness; they neither arise nor cease, are neither defiled nor pure, neither increase nor decrease. Therefore, given emptiness, there is no form, no sensation, no perception, no formation, no consciousness; no eyes, no ears, no nose, no tongue, no body, no mind; no sight, no sound, no smell, no taste, no touch, no object of mind; no realm of sight . . . no realm of mind consciousness. There is neither ignorance nor extinction of ignorance . . . neither old age and death nor extinction of old age and death; no suffering, no cause [of suffering], no cessation [of suffering], no path; no knowledge and no attainment. With nothing to attain a bodhisattva relies on prajna paramita and thus the mind is without hindrance. Without hindrance there is no fear. Far beyond all inverted views one realizes nirvana. All buddhas of past, present, and future rely on prajna paramita and thereby attain unsurpassed, complete, perfect enlightenment. Therefore know the prajna paramita as the great miraculous mantra, the great bright mantra, the supreme mantra, the incomparable mantra, which removes all suffering and is true, not false. Therefore we proclaim the prajna paramita mantra, the mantra that says: "Gate, gate, paragate; parasamgate, bodhisvaha!"

THE TIME OF Avalokiteshvara Bodhisattva practicing profound prajna paramita is the whole body clearly seeing the emptiness of all five aggregates. The five aggregates are forms, sensations, perceptions, mental formations, and consciousness; this is the fivefold prajna. Clear seeing is itself prajna.

To unfold and manifest this essential truth, [the Heart Sutra] states that "form is emptiness; emptiness is form." Form is nothing but form; emptiness is nothing but emptiness—one hundred blades of grass, ten thousand things.

The twelve sense fields are twelve instances of prajna paramita.

Also, there are eighteen instances of prajna: eye, ear, nose, tongue, body, mind; sight, sound, smell, taste, touch, objects of mind; as well as the consciousnesses of eye, ear, nose, tongue, body, and mind.

Also, there are four instances of prajna: suffering, its cause, its cessation, and the path [to cessation].

Also, there are six instances of prajna: generosity, pure precepts, calm patience, diligence, quiet meditation, and wisdom.

There is also a single instance of prajna manifesting itself right now—unsurpassable complete, perfect awakening.

Also, there are three instances of prajna: past, present, and future.

Also, there are six instances of prajna: earth, water, fire, wind, space, and consciousness.

Also, four instances of prajna are going on daily: walking, standing, sitting, and lying down.

There was a monk in the assembly of Shakyamuni Tathagata. He thought to himself, "I should venerate and make prostrations to this most profound prajna paramita. Although prajna paramita teaches that within all things there is neither arising nor extinguishing, there are practical approaches such as precepts, meditation, wisdom, emancipation, and insight resulting from emancipation. Also, there is a practical approach consisting of the ranks of entering the stream, once-returning, nonreturning, and arhat. Also, self-awakening is a practical approach. Unsurpassable perfect awakening is also a practical approach. The [Triple] Treasure of Buddha, Dharma, and Sangha is also a practical approach. Turning the wondrous dharma wheel, saving various sentient beings, is also a practical approach."

The Buddha knew the monk's thoughts, "So it is! So it is! The most profound prajna paramita is indeed subtle and difficult to fathom."

The monk realizes now that by venerating and making prostrations to all things, he is venerating and making prostrations to prajna, which teaches that even though there is neither arising nor ceasing, [there is arising and ceasing]. In this very moment of veneration and prostration, prajna manifests itself in practical approaches such as precepts, meditation, wisdom, and so forth until[57] saving various sentient beings. This [moment of veneration] is called nothingness. The approaches to nothingness thus become practical. This [veneration] is the most profound prajna paramita, subtle and difficult to fathom.

Indra asked the elder Subhuti, "Venerable One, when bodhisattva mahasattvas want to study the most profound prajna paramita, how should they do it?" Subhuti replied, "Kausika, when bodhisattva mahasattvas want to study the most profound prajna paramita, they should study it as empty space."

Therefore, to study prajna is itself empty space. Empty space is studying prajna.

Indra spoke again to the Buddha, "World Honored One, when good men and women accept and keep, read and recite, ponder in accord with reality, and expound to others this profound prajna paramita [which you have just] presented, how can I protect them? World Honored One, I simply wish that you bestow your compassion and teach me."

At that time, the elder Subhuti said to Indra, "Kausika, do you see a dharma that can be protected, or not?"

Indra replied, "No! Venerable One, I don't see any dharma that I can protect."

Subhuti said, "Kausika, when good men and women speak as you have, the most profound prajna paramita is itself protection. If good men and women act as you said, they are never separate from the most profound prajna paramita. You should know that, even if all human and nonhuman beings wanted to harm them, it would not be possible to do so. Kausika, if you want to protect them, you should do as you said. Wanting to protect the most profound prajna paramita and all bodhisattvas is not different from wanting to protect empty space."

You should know that accepting and keeping, reading and reciting, and pondering in accord with reality are nothing other than protecting prajna. The desire to protect is accepting and keeping, reading and reciting, and so on.

My late master, the ancient buddha, said,

> The whole body is like a mouth hanging in empty space.
> Not questioning the winds from east, west, south, or north,
> Equally with all of them, speaking of prajna:
> Ding-dong-a-ling ding-dong.

This is how the prajna has been expressed authentically through buddhas and ancestors. The whole body is prajna. All others [which include the self] are prajna. The whole self [which includes others] is prajna. The entire universe—east, west, south, and north—is prajna.

Shakyamuni Buddha said, "Shariputra, all these sentient beings should make offerings and prostrations to prajna paramita as they do to a living buddha. They should contemplate prajna paramita just as they make offerings and prostrations to Buddha Bhagavat. What is the reason? Prajna paramita is not different from Buddha Bhagavat. Buddha Bhagavat is not different from prajna paramita. Prajna paramita is itself Buddha Bhagavat. Buddha Bhagavat is itself prajna paramita. What is the reason? Shariputra! This is because all supreme, awakened tathagatas issue from prajna paramita. Shariputra! This is because all bodhisattva-mahasattvas, pratyekabuddhas, arhats, nonreturners, once-returners, stream-enterers, and so on issue from prajna paramita. Shariputra! This is because the way of the ten good deeds in the world, the four quiet meditations, the four formless samadhis, and the five divine powers all issue from prajna paramita."

Therefore, Buddha Bhagavat is itself prajna paramita. Prajna paramita is nothing other than all beings. All these beings are empty in form, without arising or extinguishing, neither defiled nor pure, neither increasing nor decreasing. Actualizing this prajna paramita is to actualize Buddha Bhagavat. Inquire into it! Practice it! Making offerings and prostrations [to prajna paramita] is attending and serving Buddha Bhagavat. Attending and serving [all beings] is itself Buddha Bhagavat.

*Note: I deeply appreciate the generosity of Wisdom Publications in granting permission to reprint chapter 2 of Hee-jin Kim's classic book,* Eihei Dōgen—Mystical Realist *(formerly published as* Dōgen Kigen—Mystical Realist*). Dr. Kim's book still stands as the most comprehensive overview written in English of Dōgen's life and its relevance to the history of Japanese Buddhism. I have taken the liberty to add annotations to this chapter where recent scholarship sheds new light on certain details of Dōgen's biography and teachings. Please also be aware that the Wade-Giles system is used for the names of Chinese people, books, and places in Dr. Kim's writing. In this book, we used the Pinyin system. Therefore there are differences in the way Chinese words are spelled between appendix 3 and rest of the book. For example, Dr. Kim spells Dogen's teacher's name as "Juching," but the same name is written as "Rujing" elsewhere. —S.O.*

RELIGION IS a symbolic model with symbols, values, beliefs, and practices that enable us, individually and collectively, to attain spiritual liberation and to grasp the meaning of existence. These elements of religion, in turn, are intricately interwoven with the conditions of our biological and psychological makeup, as well as with sociocultural and historical conditions. Thus, the net result is a unique fabric of an individual's symbolic reality.

Dōgen inherited the symbolic model of Buddhism through his upbringing, studies, and training in Japan and China, and accordingly his thought moved within the framework of this model. Some basic values of Buddhism, especially of Zen, were evident in his life and thought, yet were modified by his personal life as well as by the social and cultural conditions of the early Kamakura period of Japan in which he lived. In what follows, I shall attempt to review and understand some significant features of Dōgen's life so as to pave the way to understanding his thought.

Dōgen's life can be studied according to the following periods: early childhood (1200–1212); apprenticeship in Buddhism (1212–27), which may be subdivided into his spiritual struggle at Hiei and Kenninji (1212–23) and his study in China (1223–27); and the creative period in Japan, which began after his return from China in 1227 and lasted until his death in 1253, and that can be divided into the Yamashiro and Echizen periods. Before we embark on the account of Dōgen's spiritual pilgrimage, we shall briefly observe the social background of the age in which Dōgen's life and thought occurred.

## THE HISTORICAL AND SOCIAL BACKGROUND OF EARLY KAMAKURA JAPAN

The first half of the thirteenth century, namely the early Kamakura period in which Dōgen lived and died, and its immediately preceding phase of the Heian period, had several important features relevant to our investigation of Dōgen's life and thought. They can be explained in terms of the nobility warrior power struggle, the corrupted state of Buddhism, and the traditional folk movements of the masses.

There were two opposing social forces in Japan in those days: the court nobility in Kyoto and the military class in Kamakura. The court aristocracy (the imperial-Fujiwara complex) had already been advancing toward its breakdown by the end of the Heian period. Far removed from the erstwhile "glory and splendor" (*eiga*) of Fujiwara no Michinaga, they desperately clung to whatever vestiges were left of their declining power, which was formally ended by their demise in the Jōkyū War of 1221. Their life was very similar to that of the Heian aristocracy described in *Genji monogatari* (The Tale of Genji). Their activities centered exclusively around political pursuits, amorous adventures, and poetic and artistic indulgences—contingent on the wealth derived from enormous holdings of tax-free estates (*shōen*). Perhaps no society in human history emphasized aesthetic refinement and sensibility more than the Japanese court nobility in those days. As Ivan Morris aptly observes, "Upper-class Heian life was punctuated with poetry from beginning to end, and no important event was complete without it." With this aestheticism were associated two fundamentally related sentiments of the age—the sense of the affective quality of life and the world (*mono no aware*), and the sense of impermanence (*mujō*). Despite its outward pomposity, the aristocratic way of life was permeated by an awareness of beauty shadowed by a sense of sorrow due to beauty's inherently ephemeral character. The court nobles grasped something religious in the beautiful and vice versa. Beauty inspired in them a religious feeling, a sense of the ultimate limits of life, of impermanence and death. Religion, likewise, appealed to them for aesthetic, rather than ethical, reasons. The aristocratic lot in life was interpreted as resulting from karma or fate (*sukuse* or *suguse*) to which they resigned themselves. They were indifferent to the masses, as if their ethical sensibilities were incompatible with their aesthetic sensibilities. Dōgen's life and thought can be adequately understood only against this decadent, overly refined aristocratic tradition into which he was born.

After a decisive victory over the Tairas at the battle of Dannoura in 1185, the Minamoto family established hegemony over Japan with the creation of its feudal government (*bakufu*) in 1192. This set the stage for the rise of the samurai class and its gradually emerging way of life known as "the way of warriors" (*bushidō*). (In its early stage, "the way of warriors" centered strictly on greedy, predatory, and calculating business dealings with little or no sense of loyalty or sacrifice—it was a far cry from the romanticized way of life that later developed in the

Tokugawa period.) Although warriors were culturally "provincial" and looked down upon by aristocrats, their economic, military, and political powers steadily grew and consolidated—they were gradually emerging as a class separate from the aristocrats, farmers, merchants, and artisans. The martial arts were their profession, and they were acutely aware of the ultimate meaning of their profession—the destruction of human lives.

The Minamotos operated basically within the old political framework; they enforced powers delegated to them by the imperial house but were the de facto rulers of Japan without attempting to displace the imperial house. In this respect, they followed precedents that had been set by the Fujiwaras, who had created an incredibly complex political situation in which both aristocratic and military classes were helplessly enmeshed. A historian aptly described it as follows:

> One finds in thirteenth-century Japan an emperor who was a mere puppet in the hands of a retired emperor and a great court family, the Fujiwaras, who together controlled a government, completely dominated by the private government of the Shōgun—who in turn was a puppet in the hands of the Hōjō regent. The man behind the throne had become a series of men, each in turn controlled by the man behind himself.

In addition to this chaotic political situation were the infinitely complicated transactions involving tax-free estates—perhaps the most significant economic institution to mold Japanese life from the latter part of the eighth century to the end of the sixteenth century. By the end of the Heian era, some 80 percent of rice-producing lands in the country belonged to the manorial system, which was fought over by court nobles and samurai warriors.

Conspicuous in this power struggle were also the religious orders. During the Heian period, religious institutions accumulated huge tax-free estates that had to be protected by an oxymoronic Japanese institution, the armed monastics (*sōhei*). Since the middle of the tenth century, major Buddhist monasteries such as the Enryakuji temple on Mt. Hiei, the Onjōji temple in Miidera, and the Tōdaiji and Kōfukuji temples in Nara had standing armies to solve their conflicts with other religious institutions and with the government. They destroyed rival monasteries, demonstrated in the streets of the capital, presented petitions to the imperial court by force (*gōso*), and engaged in many other flagrant militant actions. Although the wealth, prestige, and power of some established monasteries undoubtedly increased, their moral, intellectual, and religious life was dangerously disintegrating. Armed monastics were very active during Dōgen's lifetime, and their entanglements in this grim situation had many sordid psychological and social ramifications.

Another characteristic of Buddhism in this period was its inseparable association with the Heian aristocracy. One of the most conspicuous examples of this was the monopolization of important posts in the monastic centers by members of the imperial house and the Fujiwara family. This resulted in the formation of clerical cliques (*monzeki*) that excluded non-Fujiwara aspirants. As political careers at court became exceedingly elusive due to the growing numbers of the Fujiwara clan, some saw the monastic profession as the next surest way to wealth and power, regardless of their religious motivation. In addition, the activities at many monastic centers revolved around magico-religious rites and prayers (*kaji-kitō*) of esoteric Buddhism that were designed for the protection of the nation and the welfare of the court aristocracy. The complete secularization (i.e., aristocratization) of Buddhism, with no distinction between Buddha-law (*buppō*) and secular law (*ōbō*), was firmly established when Dōgen entered Mt. Hiei for study in his youth.

In this period, the Buddhist doctrine of the Three Ages (*shō-zō-matsu no sanjisetsu*) was widely accepted. The Three Ages were the Age of Right Law (*shōbō*) in which the genuinely authentic Dharma (universal truth and righteousness) prevailed, the Age of Imitative Law (*zōbō*) in which mere forms of Dharma dominated, and the Age of Degenerate Law (*mappō*) in which Dharma was entirely decayed. In the first age, teaching, practice, and attainment of enlightenment prevailed; in the second, teaching and practice alone; and in the third, there was only teaching. The Age of Degenerate Law, as interpreted by some circles of Buddhism in Japan, was believed to have begun in 1052. This calculation was accepted by both the aristocrats and the general populace; the Buddhist leaders of the time based their diagnosis of the current religious situation upon this doctrine. This belief was reinforced by incessant earthquakes, fires, murders, epidemics, and famines in the late Heian and early Kamakura periods. Thus, a historical consciousness developed that was based on a sense of "apocalyptic crisis" and a conviction in the utter wretchedness and helplessness of humankind, along with a concomitant spiritual exigency that led to faith in the unfailing compassion and grace of Amida Buddha.

Dōgen, while utilizing the scheme of the Three Ages, rejected such romantic pessimism toward human nature and history, for to him human nature possessed the elements of both greatness and wretchedness, regardless of time and place. Thus he remarked:

> The ancient sages were not necessarily of sturdy build, nor were all the forebears richly endowed. It had not been long since the death of Śākyamuni Buddha, and when we consider Buddha's lifetime, not all people were superior: there were both sheep and goats. Among monastics some were unimaginable villains and others were of the lowest character.

Whether human beings were great or wretched was determined not by external conditions, but by our manner of dealing with one another. This doctrine was relevant to Dōgen to the extent that it diagnosed the mass spiritual crisis of his time and aided individuals in confronting this crisis. Otherwise, it was nothing but a symptom of human failure to deal with life and the world.

As we turn our attention from the affairs of nobles, warriors, and religionists to those of the masses, we see that the farmers, merchants, and artisans at that time were in a downtrodden state, though they had gained social and economic power. The corruption and indifference of the ruling classes, chaotic social and political conditions, and omnipresent sufferings and miseries led these disinherited people toward something radically new that promised to revitalize their spiritual life. Their primitive yearnings had been, more often than not, associated with various folk-traditional undercurrents that were deeper than Buddhist and Confucian religious ideologies. In particular, the so-called holy men (*hijiri*)—with shamanistic, magico-religious practices and beliefs—were active among the masses from the latter part of the tenth century on, disseminating "the essential importance of individual faith and unworldliness" that was at odds with institutional Buddhism. As Hori emphasizes, the *hijiri* movement was essentially folk-traditional, anti-authoritarian, and anti-secular; it paved the way for a new Kamakura Buddhism, particularly Pure Realm Buddhism. Lay monastics (*shami*) also increased in number and quietly engaged in a spiritual revitalization of the common people. In a very real sense, these holy men and lay monastics were the predecessors of Kamakura Buddhism, which could be regarded as the cultic and intellectual purification and crystallization of the passionate personal faith that they advocated.

Dōgen's Zen Buddhism was no exception in that it also was a part of this general movement taking place in medieval Japan. In addition, the folk tradition of Japan had many other features relevant to our subject matter—especially the tradition of *dōzoku* (a kind of kinship system) in the social structure of Japan, and the tradition of mountain asceticism and purification that was deeply rooted in the Japanese folk mentality. Perhaps no Kamakura Buddhist would appear more remote from folk tradition than Dōgen—antimagical, elitist, eremitic—and yet, his was a religion of the people that came into being and sustained itself by drawing its creativity and vitality from a source deeper and more indigenous than the enfeebled ideologies and adventures of the aristocratic tradition.

## EARLY CHILDHOOD:
## INITIATION INTO IMPERMANENCE

Dōgen was born in Kyoto in the first month of 1200, perhaps as an illegitimate son of Koga Michichika and the daughter of Fujiwara Motofusa. He was among eleven sons and three daughters of Michichika.[1] The Koga (or Minamoto) family was descended from Prince Tomohira, son of Emperor Murakami (r. 946–57). During the lifetime of Michichika, then the Lord Keeper of the Privy Seal, the family was at the height of its power and prosperity and controlled both the dominating power of the Fujiwara family and the pro-shōgun force within the courtly circle in Kyoto. In addition, Michichika stood unparalleled in the literary circle (the Murakami Genji's literary fame was well known) and was unfailingly devoted to the imperial family (the Murakami Genji had the tradition of fighting for the restoration of the imperial rule). His mother was a beautiful, yet ill-fated woman who, according to one account, was married to and separated from Kiso Yoshinaka[2] and subsequently married to Koga Michichika.

Michichika died suddenly in 1202, when Dōgen was only two years of age. After the death of his father, Dōgen was raised by his mother and half-brother, Michitomo, in a culturally over-refined atmosphere.[3] Many of his brothers and sisters occupied eminent positions in the imperial court and were well versed in poetry and the classics. It is not difficult to imagine that Dōgen must have been systematically educated in the Chinese and Japanese classics, and well

---

1. Today many scholars believe Minamoto Michichika (1148–1202) was actually Dōgen's grandfather and that Michichika's second son, Michitomo (1169–1227), was Dōgen's father.

2. Many scholars now believe that Dōgen's mother could not have been the person who was married to Kiso Yoshinaka.

3. Although many scholars do still believe Dōgen's mother was Fujiwara Motofusa's daughter who died when Dōgen was seven years old, many now believe that Michitomo was his father and that Dōgen was adopted by his uncle on his mother's side (see note 1 above).

trained in literary skills and techniques that were the *sine qua non* of aristocratic life. Dōgen recalled later: "In my boyhood I studied history and literature enthusiastically." He also wrote:

> As a result of my predilection for study from childhood, I am prone even now to examine the rhetorical expressions of non-Buddhist classics and to consult the *Wên-hsüan* [an anthology of classical proses and verses]. But I believe that such a thing is irrelevant and should be discarded once and for all.

Dōgen urged his disciples to pay attention not so much to the rhetoric, however notable it might be, as to the content of the writing under study. However, his sensitivity to language was cultivated in a refined literary environment, as evidenced by his poetic excellence, his fondness of the use of a flowing medieval Japanese style rather than a Chinese style, his instruction on "loving speech" (*aigo*), and his deep insight into the nature of language and symbols in human thought. Dōgen eschewed vainglorious aestheticism, but never relinquished his poetic sensibility.

At the age of seven, in 1207, Dōgen lost his mother, who at her death earnestly requested him to become a monastic to seek the truth of Buddhism and strive to relieve the tragic sufferings of humanity. Unlike his father's death, which took place when he was only two,[4] his mother's death must have been a serious blow to Dōgen's fragile and sensitive mind. We are told that in the midst of profound grief, Dōgen experienced the impermanence of all things as he watched the ascending incense at his mother's funeral service.

This experience left an indelible impression upon Dōgen, which no doubt determined the direction of his subsequent spiritual journey.

---

4. If Dōgen's father was actually Minamoto Michitomo (see note 1 above), Dōgen was not orphaned as a child since Michitomo lived until 1227, the year Dōgen returned from China. In fact many of the oldest biographic materials on Dōgen, including Keizan's *Denkōroku*, say Dōgen's father was still alive when Dōgen became a monk at age thirteen.

Later, Dōgen would emphasize, time and again, the intimate relationship between the desire for enlightenment (*bodaishin*) and the awareness of impermanence (*mujō*) and death. To Dōgen, the lucid understanding of life and the thorough penetration of death (*ryōshō-tasshi*), that is a total understanding of the meaning (*dōri*) of impermanence and death, were the alpha and omega of religion. Dōgen understood the impermanent character of life in religious and metaphysical terms rather than in psychological or aesthetic ones, and he lived out this understanding in his monastic life. Dōgen's way of life was not a sentimental flight from, but a compassionate understanding of, the intolerable reality of existence.

Five years after his mother's death, Dōgen was confronted by another crisis. After he was orphaned, Dōgen was adopted by Fujiwara Moroie, his mother's younger brother, who at over forty years of age did not yet have an heir and consequently wanted to train Dōgen for this honor. This meant the promise of a brilliant career for Dōgen in the tradition of the Fujiwara hegemony, even though the Fujiwara hegemony was in decline during this time. In the spring of 1212, Moroie planned to have a *gempuku* ceremony for Dōgen to mark his initiation into aristocratic manhood. At this juncture, Dōgen was forced to choose either to become a monastic or follow his uncle's desire. Dōgen decided to become a monastic, and visited Ryōkan, another uncle on his mother's side, in the Onjōji temple at the foot of Mt. Hiei, for an intelligent discussion of the matter. Deeply moved by Dōgen's determination and motivation, Ryōkan recommended that he study at the Senkōbō at Yokawa-Hannyadani on Mt. Hiei, one of the most renowned centers of Buddhist studies at that time. Upon hearing the news of Dōgen's decision to become a monastic, Moroie was greatly disappointed.

To Dōgen there was no conflict between his decision and his filial piety to Moroie. As he saw it, to study Buddhism was to fulfill his duty to Moroie. He wrote that filial piety should not be limited to one's parents alone but extended to all sentient beings, and further said: "To follow the Way obediently in our living from day to day and in our study from moment to moment—that is the truest filial piety." In a more revealing statement indicative of his unique style of Zen, Dōgen wrote:

> Even the Buddhas and ancestors are not without tender feelings and affections (on'ai) but they have thrown them away. The Buddhas and ancestors, too, are not lacking various bonds, yet they have renounced them. Even though you hold them dear, the direct and indirect conditions forsake the bonds of affection, they in turn shall desert you. If you must care for tender feelings, treat them with compassion; to treat them with compassion means to resolutely relinquish them.

Thus: "The students of Buddhism should not study Dharma for their own profit but only for the sake of Dharma." The Way, for the sake of the Way, heartless as it may have sounded, was the core of Dōgen's spiritual search from beginning to end.

## APPRENTICESHIP IN BUDDHISM

In the fourth month of 1213, Dōgen's ordination ceremony was administered by Kōen, abbot of the Enryakuji temple on Mt. Hiei. Thereafter Dōgen delved deeply into a systematic study of Buddhist sūtras at the Senkōbō. A more favorable educational environment could not have been found in those days than at Hiei. Dōgen devoured these studies with his gifted mind. His earnest search for truth at that time and thereafter can be seen in the emphasis he placed on the need to live seriously. Some twenty years later, Dōgen repeatedly maintained in his Shōbōgenzō Zuimonki: "The arising and decaying of all things occur swiftly; birth-and-death is gravely important" (mujō-jinsoku shōji-jidai). The impermanence of existence did not lead him to fatalism or to the pessimism that pervaded the age; on the contrary it led him to heightened vitality in the search for the Way. Dōgen admonished: "Having a transient life, you should not engage in anything other than the Way." He further wrote:

> In a Chinese classic it is said: "I shall be content even to die in the evening if only I hear the Way in the morning." Even if you were to die by starvation or by cold, you ought to follow the Way even a day or even an hour. How many times might we be born again and die again in an infinitude of aeons and rebirths? Such a hope is nothing but a blind attachment to worldly conditions. Die of starvation in following the Way once and for all in this very life, and you shall attain eternal peace and tranquility. . . . If you do not seek enlightenment here and now on the pretext of the Age of Degenerate Law or wretchedness, in what birth are you to attain it?

And: "At each moment do not rely upon tomorrow. Think of this day and this hour only, and of being faithful to the Way while given a life even just for today, for the next moment is uncertain and unknown." Elsewhere Dōgen stated:

> The student of Buddhism should think of the inevitability of dying. While the truth is too obvious to be thought in those words, you should not waste your precious time by doing useless things, but instead do worthwhile things. Of many worthwhile things, just one—indeed all else is futile—is vitally important: the way of life of the Buddhas and ancestors (*busso no anri*).

"Today's life does not guarantee tomorrow's. The possibility and danger of dying are always at hand." These statements, though written much later in his life, unmistakably reflected the seriousness of the religious enterprise Dōgen undertook at the Senkōbō after his initiation into Buddhism.

While he was studying the sūtras at the Senkōbō, Dōgen was confronted with an apparently insoluble question that, according to the biographies of Dōgen, was as follows:

> As I study both the exoteric and the esoteric schools of Buddhism, they maintain that human beings are endowed with Dharma-nature by birth. If this is the case, why did the Buddhas of all ages—undoubtedly in possession of enlightenment—find it necessary to seek enlightenment and engage in spiritual practice?

No one on Mt. Hiei could give a satisfactory answer to this spiritual problem. The question itself, however, was of such magnitude in Dōgen's religious struggle that he was thereafter restless until he finally found an answer in 1225 from Ju-ching at the T'ien-t'ung monastery.

Dōgen's question was concerned with the time-honored Mahāyāna doctrines of original enlightenment (*hongaku*) and acquired enlightenment (*shikaku*). The doctrine of original enlightenment was propounded primarily by Tendai Buddhism, which was responsible for the synthesis of diverse currents of Buddhist thought, such as Tendai, Kegon, Shingon, and Zen. Although the doctrine itself was as old as the early history of Mahāyāna Buddhism, its most radical interpretation was formulated in Japan during the Heian and Kamakura periods, for the most part by Tendai thinkers, who pressed the doctrine to its logical extremity. Several aspects of the doctrine were as follows: Original enlightenment was eternal in that it was not a temporal occurrence that had a beginning and an end in time. Opposites, such as enlightenment and delusion, life and death, being and nonbeing, one and many, were dialectically negated and in turn affirmed, without minimizing their respective absolute status. Related to this was the unity of enlightenment and practice, in which emphasis was placed not so much on special forms of religious discipline as it was on activities of daily life. The metaphysical status of phenomenon (*ji*) was now construed as primary, in contrast to that of principle (*ri*); accordingly, the existential actualities of a given situation acquired supreme importance. Things, events, and values as they existed in actuality were eternalized not as the manifestations of principle, but precisely by virtue of the intrinsic status of the phenomena themselves. Doctrinal studies were held in disrepute, and instead, an instantaneous liberation here and now through faith in original enlightenment was assured.

In addition, the doctrine of original enlightenment was accompanied by a cognate doctrine of "this body itself is Buddha" (*sokushin-jōbutsu*), which was likewise radicalized by Japanese Buddhism. This tenet accepted the immediate enlightenment of the psycho-physical existence with all its particularities, which were not, as Zen Buddhists would say, "a finger pointing to the moon," but the moon itself, or to put it differently, not the accommodative manifestations of the Body of Law (*dharmakāya; hosshin*), but the Body of Law itself. This doctrine of esoteric Buddhism, both the Shingon and Tendai versions, influenced the ethos of the time. Mundane existence was sanctified, as it was by the doctrine of original enlightenment.

The doctrines of original enlightenment and of "this-body-itself-is-Buddha" went hand-in-hand in reinforcing the efficacy of faith, the absolutization of phenomena, and the instantaneous attainment of liberation. When one denied any metaphysical hiatus between principle and phenomenon, however, even the profoundest Mahāyāna doctrines became dangerously indistinguishable from a crude and irresponsible acceptance of whatever existed in the world, at the sacrifice of spiritual exertions. In fact, a number of dangerous misinterpretations of these doctrines were rampant toward the close of the Heian period, and were especially flagrant among worldly minded Buddhist monastics who attempted to rationalize the pursuit of their selfish interests. Furthermore, an exclusive claim of faith, which required no strenuous religious or moral exertion, became readily associated with the antinomian cynicism inspired by the Age of Degenerate Law.

It is worth noting that this moral, intellectual, and religious crisis coincided with the popularity of the doctrines of original enlightenment and "this-body-itself-is-Buddha." The latter unwittingly served to rationalize the apathetic state of affairs. The significance of Dōgen's original question at Mt. Hiei and his endeavors thereafter can only be properly understood in light of his acute sense of this crisis of the age in which he lived.

If we are primordially enlightened and consequently liberated here and now within this body-mind existence, then why do we have to exert ourselves at all? What is the significance of intellectual, moral, cultic, and religious activities and endeavors? Dōgen did not question the truth of original enlightenment, but believed it with his whole heart and mind. However, he did question the significance of the activities that constituted human existence, which amounted to asking, "What is the meaning of existence?"[5]

With his question unanswered, Dōgen finally left Hiei when Kōen resigned as abbot. He brought the question to Kōin (1145–1216) at the Onjōji temple in Miidera in the province of Ōmi. However, Kōin was unable to answer his question; instead, the latter referred the young man to Eisai (1141–1215),[6] who had returned from China to found Rinzai Zen and who resided at the Kenninji temple in Kyoto. Dōgen later wrote:

5. Since the 1980s Sōtō Zen scholars have debated both the nature of Dōgen's key doctrinal question raised at Mt. Hiei and his view of the theory of original enlightenment. The discussion began with Komazawa University scholars who propounded the Critical Buddhism hypothesis. They insisted that the Tathagata-garbha (Buddha nature) theory, a variation of the theory of original enlightenment, is incompatible with authentic Buddhist teaching. Within this context Professor Yamauchi Shunyū, an expert in both Chinese Tendai teachings and the medieval Japanese Tendai theory of original enlightenment, said the question introduced in Dōgen's biography was very elementary and common to the period, there being many examples of answers to such questions in Tendai teachings of the day. Yamauchi suggested the question was invented by an author of one of Dōgen's biographies in order to explain why Dōgen left Mt. Hiei at such a young age. Yamauchi also suggested Dōgen was persistently critical of the theory of original enlightenment.

6. In the oldest biographical sources Kōin advises the young Dōgen to travel to China to study Zen Buddhism; he does not encourage him to visit Eisai at Kenninji. In Shōbōgenzō Zuimonki, Dōgen himself quotes general advice he received from Kōin: "Bodhi-mind is studying the dharma-gate (teachings) of 'the three-thousand worlds in a single moment of thought,' and keeping them in one's mind. This is called bodhi-mind. To meaninglessly wander around in confusion with a bamboo hat hanging around one's neck is called a deed influenced by a demon."

As a result of the desire for enlightenment which was first aroused in my mind through the awareness of the impermanence of existence, I traveled extensively to various places and, finally having descended Mt. Hiei to practice the Way, settled at the Kenninji temple. Until then I had met neither a right teacher nor a good friend and consequently had gone astray and had erroneous thoughts.

Dōgen apparently visited Eisai at the Kenninji temple in 1214. Founded by Eisai in 1202, the Kenninji temple was at the time not only the center of Zen, but was also the center of studies for Tendai, Shingon, and other schools of Buddhism. Indeed, Kenninji was a rival of Hiei and visiting Eisai under such circumstances was a bold venture for a young man of only fourteen. At any rate, "Dōgen entered Eisai's school and heard Rinzai Zen Buddhism for the first time." Despite the fact that there was an extremely short length of time between Dōgen's visit in 1214 and Eisai's death in 1215, and that Dōgen probably could not have had frequent and intimate personal contact with Eisai,[7] given the latter's constant travel between Kyoto and Kamakura to propagate Zen, Eisai's lasting influence on Dōgen cannot be denied. However, the Kenninji visit was only one stop among many in Dōgen's extensive traveling. His willingness to learn from a variety of sources was indicative of his moral courage and intellectual openness, and revealed his "intersectarian" approach to Buddhism, which would later revitalize the religion in his time.

7. It is uncertain that Dōgen and Eisai actually ever met, and many scholars especially doubt the possibility of their meeting at Kenninji. Menzan's revised Kenzeiki states that Dōgen went to Mt. Hiei in 1212, raised his famous question within a year of his ordination in 1213, visited Kōin in 1214, and visited Eisai later in 1214 at Kenninji where he began to practice under Eisai's guidance. The account says that after Eisai's death in 1215, Dōgen continued to practice at Kenninji with Eisai's disciple Myōzen until 1223. However, older sources state that it was not until 1217 that Dōgen left Mt. Hiei to begin his Zen practice with Myōzen at Kenninji. Although we cannot completely dismiss the possibility that while still living at Mt. Hiei Dōgen visited Eisai, it is certain that Dōgen did not move to Kenninji in 1214. Even if Dōgen and Eisai did meet during the time Dōgen resided at Mt. Hiei, the meeting was likely of little significance to Dōgen since he undoubtedly met many high-ranking teachers during his stay at the Tendai monastery.

After three years' wandering,[8] Dōgen again settled at the Kenninji temple in 1217 to receive the instructions of Myōzen (1184–1225) and stayed there until 1223, when he left to study in China. During this period, Dōgen studied Rinzai Zen systematically; at the same time a warm relationship between Myōzen and Dōgen developed as they studied together as teacher and disciple. It may be fair to say that Dōgen's knowledge about Zen Buddhism was acquired from Myōzen, who was the highest-ranking disciple of Eisai and his successor. Some ten years later, Dōgen wrote about Myōzen with respect and affection: "Myōzen Zenji, the chief disciple of the founder Eisai—he alone transmitted the supreme Dharma rightly. None of the others could equal him in this respect." Undoubtedly, Dōgen's six years of study under Myōzen, during which he was constantly encouraged and assisted by his teacher, must have been as momentous as the study he had had at Hiei.

Yet still, Dōgen could not erase a feeling of dissatisfaction. He reminisced later:

> Although my teachers were just as distinguished as any others in the world of Buddhist scholarship, they taught me to become famous in the nation and to bring honor to the whole country. Thus in my study of Buddhism, I thought, above all, to become equal to ancient wise ones of this country and to those who held the title of Great Teacher (*daishi*). As I read in this connection [Hui-chao's] *Kao-sêng ch'uan* (Biographies of Eminent Buddhist Monastics) and [Tao-hsüan's] *Hsü kao-sêng ch'uan* (Further Biographies of Eminent Buddhist Monastics) and others, and studied eminent Buddhist monastics and scholars of the great T'ang dynasty, I came to realize

8. Current scholarship indicates it is unlikely Dōgen wandered for three years during this time (see note 7 above). The oldest biographical sources state that he practiced in the Tendai tradition for six years at Mt. Hiei from 1212 until 1217, and Dōgen's thorough knowledge and understanding of the Lotus Sutra and Tendai teachings seem to corroborate this evidence.

that they differed from what my teachers taught. What is more, I realized that thoughts such as mine, according to their treatises and biographies, were loathed by these people. Having contemplated the nature of the matter at last, I thought to myself I should have rather felt humbled by ancient sages and future good men and women instead of elated by the praise of despicable contemporaries. As for an aspiration for greatness, I wished to emulate the greatness of Indian and Chinese monastics and scholars rather than my countryfolk. Also I should have aspired to be equal to the gods of heavens and invisible worlds, Buddhas and bodhisattvas. In view of such a realization, the holders of the title of Great Teacher in this country seemed to me worthless, like earthen tiles, and my whole life was changed completely.

This passage summarized Dōgen's ten-plus years of spiritual struggle at Hiei and Kenninji. His original question remained unanswered; he could not find a right teacher, and the general circumstances of Japanese Buddhism at the time were unfavorable to him. Regarding his failure to find a right teacher (*shōshi*), Dōgen wrote:

Right teachers have not appeared in our country since olden times. How can we tell this? Observe their utterances. They are like those who try to fathom the source of a stream by scooping up a handful of water. Although the ancient teachers of this country wrote books, taught disciples, and expounded teachings to humans and gods, their speeches were green and their expression yet immature. They did not attain the summit of an intellectual grasp of doctrines, much less the neighborhood of enlightenment. They merely transmitted words and letters, while their disciples recited names and sounds. Day and night they counted others' riches for nothing. Herein lies my charge against the ancient teachers. Some led people to seek enlightenment outside the conditions of mind, while still others led them to desire rebirth in other lands. Confusions arise from and delusions originate in this. . . . Alas, Buddhism has not yet been disseminated in this tiny remote country, and right teachers have not yet appeared. If you want to study the best of Buddhism, you should consult the scholarship of China far away and reflect thoroughly on the living path that transcends the deluded mind. When you don't meet a right teacher, it is better not to study Buddhism at all.

Uttered by a man with an essentially conservative frame of mind, these words were a startling attack on the immaturity of contemporary Japanese Buddhism.

Perhaps as a result of this disillusionment, the possibility (or more appropriately the necessity) of study in China, which had been originally suggested by Kōin, might have emerged in Dōgen's mind as the next step necessary for the fulfillment of his search for truth. Or as Takeuchi surmises, the Jōkyū (or Shōkyū)War in 1221 with all its miseries and sufferings—especially the banishment of three ex-emperors (all of whom were related to Dōgen's family), countless bloody executions, and the involvement of armed monastics—may have prompted Dōgen's decision to study in China. Dōgen brought the matter to Myōzen, and both began preparing to study abroad immediately after the Jōkyū War. In the second month of 1223, after due formalities, a party of Myōzen, Dōgen, and others left the Kenninji temple and toward the end of the third month set sail for China from Hakata in Chikuzen.

The group's voyage on the East China Sea was not always smooth. Particularly for Dōgen—a man of frail physical frame who probably had not had any previous experience on a ship, the voyage must have been a tough one. Early in the fourth month, the ship arrived at Ch'ing-yüan-fu in Mingchou (now the province of Chekiang).

While Myōzen immediately entered the Ching-tê-ssû temple on Mt. T'ien-t'ung, Dōgen lived on the ship, visited various other temples, and observed the Chinese customs until early in the seventh month, when he was able to enroll at the Ching-tê-ssû temple.

While Dōgen was living on the ship, an old Chinese monk who was sixty-one years of age came on board to get Japanese *shiitake* (a kind of mushroom for soup). He was the chief cook at the monastery on Mt. A-yü-wang (Yüwang), situated some eighty-five miles from where the ship was anchored. In the course of a lively conversation, Dōgen, paying courtesy to the old man, asked him to stay overnight and talk some more. The old man, however, declined and insisted on returning to the monastery immediately after he bought the *shiitake*. Dōgen apparently could not understand why this man had to return in such a hurry, despite the fact that the monastic food, in Dōgen's view, could readily be prepared by other cooks without him. In response to Dōgen's puzzlement, the old man said: "The reason for my being the chief cook at such an old age is that I regard this duty as the practice of the Way (*bendō*) for the rest of my life. How can I leave my practice to other persons? Besides I did not obtain permission for staying out." Then Dōgen asked: "Why are you, a person of advanced age, engaged in such a troublesome task as the chief cook rather than in practicing zazen or reading the kōans of old masters? Is there any worthwhile thing in your work?" To this question, the old monk laughed loudly and said: "You, a good man from a foreign country, perhaps do not understand what the practice of the Way is, nor what words and letters (*monji*) are." Upon hearing this old man's remark, Dōgen was "all of a sudden shocked and ashamed profoundly." Promising Dōgen that he would discuss the matter some day in the future, the old man disappeared hurriedly into the gathering dusk.

In the seventh month of 1223, Dōgen at last left the ship and enrolled at the Ching-tê-ssû temple on Mt. T'ien-t'ung where Wu-chi Liao-p'ai (d. 1224) was abbot. This was the same temple where Eisai had studied and, as one of the "Five Mountains," was a leading center of Zen Buddhism in China. It was supported by the Chinese royal court and had a population of monastics that was reportedly never fewer than one thousand.

One day in the seventh month, soon after Dōgen's enrollment at the Ching-tê-ssû temple, a second meeting took place between Dōgen and the old chief cook. The old man was about to retire from his post at the A-yü-wang monastery and was going to leave for his native village. The two picked up their discussion where they had left off previously. Dōgen asked: "What are words and letters?" The answer came: "One, two, three, four, five." "What is the practice of the Way, then?" asked Dōgen. "Nothing throughout the entire universe is concealed" (*henkai-fuzōzō*) was the old man's reply. Their lively discussion continued without their knowing where to end it. Dōgen wrote later:

> Just as the words and letters I have seen thus far are one, two, three, four, and five, so the words and letters I see now are also six, seven, eight, nine, and ten. The monastics of future generations will be able to understand a nondiscriminative Zen (*ichimizen*) based on words and letters, if they devote efforts to spiritual practice by seeing the universe through words and letters, and words and letters through the universe.

Dōgen's encounters with the old chief cook on these two occasions were decisive events in his subsequent life and thought. It was during these discussions that he realized he had been pondering the relationship between practice and language, between deeds and words, between activities and expressions—specifically with respect to the place of words and letters (*monji*) in the scheme of things. Unlike other Zen Buddhists of the time, Dōgen recognized the limits and dangers of language as well as, and more important, the possibility of using it for spiritual liberation by understanding the "reason of words and letters" (*monji no dōri*). To him, language and symbols held the potential of opening, rather than circumscribing, reality;

consequently, they needed to be reinstated in their legitimate place within the total context of human spiritual endeavors.

At this juncture it is worthwhile to review the place of Buddhism in general, and Zen (Ch'an) in particular, during the Sung period. When Dōgen visited China, it was nearly a century after the establishment of Southern Sung (1127–1279) with its capital in Hangchow (Lin-an), which governed central and southern China. (Northern China was controlled by the Chin.) China suffered constant threats of foreign invasion, internal political factionalism, and military weakness, while at the same time it enjoyed unprecedented economic, technological, and cultural advances. Neo-Confucianism was the predominant ideology of the day and was destined to become the official learning of China. Buddhism had been steadily declining in those days in contrast to its golden age during the Sui-T'ang period (581–907).

This was due to several factors, as observed by Ch'en: (1) the moral degeneration of monastic communities due to the sale of monasterial certificates and honorary clerical titles by the Chinese government in order to cope with its severe financial difficulties; (2) the rise of Neo-Confucianism to intellectual eminence; (3) the civil service examination system that lured many able men to the study of the Confucian classics for prestige and power; (4) the popularity of the Zen and Pure Realm schools of Buddhism, which tended to be anti-textual and anti-scholastic and did not produce great thinkers comparable to those of the T'ang period; and (5) the decline of Buddhism in India during the eleventh and twelfth centuries, which resulted in the end of cultural exchange between Indian and Chinese Buddhists. Despite all this, the Zen and Pure Realm schools were still active, and Zen in particular was held in the highest esteem. Although Neo-Confucianists rejected Zen, their thought contained Buddhist and Zen elements, and the culture of the period owed as much to Zen Buddhism as to Neo-Confucianism. Yet although Zen communities were expanding physically and their economic activities were vigorous, Zen lacked the rigor, authenticity, and brilliance it had had in the previous period and showed its inner impoverishment and decay.

Moreover, Zen teachers began to meddle with politics, and Zen monasteries soon became centers of social and political life.

On various occasions, Dōgen himself wrote about the state of affairs of Zen Buddhism, which he witnessed during his stay in China. For example:

> Those who allegedly study vinaya today in the great country of Sung drink heavily and are intoxicated, in contradiction to the name of śrāvaka—yet they neither are ashamed of, nor have regret for, nor are aware of, the fact that they are transmitting a family heritage entirely foreign to their own tradition.

> Although there are in China a great number of those who proclaim themselves to be the descendants of the Buddhas and ancestors, there are few who study the truth and accordingly there are few who teach the truth. . . . Thus those people who have not the slightest idea of what the great Way of the Buddhas and ancestors is now become the teachers of monastics.

> . . . In the country of Sung lately there are those who call themselves Zen teachers. However, they do not understand the wealth and depth of Dharma and are inexperienced. Reciting a few words of Lin-chi and Yün-mên, they take them for the whole truth of Buddhism. If Buddhism had been exhausted by a few words of Lin-chi and Yünmên, it would not have survived until today. . . . These people, stupid and foolish, cannot comprehend the spirit of the sūtras, slander them arbitrarily, and neglect to study them. They are truly a group of non-Buddhists.

These forthright criticisms were made as a result of Dōgen's keen observations of Zen Buddhism in China. As these quotations amply show, the religious situation in China was not too far from what Dōgen had experienced in his own country.

Another aspect of contemporary Buddhism and Zen criticized by Dōgen was a theory of "the unity of three religions" (sankyō-itchi) of Confucianism, Taoism, and Buddhism. This theory was advocated not only outside, but even within, the Buddhist circle, probably because the survival of Buddhism was guaranteed only by its coming to terms with Confucianism and Taoism under extremely unfavorable conditions. Dōgen witnessed a number of those who held this popular view:

> Lately, a number of the shallow-minded in the country of Sung do not understand the purport and substance [of the doctrine of "All things themselves are ultimate reality" (shohō-jissō)] and regard the statements of ultimate reality (jissō) as false. Furthermore, they study the doctrines of Lao-tzû and Chuang-tzû, maintaining that they are the same as the Way of the Buddhas and ancestors. Also, there is a view of the unity of Confucianism, Taoism, and Buddhism. Some say that the three are just like the three legs of a tripod kettle which cannot stand upright if it lacks even one leg. There is nothing comparable to the foolishness of such a view.

Apart from the general state of Buddhism and Zen, Dōgen's criticism was directed primarily at the Lin-chi (Rinzai) sect popular at the time. As Dōgen wrote, "In the country of Sung today the Lin-chi sect alone prevails everywhere." Of the two separate lines of transmission in the sect, the line of Huang-lung Hui-nan (1002–69) and the line of Yang-ch'i Fang-hui (992–1049), the latter brought forth the highest development in Chinese Zen Buddhism. Although Dōgen was already familiar with the Huang-lung line transmitted by Eisai, which he had studied at the Kenninji temple, what he encountered in China was the Yang-ch'i tradition, whose best-known representative was Ta-hui Tsung-kao (1089–1163). Dōgen denounced him and his followers relentlessly; he may have been prejudiced to some degree, yet his primary reason seems to have been their involvement with political and other secular interests and concerns, and their transcendentalistic interpretation of Zen, which we shall have an occasion to investigate later.

It is easy to understand Dōgen's great disappointment with the general condition of Buddhism and especially that of Zen in China. Although he stayed at the Ching-tê-ssû temple for nearly two years under Wu-chi Liaop'ai, Dōgen's spiritual needs were not fully satisfied. Thus, while he was at the Ching-tê-ssû temple, Dōgen seems to have visited various nearby Zen monasteries. Upon Wu-chi's death toward the end of 1224, Dōgen left Mt. T'ien-t'ung and began traveling extensively, visiting the various temples and monasteries of the "Five Mountains" and studying the characteristics of the "Five Houses" of Chinese Zen Buddhism. As a result of this wandering, Dōgen gained firsthand acquaintance with Chinese Buddhism but still did not find a right teacher.

With a thoroughly discontented heart, Dōgen decided to return home after realizing the futility of staying in China any longer, and set out to pay his last visit to Mt. T'ien-t'ung where Myōzen had been ill for some time. On the way to T'ien-t'ung, Dōgen learned of the death of his former teacher, Wu-chi Liao-p'ai, and his heart was greatly saddened. While revisiting the Ching-shan Wan-shou-ssû temple, Dōgen met an old monk who informed him of Ju-ching (1163–1228), well known as a peerless master in Zen Buddhism, who had been appointed abbot of the Mt. T'ien-t'ung monastery by the Chinese royal court and whom the old monk urged Dōgen to see as soon as possible.

It was early in the fifth month of 1225 when Dōgen met Ju-ching at long last at Miao-kao-t'ai, the latter's private quarters. "I met Master Ju-ching face to face. This was an encounter between a man and a man," Dōgen later wrote. Ju-ching's warm reception of Dōgen was that of a loving father welcoming his beloved son; he told Dōgen to visit him and freely ask questions at his own private quarters at any time without the slightest ceremony. This availability of the great teacher rekindled in the young inquiring mind a burning desire for truth. How earnestly Dōgen had longed for such a meeting! As we have observed before, Dōgen once went so far as to say: "When you don't meet a right teacher, it is better not to study Buddhism at all."

He also wrote: "Without meeting a right teacher, you do not hear the right Dharma." Dōgen was convinced that the actualization or perfection of Dharma largely depended upon the ability and competence of a teacher to shape the disciple as an artisan shapes raw material.

More important, however, the personal encounter was absolutely necessary in Dōgen's view, for Dharma did not emerge in a vacuum, but invariably emerged in a concrete social context, in which persons were significantly related to one another. "When a person meets a person, intimate words are heard and deciphered." The season was ripe for the mystery of Dharma to decisively unfold itself in the meeting between Ju-ching and Dōgen on Mt. T'ien-t'ung.

Let me digress a little at this point. Ju-ching, a native of Yüeh-chou, left there at the age of nineteen, traveled all over China, visited Zen temples and monasteries, and studied Buddhism under various teachers. Later he became a disciple of Tsu-an (or Chih-chien) on Mt. Hsüeh-t'ou and attained enlightenment. Then he went on a pilgrimage throughout the country for nearly forty years and presided over various famous monasteries such as Ch'ingliang in Chien-k'ang, Shui-yen in T'ai-chou, Ching-tz'ŭ in Lin-an, Shuiyen in Ming-chou, Ching-tz'ŭ again, and lastly T'ien-t'ung. Although the T'ien-t'ung monastery was traditionally presided over by abbots of the Linchi sect, Ju-ching belonged to the tradition of the Ts'ao-tung (Sōtō) sect, and more specifically, to the Chen-hsieh line of that sect in China.

We are told that during this period, Ju-ching never failed, even for a single day, to practice zazen, the traditional form of Buddhist meditation that emphasized the upright lotus posture, steady breathing, and mental freedom from all attachments, desires, concepts, and judgments. Ju-ching devoted so much time to zazen that the flesh of his buttocks repeatedly broke out in sores; yet when this happened, he would practice it more earnestly. Ju-ching's educational method reflected this disciplinary rigorism and monastic asceticism. As Dōgen wrote:

> When I stayed once at the T'ien-t'ung monastery, I saw that Ju-ching, accompanied by other elders in the monastics' hall, used to practice zazen until eleven o'clock in the evening and begin at dawn as early as two-thirty or three; he never failed to practice this even a single night.

This uncompromising rigor, whether toward himself or his disciples, was combined with utter sincerity and personal warmth. Dōgen recounted the following moving episode:

> Ju-ching, my former teacher and abbot of the T'ien-t'ung monastery, admonished those who had fallen asleep during zazen practice in the monastics' hall, striking them with his shoe and scolding them with harsh words. Nevertheless monks rejoiced in being struck by the teacher and admired him. Once he spoke to the congregation in the hall: "At such an advanced age, I should now retire from the monastic community, seclude myself in a cottage, and care for my remaining days. However, I am in the office of abbot as your leader in order to help each of you break delusions and find the Way. For this reason I sometimes utter scolding words and strike with a bamboo rod, although I do this very carefully. It is a method to educate people in the place of Buddha. So brothers, forgive me with compassion." Thereupon all the monks wept.

Thus, Dōgen had an unreservedly high regard for his teacher who advocated "zazen-only" (*shikan-taza*), which later became the heart of Dōgen's religion and philosophy:

> There are throughout the country of great Sung not merely a hundred or two, but thousands, of those who allegedly advocate the practice of meditation and thereby profess to be remote descendants of the ancestors. However, I hear of none who exhort zazen-only. Throughout China, only Master Ju-ching [is an exception].

The central religious and philosophical idea of Ju-ching's zazen-only was the "body-mind cast off " (*shinjin-datsuraku*)—the phrase repeated tirelessly by Dōgen throughout his works.

Ju-ching was also famous for his rare uninterest in worldly fame and gain, which had corrupted Buddhism of the time to the marrow. Dōgen observed:

> My former teacher neither approached an emperor nor met one. No intimate acquaintance with ministers and governmental officials was made. Not only did he decline the purple robe and the title of Great Teacher but he also did not wear colorful robes—instead, he always wore a black robe or a simple one-piece gown, whether during lectures or private sessions.

Ju-ching was utterly indifferent to pecuniary gains; Dōgen professed to witness this quality in his teacher alone and in no one else.

During the Sung period, the so-called Five Houses of Zen were feuding, although the Lin-chi sect dominated over all others. Ju-ching, although nurtured in the Ts'ao-tung tradition, detested sectarian biases and divisions and even disliked using the name of Zen, as opposed to other Buddhist sects and schools. He aimed at the catholicity of Buddhism at large. We can glimpse Ju-ching's thought from the following descriptions of Dōgen:

> My former teacher, Ju-ching, once gave a sermon to monastics: "In recent times people assert seriously that there are distinct traditions of Yün-mên, Fa-yen, Wei-yang, Lin-chi, and Ts'ao-tung. This is neither Buddhism, nor the teaching of the Buddhas and ancestors. Such a realization of the Way can be found not even once in a millennium, but Teacher alone comprehends it. Nor is it heard in the ten directions of the universe, but Teacher alone hears it."

And then:

> It ought to be clear that nothing could be more seriously mistaken than to call it "a school of Zen." Foolish persons lament as if they failed in Buddhist scholarship on account of not having the designation of a school or a sect after the fashion of the "school of realism," the "school of nihilism," etc. Such is not the Way of Buddhism. No one ever called it "the school of Zen." Nevertheless, mediocre persons in recent times are foolish enough to disregard the old tradition and, having no instructions from Buddhas, maintain erroneously that there are five distinct traditions in [Zen] Buddhism. This shows its natural decline. And no one has yet come to save this situation except my teacher, Ju-ching, who was the first one to be greatly concerned with it. Thus humanity has been fortunate; Dharma has deepened.

Ju-ching also opposed the popular view of the unity of three religions. Its syncretistic tendencies must have been quite unpalatable to his purist religious principles.

What emerges from our examination of Dōgen's *Hōkyōki*, Shō-bōgenzō, and other works concerning Ju-ching's character and thought is clear. He was a strong, dynamic, charismatic personality who had an uncompromising passion for the monastic asceticism of zazen-only as the *sine qua non* of Buddhism. For him, Buddhism was subservient to neither worldly power nor glory; it was content with the virtue of poverty and lived quietly deep in the mountains. Dharma was sought for the sake of Dharma. He strongly opposed the prevalent sectarianism of Buddhism in general and Zen in particular. Ju-ching sought a catholic Buddhism free from sectarian divisions. In brief, he was the embodiment of the idealism and purity of Zen monasticism that was the rightly transmitted Buddha-dharma (*shōden no buppō*). These tenets (though no doubt selected and emphasized by Dōgen) were very likely Ju-ching's,[9] and Dōgen enthusiastically accepted and faithfully transmitted them, transforming them through his own distinctively Japanese ethos.

Dōgen deemed Ju-ching the right teacher he had been seeking. According to Dōgen, a right teacher was described as follows:

> A right teacher is one who, regardless of old age or stature, comprehends the right Dharma clearly and receives the certification of a true teacher. He/she gives no precedence to words and letters or to intellectual understanding. With an unusual ability and an extraordinary will power, he/she neither clings to selfishness nor indulges in sentimentality. He/she is the individual in whom living and understanding complement one another (*gyōge-sōō*).

9. Professor Kagamishima Genryū says in his book *Tendō Nyojō Zenji no Kenkyū* (Study on Tendō Nyojō Zenji) that Rujing's teachings as presented in *Recorded Sayings of Tiantong Rujing*, compiled in China near the time of Rujing's death, and Rujing's teachings as presented in Dōgen's Shōbōgenzō, Eihei Kōroku, and *Hōkyōki*, are very different. The Chinese text presents Rujing's teachings as essentially similar to those of other Zen masters in Song China. Kagamishima suggested that the image of Rujing as the ancient-buddha (*kobutsu*) was created by Dōgen.

Dōgen must have recollected his mentor's character and thought as he wrote these statements some ten years later. True, Ju-ching fitted the foregoing criteria for the right teacher, or perhaps vice versa. In any case, Dōgen exalted and adored his teacher—with tears of gratitude and joy—so much so that his rhetoric may have superseded any factual descriptions of Ju-ching. Nevertheless, we cannot but acknowledge the picture of a towering personality who decisively shaped the destiny of Dōgen's subsequent life.

What is significant is Dōgen's absolute devotion to the person whom he considered the right teacher, and consequently the authority and tradition the teacher represented. Such was the case in spite of Dōgen's equally indomitable defiance of political power and authority, and his respect for intellectual independence.

In turn, Ju-ching admired his Japanese disciple and once asked him to become his assistant, saying: "In spite of being a foreigner, you, Dōgen, are a man of superior character." Dōgen, however, "positively declined the offer."

As such, the teacher and disciple studied and practiced together for two years (1225–27) in almost ideal rapport. This, however, should not suggest that there was a complete absence of conflicts between them. Dōgen later acknowledged that conflicts between teacher and disciple were a necessary condition for the right transmission of Dharma. He wrote: "The common endeavor of teacher and disciple in practice and understanding constitute the entwined vines of the Buddhas and ancestors (busso no kattō), that is, the life force of the skin-flesh-bones-marrow of Dharma (hiniku-kotsuzui no meimyaku)." "Entwined vines" in the traditional Zen parlance referred to doctrinal sophistries, intellectual entanglements, and conflicts. Dōgen saw, contrary to the Zen tradition, the positive values of such conflicts in the personal encounter of teacher and disciple. Both teacher and disciple grew together through such entwined vines.

Under Ju-ching, Dōgen studied and practiced meditation without sparing himself. Dōgen later recalled:

After hearing this truth [the sole importance of zazen] from the instruction of my former teacher of T'ien-t'ung, I practiced zazen day and night. When other monastics gave up zazen temporarily for fear that they might fall ill at the time of extreme heat or cold, I thought to myself: "I should still devote myself to zazen even to the point of death from disease. If I do not practice zazen even without illness, what is the use of taking care of my body? I shall be quite satisfied to die of a disease. What good fortune it is to practice zazen under such a great teacher of the great country of Sung, to end my life, and to be disposed by good monastics . . ." Thinking thus continually, I resolutely sat in zazen day and night, and no illness came at all.

Dōgen's apprenticeship matured daily in such an uncompromising asceticism.

In 1225, a decisive moment of enlightenment in Dōgen's life came at long last during an early morning zazen session at *geango* (i.e., the three-month intensive meditational retreat). In the course of meditation, a monk next to Dōgen inadvertently had fallen asleep. Upon noticing the monk, Ju-ching thundered at him: "In zazen it is imperative to cast off the body and mind. How could you indulge in sleeping?" This remark shook Dōgen's whole being to its very core, and then an inexpressible, ecstatic joy engulfed his heart. In Ju-ching's private quarters that same morning, Dōgen offered incense and worshiped Buddha. This unusual action of Dōgen prompted Ju-ching to ask: "What is the incense-burning for?" The disciple exuberantly answered: "My body and mind are cast off!"[10] "The body and mind

---

10. One of the most intensely debated topics among Dōgen scholars is the nature and time of Dōgen's experience of dropping off body and mind. The traditional account of Dōgen's experience while sitting next to the scolded monk, above retold by professor Kim, is said to have occurred in 1225 or 1226, while in his book, *Dōgen Zenji*, Kagamishima Genryū says it happened in 1227, the year Dōgen received Dharma transmission from Rujing and returned to Japan.

are cast off" (*shinjin-datsuraku*), joined the teacher, "cast off are the body and mind" (*datsuraku-shinjin*). Thus, Ju-ching acknowledged the authenticity of Dōgen's enlightenment.

This event, sudden and transformative, was not an isolated one but the necessary fruition of Dōgen's long spiritual struggle. What Dōgen's mind had consciously and unconsciously groped for and reflected upon finally took shape dramatically in these unique circumstances. It was at this moment that Dōgen's question, with which he had lived since his residence on Mt. Hiei, was finally resolved. The significance of the key notion of "casting off the body-mind" in the context of Dōgen's life and thought was that zazen-only, as the mythic-cultic archetype, symbolized the totality of the self and the world and represented that in which Buddha-nature became embodied. To cast off the body-mind did not nullify historical and

---

Sugio Genyū of Yamaguchi University questioned the story suggesting it is a fictitious account created by Dōgen's early biographers. Sugio asserts that Dōgen attained dropping off body and mind at his first meeting with Rujing, as Dōgen himself wrote in the conclusion of Shōbōgenzō Menju (Face-to-face Transmission): "[I,] Dōgen, on the first day of the fifth month, in the first year of Baoqing (Hōkyō) era in Great Song China, prostrated myself to my late Master Tiantong, the ancient buddha, and received his face-to-face transmission for the first time. I was then allowed to enter his innermost sanctum. [Only] Slightly dropping off body and mind, yet [none-the-less] being able to uphold and maintain the face-to-face transmission, I came back to Japan."

Professor Ishii Shūdō criticizes the traditional account as a blatant fabrication saying "I don't believe the story of [Dōgen's] dropping off body and mind at the time of Rujing's scolding is historically true. I hold the view that this story causes much misunderstanding concerning the core of Dōgen's Zen. Nowhere in Dōgen's writings, I believe, is there a single sentence that reveals an intention to suggest the underlying message the story conveys." Ishii says that unlike the kenshō experience of Rinzai Zen practice, Dōgen's dropping off body and mind is not a one-time psychological enlightenment experience, and therefore no particular event in Dōgen's biography can be singled out as the definitive occasion of his dropping off body and mind.

Matsuoka Yukako of Hanazono University basically agrees with Ishii about the fictitious nature of the story, however she says that although his dropping off body and mind was not a one-time experience, there must have been some point at which Dōgen first clearly understood what dropping off body and mind meant. She believes this understanding occurred when Dōgen received Rujing's teachings on the subject, as recorded by Dōgen himself in *Hōkyōki*. I introduce Dōgen's record of his discussions with Rujing about dropping off body and mind in chapter 6 of this book.

Many scholars have presented differing ideas of what the phrase "dropping off body and mind" means, but no single hypothesis has been universally accepted.

social existence so much as to put it into action so that it could be the self-creative and self-expressive embodiment of Buddha-nature. In being "cast off," however, concrete human existence was fashioned in the mode of radical freedom—purposeless, goalless, objectless, and meaningless. Buddha-nature was not to be enfolded in, but was to unfold through, human activities and expressions. The meaning of existence was finally freed from and authenticated by its all-too-human conditions only if, and when, it lived co-eternally with ultimate meaninglessness.

What was taking place then in Dōgen's mind was a radical demythologizing and, in turn, remythologizing of the whole Buddhist symbol-complex of original enlightenment, Buddha-nature, emptiness, and other related ideas and practices. The crux of his vision lay in a realistic affirmation and transformation of what was relative, finite, and temporal in a nondualistic vision of the self and the world. To understand duality lucidly and to penetrate it thoroughly within a nondualistic mode of existence was Dōgen's final solution. His remaining life consisted of his intellectual, moral, and cultic efforts to enact and elucidate this vision in the specific historical and social conditions of his time.

In the ninth month of 1225, Ju-ching conferred upon Dōgen the official certificate of the ancestral succession to the Chen-hsieh line of the Ts'aotung sect. On this day, the sect saw the succession of a Japanese monk for the first time in the history of Chinese Buddhism.

One day in 1227, Dōgen told Ju-ching his intention to return to Japan; the latter gave him the sacerdotal robe transmitted from the time of Fuyung Tao-chiai (1043–1118), the genealogical document of ancestral succession, his own portrait, and other precious objects. Except for these objects that he received from Ju-ching, Dōgen returned to Japan "empty handed" (*kūshu-genkyō*). Unlike other Buddhists who had previously studied in China, Dōgen brought home with him no sūtras, images, or documents. His sole "souvenir" presented to his countrymen was his body, mind, and total existence, now completely liberated and transformed. He himself was the surest evidence of Dharma and as such, Dōgen transmitted the Chen-hsieh line of Sōtō Zen to Japan. The date of Dōgen's return to Japan was probably sometime in the fall of 1227. Ju-ching died a year later in 1228.[11]

Meanwhile, Myōzen, who had been studying at the T'ien-t'ung monastery ever since his arrival in China, died in 1225, soon after Dōgen met Ju-ching. Dōgen brought Myōzen's remains to Japan with him and very soon thereafter wrote the *Sharisōdenki* (Account of the Death of Myōzen Zenji). Dōgen concluded the period of his apprenticeship with the following:

> Further, I went to great Sung, visited good teachers throughout the province of Chekiang, and investigated the various traditions of the Five Houses. Finally, I became the disciple of Ju-ching on T'ai-pai fêng [the Ching-tê-ssû temple on Mt. T'ien-t'ung], and the great matter of my entire life (*isshō sangaku no daiji*) was thus resolved.

## TRANSMISSION AND TRANSFORMATION OF THE WAY IN JAPAN

Upon his arrival in Japan, Dōgen immediately returned to the Kenninji temple after a four-year absence. The chaotic situation he had witnessed before had not changed much. In fact, it had worsened in every respect. Dōgen, however, expressed his sense of mission this way: "In the first year of the Shao-ting era [1228–33] of the Sung dynasty I returned to my native place [Kyoto] and vowed to propagate Dharma and save all beings of the world. I felt then that a heavy load was on my shoulders." In the fall of the same year, Dōgen wrote

11. Menzan's revised Kenzeiki states that Rujing died in 1228, one year after Dōgen's return to Japan. However, after studying the recorded sayings of Rujing and those of other Chinese Zen masters of his time, Satō Shūkō of Komazawa suggests that Rujing's death occurred on the seventeenth day of the seventh month in 1227. That was very close to the time of Dōgen's return to Japan, likely a month or so after his leaving China.

the Fukanzazengi (General Advice on the Principles of Zazen), which might have been regarded as the manifesto of Dōgen's "new" Buddhism vis-à-vis the established Buddhism of Japan. At the beginning of the book, Dōgen proclaimed:

> If the Way is originally perfect and ubiquitous, why do we distinguish between practice and enlightenment? If the supreme Dharma is free, why do we need our efforts to attain it? Inasmuch as the whole truth has nothing to do with the world's dust, why do we believe in the means of wiping it away? The Way is not separate from here and now; so what is the use of getting a foothold in practice? However, when there is even the slightest gap between two opposites, they are poles asunder like heaven and earth. When "for" and "against" are differentiated, even unconsciously, we are doomed to lose the Buddha-mind. It should be perfectly clear that infinite recurrences of rebirth is due to our mental discrimination, while delusions of this world arise from an incessant persistence of selfish deliberation. If you wish to surpass even the pinnacle of spiritual advancement, you should understand clearly the here and now as it is (*jikige no jōtō*). Even if you boast of your understanding of Dharma and are richly gifted in enlightenment, even if you attain the Way and illuminate your mind, even if you are about to enter the realm of enlightenment with a soaring spirit, you are still short of the total freedom in which enlightenment itself is transcended (*shusshin no ro*). Although Buddha was endowed with natural knowledge, he sat in zazen for six years. Bodhidharma bequeathed us the legacy of the Buddhamind, yet still sat facing a wall for nine years. Such were the ancient sages. Why can we not practice like them? Therefore, desist from pursuing words and letters intellectually and reflect upon your self inwardly (*ekō-henshō*). Thus your body and mind

shall be cast off naturally and your original nature (*honrai no memmoku*) shall be realized. If you wish to attain it, be diligent in zazen at once.

The above statement indicated the direction and character of Dōgen's thought and activity in the subsequent period of his life. In the simplest and purest form of zazen-only, Dōgen found the essence and prototype of Buddhist *cultus* as well as *mythos*, and the crystallization of practice and enlightenment.

Dōgen stayed at the Kenninji temple for three years. In the meantime, as the peculiarities of his Zen manifested themselves in his teaching and education of disciples, and his name became evermore famous, enmity from both Hiei and Kenninji seems to have been aggravated. It was perhaps this antagonism that led Dōgen eventually to move in 1230 to an abandoned temple called An'yōin in Fukakusa. While at An'yōin, Dōgen wrote the Shōbōgenzō, "Bendōwa,"[12] which expounded his basic tenets in the form of eighteen questions and answers. Expanding the basic thought of the Fukanzazengi, Dōgen clarified the purpose of writing this chapter, which also applied to all his subsequent writings:

> In our country, principles of zazen practice have not yet been transmitted. This is a sad situation for those who try to understand zazen. For this reason I have endeavored to organize what I learned in China, to transcribe some wise teachers' teachings, and thereby to impart them to those who wish to practice and understand zazen.

---

12. Bendōwa was originally not considered part of the Shōbōgenzō collection, having not been discovered until the seventeenth century. When the Sōtō master Manzan Dōhaku (1636–1715) compiled the eighty-four-fascicle Shōbōgenzō collection, for example, it was added as an addendum. It was included as the first fascicle of the ninety-five-fascicle Shōbōgenzō of 1816, the first woodblock print publication of Shōbōgenzō, and since then, until quite recently, Bendōwa has been considered the first fascicle of Dōgen's great philosophical work. Today scholars do not consider Bendōwa to be a part of the Shōbōgenzō collection and treat it as an addendum.

Thus with the Fukanzazengi and the "Bendōwa" chapter, Dōgen laid the cornerstone of his religious and philosophical citadel. Upon this foundation Dōgen's Zen Buddhism, though initially transplanted from China, gradually developed into a distinctively Japanese form that was the product of the symbolic model Dōgen had inherited from Buddhist traditions (which will be greatly elaborated later on), his own idiosyncracies, and the social and historical peculiarities of thirteenth-century Japan. The Way was transmitted and transformed.

As the number of his followers had increased steadily, Dōgen moved again in 1233, this time to the Kannon-dōriin temple in Fukakusa which had been built as the Gokurakuji temple and maintained by the Fujiwara family for generations. Dōgen's life at Kannon-dōriin for the following ten years (1233–43) was his most creative period, literarily and otherwise: he expanded the original Kannon-dōriin into the Kōshō-hōrinji temple, accepted Koun Ejō (1198–1280) as his disciple and the headmonk (*shuso*) of the temple, and wrote forty-four chapters of the Shōbōgenzō, including such crucially important chapters as "Genjō-kōan" and "Busshō," and the *Eihei shoso gakudō yōjinshū*, and the Tenzo-Kyōkun. These events were intimately interconnected with one another.

In the winter of 1234, Ejō became a disciple of Dōgen. From the age of seventeen Ejō had studied such schools of Buddhism as Tendai, Shingon, Kusha (Abhidharmakośa), Jōjitsu (Satyasiddhi), and Hossō (Yogācāra), on Mt. Hiei, and later the Pure Realm school from Shōkū (1147–1247), and Zen Buddhism from Kakuan of Tōnomine. Thus Ejō was already well versed in Buddhism in general. He probably met Dōgen for the first time immediately after the latter returned from China. Although Ejō was two years older than Dōgen, he must have been impressed by Dōgen's fresh interpretation of Buddhism in general and Zen in particular. Two years after this first meeting, Ejō became Dōgen's disciple. For nearly twenty years thereafter, until Dōgen's death, teacher and disciple worked together to found Sōtō Zen in Japan. The timing of Ejō's discipleship was crucially important as Dōgen needed an able co-worker for the education of disciples, administration of the temple, and also for the impending founding of the Kōshōji temple.

In the twelfth month of 1235, Dōgen started a fund-raising campaign for the building of a new monastics' hall (*sōdō*), the center of monastic activities. In light of the calamitous circumstances of the time, this drive must have been far from easy; yet the completion of the monastics' hall was accomplished in the fall of the following year. In the Shōbōgenzō Zuimonki, Ejō reported the following remarks made by Dōgen:

> It should not be thought to be necessarily for the growth of Buddhism that we now campaign for the building fund of the monastics' hall and take pains with that project. At present the number of students is still small, so, instead of doing nothing and wasting time, I want to offer an opportunity for those who have gone astray to get acquainted with Buddhism and, at the same time, to provide a place for monastics to practice zazen. Also there should be no regret even if the original project is not completed. I will not be distressed even if people in the future, seeing just one pillar built, think that despite my intentions, I failed to finish it.

In the tenth month of 1236, the opening ceremony of the monastics' hall was successfully held and the temple was officially named Kōshō-hōrinji temple. As we shall see, this was an epoch-making event in the history of Japanese Zen Buddhism, because it was the realization of Po-chang's envisionment in which the monastics' hall was the center of Zen monastic life. In the twelfth month, Dōgen appointed Ejō as head monk whose function was to assist the abbot in all educational and religious matters in the monastic community. At the same time, Ejō delivered his first sermon in place of Dōgen. About a year later, the Dharma hall (*hattō*) was added to the temple through the efforts of Shōgaku Zenni. This, combined with the Buddha hall (*but-suden*) that had existed from the beginning, marked the realization of Dōgen's dream in which the monastics' hall, the Dharma hall, and the Buddha hall became the three most important buildings of a monastic community. The Kōshō-hōrinji temple was gradually shaping up as one of the most powerful centers of Buddhism in Japan.

Dōgen opened his monastic community for everyone, regardless of intelligence, social status, sex, or profession. His religion was through and through the religion of the people, as were other "new" Kamakura Buddhist sects. His logic of universalism was thorough, if not always consistent. Dōgen wrote: "In their excess of mercy the Buddhas and ancestors have opened the boundless gate of compassion (*kōdai no jimon*) so that all sentient beings may be led into enlightenment. Who in the heavens and on earth cannot enter it?" Dōgen, like Shinran, proclaimed: "There is a very easy way to become a Buddha," and "Zazen-only is of the foremost importance for the growth of a Zen monastic. Through the practice of zazen, irrespective of intelligence, one will mature naturally." He also said:

> The true learning of the Way is not dependent on one's native intelligence or acquired learning, nor on cleverness or quickness. This should not be construed as an exhortation to become like the blind, the deaf, or the fool. Truth does not employ erudition and high intelligence; so do not despair of being endowed with slowness and inferior intelligence. For the true learning of the Way should be easy.

Similar statements are replete in Dōgen's works. Despite his aristocratic origin and philosophical erudition, nothing was more alien to his thought than social condescension or intellectual arrogance.

Dōgen's religion abolished the separation between monastics and lay persons. "Those who regard mundane activity as an obstacle to the Buddhadharma know only that there is no Buddha-dharma in the mundane life; they do not yet know that there is no mundane life in the Buddha-dharma." Monastics and laity are in essence one and the same. "It [enlightenment] depends," wrote Dōgen, "solely upon whether you have a sincere desire to seek it, not upon whether you live in a monastery or in the secular world."

Nevertheless Dōgen also stated:

> Of all the Buddhas in the three periods and ten directions, not a single Buddha attained Buddhahood through the secular life. Because of those Buddhas of the past, monasticism and ordination have their merits. Sentient beings' attainment of the Way necessarily depends upon entering into the monastic's life and receiving the precepts. Indeed the monastic's life and the vow to observe the precepts, being the unchanging law of Buddhas, are possessed of boundless merits. Although in the holy teachings there is the view that advocates the attainment of Buddhahood through the secular life, it is not the rightly transmitted teaching. . . . What the Buddhas and ancestors have rightly transmitted is to become a Buddha through the monastic's life.

Dōgen went so far as to say that "even if a monastic violates the precepts, he/she is superior to a lay person who does not break his/her precepts." Herein lies one of the thorniest problems in Dōgen studies—his view on monasticism and laity. However, as we shall see in more detail later, Dōgen held from beginning to end that "homelessness" was the ideal possibility or model of rightly transmitted Buddhism and transcended both the monastic's and the layperson's lives in their ordinary senses. Dōgen's universalism was envisioned in terms of this monastic elitism, that is to say, Dōgen held up the monastic life as a challenge to his Buddhist contemporaries as well as to the secularists of the time. The monastic life was not a withdrawal from the world, but a protest, an invitation, a recommendation to the world. It is in this light that we understand Dōgen's idealization of monasticism and his relentless demand that his disciples pursue the Way for the sake of the Way, without accommodating themselves to worldly interests and concerns. Fundamentally speaking, the ideal of monasticism was the ideal of every human being—to be born was one's initiation into monastic life. He wrote:

> Therefore, whether you are a heavenly being, human, ruler, or public official, whether you are a layperson, monastic, servant, or brute, you should uphold the Buddhist precepts and rightly transmit the monastics' robes in order to become a child of Buddha. Indeed this is the shortest way to rightly enter the rank of Buddha.

This was quite different from approaches taken by his contemporaries such as Shinran and Nichiren, who while equally anti-secular and antiauthoritarian, approached the matter of liberation by adapting the Way to the levels of the common people (*taiki-seppō*) who were living in the Age of Degenerate Law. The easy path (*igyō*), which called for the recitation of "Namu-Amida-Butsu" (*myōgō*) and "Namu-Myōhō-Rengekyō" (*daimoku*), was "superior" to other methods precisely because it was superlatively adapted to the religious situation of the age. It was the means by which these leaders involved themselves in human existence.

On the other hand, accommodating himself to inferior and mediocre minds appealed little to Dōgen. In this respect, Dōgen retained his aristocratic elitism while at the same time detesting any flattering association with power and authority. It must be remembered that at this time incessant earthquakes, epidemics, fires, famines, social unrest, and so forth, had brought incalculable suffering upon the entire populace. Yet, unlike Shinran and Nichiren, Dōgen seems to have been impervious to this, not because he lacked compassion but because his compassion was modulated in a different key, although some may undoubtedly interpret it as misplaced and inhumane.

Dōgen repudiated, at least in principle, religious discrimination between the sexes. Regarding the question of whether zazen can be practiced by men and women in the secular life or only practiced by monks, Dōgen answered: "The understanding of Dharma, as the ancestors taught, does not depend on differences in sex and in rank." His case for the equality of sexes was most eloquently stated in the following:

> Some people, foolish to the extreme, think of a woman as nothing but the object of sensual pleasures, and see her in this way without ever correcting their view. A Buddhist should not do so. If a man detests a woman as a sexual object, she must detest him for the same reason. Both man and woman become objects, and thus become equally involved in defilement.

Dōgen continues:

> What charge is there against woman? What virtue is there in man? There are wicked men in the world; there are virtuous women in the world. The desire to hear Dharma and the search for enlightenment do not necessarily rely on the difference in sex.

Thus, Dōgen ridicules the Buddhist practice of "no admittance to women" (*nyonin-kinzei*) as "a laughable matter in Japan." The rapid expansion of Dōgen's Buddhism can be seen in the fact that an annex (*jūundō*) soon had to be added to the monastics' hall in 1239. In commemoration of this event, Dōgen wrote twenty-one instructions on life in the annex in his *Kannon-dōri Kōshō-gokokuji jūundōshiki*, which begins with the statement: "Those who have believing minds and give up desire for worldly fame and gain shall enter. Those who lack sincerity shall not join; entering mistakenly, they shall depart after due deliberation." And: "The congregation in the hall should be in harmony with one another just like milk and water, and endeavor to live by the Way." The book ends with this remark: "The foregoing instructions are the body and mind of the Buddhas and ancestors: revere and follow them."

In 1241, such able disciples as Ekan, Gikai (1219–1309), Giin, Gien, Gijun, and others (who had been the disciples of Dainichibō Nōnin) joined Dōgen's community.[13] It is significant to note that Dainichibō Nōnin was the favorite among Japanese Buddhists to establish a "pure Zen" (*junsui-zen*) in the country over the traditional "mixed Zen" (*kenju-zen*)—this task, however, came to be fulfilled by Dōgen and his disciples.[14]

13. Ekan was not Dainichi Nōnin's disciple. Ekan and Koun Ejō were dharma brothers, both ordained disciples of Bucchi Kakuan, a dharma heir of Nōnin. Gikai, Giin, Gien, Gijun, and the "other monks" mentioned above were Ekan's disciples.

14. It appears that Dōgen did not actually consider the teaching and practice of Dainichi Nōnin and his lineage, the Nihon Daruma-shū (Japanese Daruma School), as authentic.

In studying a Nihon Daruma-shū text entitled Jōshōtōkakuron (Thesis on Accomplishing Ultimate Awakening), Ishii Shūdō found that Dainichi Nōnin's teaching was primarily based on Zongjinglu (Jap.: Sugyōroku;True Mirror Source Collection) by Yongming Yanshou (Jap.: Yōmyō Enju, 904–75). Yongming advocated unifying the teaching schools with the Zen school, a prescription that Dōgen criticized.

Also, Nōnin received Dharma transmission from the Chinese Rinzai Zen master Zhuoan Deguang (Jap.: Setsuan Tokkō, 1121–1203), a Dharma heir of Dahui Zonggao (Jap.: Daie Sōkō, 1089–1163) who was an advocate of kenshō Zen and critic of the silent illumination practice of the Sōtō School. Dōgen was very critical of Dahui's lineage and its practice of kenshō jōbutsu (becoming buddha by seeing the nature). In his Denkōroku (Transmission of Light), Keizan Jōkin described the first meeting between Koun Ejō, who at that time was of the Daruma-shū lineage, and Dōgen, who had just returned from China. According to the account, Ejō thought to himself, "I understand the [Tendai] teaching of the three cessations and three contemplations and have grasped the essential practice of the one approach of Pure Land Buddhism. Moreover, I studied at Tōnomine [with Kakuan] and grasped the essence of seeing essential nature, becoming a Buddha at once. What could Dōgen have brought [from China]?" (*The Record of Transmitting the Light: Zen Master Keizan's Denkōroku*, p. 267).

During the meeting, Dōgen's initial statements were in accordance with Ejō's understanding, but after several days of discussion Dōgen shifted his perspective radically. The account states that Ejō attempted to dispute Dōgen's assertions but soon realized that Dōgen's understanding of the Dharma was superior to his own. As a result of this meeting Ejō asked Dōgen to accept him as a disciple. This account, and indeed Dōgen's own writings, clearly illustrate that Dōgen was critical of kenshō oriented practices such as the kenshō jōbutsu practice of the Nihon Daruma-shū.

The acceptance of Ekan and his disciples strengthened Dōgen's sangha, yet after Dōgen's

Thus the primitive order of the Sōtō sect in Japan was formed with a deep commitment to pure Zen. As we shall see, Dōgen wished to establish an unadulterated, full-fledged Zen Buddhism that was clearly distinguished from all non-Zen schools of Buddhism as well as from those Zen schools that had blended with esoteric Buddhism. Dōgen, like Dainichibō Nōnin, was passionately puristic in this respect and indomitably independent of all Buddhist schools.

We should also note that Hatano Yoshishige, a well-known member of the supreme court of the shogunate in Rokuhara, became a devout follower of Dōgen and himself entered into monkhood eventually. Hatano would play an important role in the future development of Dōgen's religion.

The founding of the Kōshō-hōrinji temple and Ejō's assistance gave Dōgen a favorable opportunity for the unfolding of his creative literary activity, which I referred to previously. The core of Dōgen's thought matured during this period.

As time went on, Dōgen himself felt compelled to articulate his position more definitively, in order to distinguish it from other schools of Buddhism. As I have noted already, he criticized both established and new Buddhism unflinchingly. Early in his career, he criticized Pure Realm Buddhism in the following:

> Do you know the merits attained by the reading of the sūtras and the practice of nembutsu? It is most pitiful that some believe in the virtue of just moving the tongue or of raising the voice. Taking them for Dharma, they become more and more remote from it. . . . To try to realize the Way by way of nembutsu—moving the mouth foolishly ten million times—can be compared to the attempt to leave for Yüeh [south] by orienting the wheel of your cart toward the north. . . . Lifting the voice incessantly is

---

death disharmony and disputes erupted among his disciples, eventually splitting the sangha into several factions.

just like a frog croaking day and night in a rice pad in the springtime. It is, after all, futile.

In the context of his criticism of such schools as Hokke, Kegon, and Shingon, Dōgen wrote: "A Buddhist should neither argue superiority or inferiority of doctrines, nor settle disputes over depth or shallowness of teachings, but only know authenticity or inauthenticity of practice." Dōgen relentlessly criticized the Buddhists of these schools, calling them "the scholars who count words and letters" (*monji o kazouru gakusha*). Dōgen sharply set himself apart from scholastically oriented Buddhism by characterizing his own religion as intent on the authenticity of practice, for which he had a burning sense of mission and a stubborn purism.

Coupled with his rising popularity, this stubbornness and sense of mission did not fail to irritate the traditionally-minded Buddhists, especially those on Mt. Hiei. Dōgen's position at the Kōshō-hōrinji temple became increasingly threatened by these traditionalists. At the same time, however, Dōgen was offered an attractive invitation by Hōjō Yasutoki to visit Kamakura although he flatly refused it, perhaps because his anti-authoritarian spirit would not allow him to accept.[15]

Despite this, Dōgen dedicated the *Gokoku shōbōgi* (Significance of the Right Dharma for the Protection of the Nation) to the imperial authority, which sparked Hiei's furies against him. In doing so, Dōgen followed the footsteps of other Japanese Buddhists and/or the loyal family tradition of the Murakami Genji, which revealed his deep involvement with other religionists, nobles, and warriors—the well-known tripartite camps of the upper echelon of Kamakura Japan.

A proposal to move the monastic headquarters to the province of Echizen was made by Hatano Yoshishige, who offered his own property in the province for the site of a new monastery. Dōgen's accep-

---

15. No evidence can be found in any biographical material to indicate that Hōjō Yasutoki, the regent of the Kamakura shogunate government, invited Dōgen to Kamakura. In Shōbōgenzō Zuimonki Dōgen simply states that someone had encouraged him to visit Kamakura.

tance of this offer seems to have been hastened by several factors:[16] (1) As we have seen, the pressures of established Buddhism led Dōgen to the realization that the original vision of his monastic ideal was insurmountably difficult to carry out in his current surroundings. (2) As Furuta contends, his sense of rivalry with the Rinzai sect, particularly with Enni Ben'en (1202–80) of the Tōfukuji temple—Dōgen's most powerful contemporary—might have driven him to a more self-conscious effort to establish Sōtō Zen, as opposed to Rinzai Zen, despite his advocacy of a catholic Buddhism. Significantly enough, his anti-Rinzai remarks became especially frequent around 1243 and thereafter. (3) Dōgen was increasingly mindful of Ju-ching's instruction: "Do not stay in the center of cities or towns. Do not be friendly with rulers and state ministers. Dwell in the deep mountains and valleys to realize the true nature of humanity." (4) Dōgen's unquenchable yearnings for nature rather than urban commotion grew in this period as expressed in his exaltation of mountains and waters (*sansui*): "From the timeless beginning have mountains been the habitat of great sages. Wise ones and sages have all made mountains their secret chambers and their bodies and minds; by them mountains are realized." And finally: (5) These circumstances and factors reinforced his original belief in monastic Buddhism (*shukke-Bukkyō*), rather than lay Buddhism (*zaike-Bukkyō*). Monastic Buddhism had consistently been the model of Buddhism for Dōgen from the very beginning. Sadly, Dōgen must have realized the impracticability of his ideal of universal monasticism in the mundane world. Perhaps a bit pessimistically, he was increasingly attracted to the community of a select few in order to achieve his utopian vision.

This shift in emphasis, although not in principle, contrasted significantly with his earlier position, namely the widest possible dissemination and popularization of zazen in Japan. Nevertheless, his new stress on elitism, rather than universalism, did not imply in the slightest the

16. Steve Heine discusses several recent hypotheses of Dōgen scholars concerning the reasons for Dōgen's move from Kyoto to Echizen in his book *Did Dōgen Go to China?* (Oxford: Oxford University Press, 2006), p. 155, section 5.

abandonment of his mission to change the world as much as the self. We must not minimize the social significance of monastic asceticism in this respect.

In the seventh month of 1243, Dōgen left the care of the Kōshōji temple to his disciple Gijun and arrived in the province of Echizen. He immediately entered a small temple called Kippōji, which had long been in a state of disrepair. Dōgen stayed at Kippōji and occasionally went to Yamashibu to preach. Although the Kippōji period lasted only about a year, Dōgen, secluded from the world by heavy snow, preached and worked as energetically as ever and produced twenty-nine chapters of the Shōbōgenzō. He was unquestionably still at the height of his literary productivity.

In the meantime, Hatano Yoshishige and other lay disciples had been engaged in the construction of the Daibutsuji temple, to which Dōgen moved in the seventh month of 1244. The Dharma hall and the monastics' hall were built in rapid succession, and in 1245, Dōgen announced the observance of the *geango* period for the first time in the history of the new headquarters.

In 1246, Dōgen changed the name of the Daibutsuji to the Eiheiji temple. "Eihei" means "eternal peace" and was the name of the era in the Later Han dynasty during which Buddhism was said to have been introduced to China. With this naming, Dōgen signaled the introduction of the eternal peace of Buddhism in Japan. He had finally realized his long-cherished dream—the establishment of an ideal monastic community, as envisioned by Po-chang Huai-hai (720–814), in the bosom of the mountains and waters. Echizen was an ideal place for such a community, for it was physically remote from Kyoto and Kamakura and therefore free from the established Buddhism, the imperial-Fujiwara power complex, and the warrior class. The Eiheiji temple became the symbol of the "center of the world" (*axis mundi*) in the religion of Dōgen and his followers.

In the Daibutsuji-Eiheiji period (1244–53), Dōgen wrote only eight chapters of the Shōbōgenzō. He directed his efforts primarily to the formulation and guidance of moral precepts and disciplinary rules for the monastic community, rather than the exposition of his thought.[17] This period was characterized by his concentration on the ritualization of every aspect of monastic life. He wrote, for example, the *Taidaiko goge jarihō* (1244), which established the sixty-two rules of behavior for junior members of the monastic community (as opposed to senior members who received training for five years or more); the *Nihonkoku Echizen Eiheiji chiji shingi* (1246), in which the six administrative leaders were instructed in their treatment of inferiors (in contrast to the *Taidaiko goge jarihō*, which was written for monastic leaders); the *Bendōhō* (circa 1244–46), containing minute instructions on early morning, morning, early evening, and evening zazen, all aspects of daily life in the monastics' hall such as washing the face, wearing the robe, and sleeping; the *Eiheiji jikuimmon* (1246), in which Dōgen exalted the spiritual significance of preparing and taking a meal (his instructions were permeated by his belief that eating itself was a spiritual matter); the *Fushuku hampō* (circa 1246–53), which specified in minute detail mealtime manners and rules following Dōgen's metaphysics of eating, in which food and Dharma were nondually one; the *Kichijōzan Eiheiji shuryō shingi* (1249), in which Dōgen formulated the code of conduct for the monastic library, which he regarded as the center of intellectual life; and the *Eiheiji jūryo seiki* (1249) in which he admonished disciples to not involve themselves in or cater to political and religious powers. Such moral and cultic formulations were derived directly from his conception of the sanctity of every aspect of life; they were regarded as free expressions of Buddha-nature and not just rules and codes that bound the lives of ordinary monastics.

---

17. For any particular period of Dōgen's life, one can measure the level of his teaching activities by studying the number of dharma discourses recorded in Eihei Kōroku (Dōgen's Extensive Record). Of 531 dharma discourses recorded in Eihei Kōroku, only 126 were delivered at Kōshōji before his assembly moved to Echizen. The other 405 were given during the Daibutsuji/Eiheiji period from 1245 to 1252. In 1246 alone, for example, he gave seventy-four dharma discourses, about one every five days. Dōgen also revised the older fascicles of Shōbōgenzō during this period and wrote twelve new ones (later named the twelve-fascicle version Shōbōgenzō). It is therefore clear that his productivity did not decline after he moved to Echizen.

Thus the Eiheiji monastery was an exclusive religious and educational community of the very best seekers who had an unflinching determination to grow in the wisdom and compassion of the bodhisattva way and therein become members of the family tradition of the Buddhas and ancestors (*busso no kafū*). This community was also designated as the community of truth(*shinjitsu-sō*), the community of peace and harmony (*wagō-sō*), and the community of purity (*shōjō-sō*).

For about seven months between the eighth month of 1247 and the third month of 1248, Dōgen preached before Hōjō Tokiyori of the Kamakura government, but declined his offer of property in the Echizen province. In light of his rejection of Yasutoki's invitation, Dōgen's Kamakura visit could have been construed as self-contradictory; his compliance was most likely due to a request from Hatano Yoshishige. There are different speculations as to what Dōgen recommended to or discussed with Tokiyori during his stay in Kamakura; the question is still open to further investigation.

In 1250, the ex-emperor Gosaga sent an offer to Dōgen to bestow a purple robe upon him.[18] Dōgen declined more than once, but finally accepted on imperial insistence. However, Dōgen did not wear the robe until the end of his life. From about 1250 on, he suffered from ill health, and his participation in monastic activities was greatly hampered.[19] His condition worsened around the summer of 1252. Nevertheless in the first month of 1253, Dōgen wrote the Shōbōgenzō, "Hachi-dainingaku," which was his last message to his disciples in anticipation of his approaching death. According to remarks by Gien and Ejō, inserted at the end of this chapter, Dōgen wanted to compose

18. The story of Dōgen receiving a purple robe from the ex-emperor appears only in Menzan's revised Kenzeiki. No older biographical materials mention the story and scholars now consider it fictitious.

19. According to Eihei Kōroku, Dōgen gave fifty-one Dharma discourses in 1252, and the last formal dharma discourse it records with a date was delivered on Buddha's enlightenment day, the eighth day of the twelfth month of 1252. It appears Dōgen was active up until that occasion, and he wrote Hachi-dainingaku (Eight Awakenings of Great Beings) the following month.

a total of one hundred chapters for the Shōbōgenzō, but was unable to. Ejō wrote: "Unfortunately we cannot see a one-hundred-chapter version. This is a matter for deep regret."

In the seventh month, Dōgen appointed Ejō his successor as the head of the Eiheiji monastery. Following Hatano Yoshishige's advice, Dōgen reluctantly left Echizen for Kyoto in the following month to seek medical care, accompanied by Ejō and several other disciples. He was treated at the home of his lay disciple Kakunen in Kyoto; however, his illness, perhaps aggravated by the journey, was already too advanced to be cured by any medical treatment.

In the eighth month of 1253, Dōgen bade farewell to his grieving disciples and died in the posture of zazen.

# BIBLIOGRAPHY

Cook, Francis, trans., *The Record of Transmitting the Light: Zen Master Keizan's Denkōroku* (Boston: Wisdom, 2003), pp. 266–73.

Heine, Steve, *Did Dōgen Go to China?* (Oxford: Oxford University Press, 2006), section 5, pp. 155–88.

Ishii, Shūdō, *Dōgen-Zen no seiritsusiteki kenkyū* (Tokyo: Daizōshuppan, 1991), pp. 415–85; 625–714

Kagamishima, Genryū, *Dōgen Zenji* (Tokyo: Shunjusha, 1997), pp. 143–50

Kagamishima, Genryū, *Tendō Nyojō Zenji no Kenkyū* (Tokyo: Shunjūsha, 1973), pp. 122–33.

Kim, Hee-Jin, *Eihei Dōgen, Mystical Realist* (Boston: Wisdom, 2004), pp. 13–49.

Matsuoka Yukako, *Dōgen no sinjin-datsuraku jōtō no toki* (Shūgaku Kenkyū No. 37, 1995).

McRae, John, *Seeing Through Zen* (Berkeley: University of California Press, 2003), p. 121.

Okumura, Shohaku, trans., *Shōbōgenzō Zuimonki* (Tokyo: Sotoshu Shumucho, 1988), 2–5, p. 75.

Satō, Shūkō, *Nyojō zenji jijaku no shūhen* (Indogaku Bukkyōgaku Kenkyū 34–1, 1985).

Sugio, Genryū, *Gokyōji wo aogitaki mondai—Menjuji datsuraku no koto oyobi fukanzazengi no shofū no koto* (Shūgaku Kenkyū No. 19, 1977).

Yamauchi, Shunyū, *Dōgen Zen to Tendai Hongaku Hōmon* (Tokyo: Daizō Shuppan, 1985), pp. 88–99; 642–73.

## Terms

Note: Foreign terms are Japanese unless otherwise noted.

**absolute reality**: Interdependence and interconnection; reality beyond the dichotomy of individuality and unity. *See also* network of interdependent origination and Two Truths.

**alaya consciousness (Skt.)**: Storehouse consciousness. In Yogacara philosophy, the eighth and deepest level of consciousness that contains the seeds of all experience. All karmic tendencies and past experiences of an individual are stored in the alaya, and particular seeds arise when a person encounters particular circumstances, resulting in the formation of particular thoughts and behaviors. In other words, the alaya consciousness is thought to be the source of a person's karma. *See also* karma, manas consciousness, and Yogacara school of Buddhism.

**all dharmas**: All sentient and insentient beings and all phenomena. *See also* banpō.

**anatman (Skt.)**: No soul or no fixed self. The teaching of the Buddha that denies the existence of the atman as the essence of a being. The Buddha taught that all beings are simply an aggregation of the five skandhas and are therefore empty of any fixed, unchanging essence. *See also* atman *and* skandha.

**anuttara-samyak-sambodhi** (Skt.): Unsurpassable complete awakening. This phrase is an epithet for Shakyamuni Buddha's awakening under the bodhi tree.

**atman** (Skt.): Self. The Buddhist definition of atman in Japanese is *jō-itsu-shu-sai*, "the (mistakenly imagined) permanent (*jō*) and only (*itsu*) owner of the body and mind (*shu*), which controls and operates the body and mind (*sai*)." The word is sometimes compared to the English words "soul" or "ego." Buddhism denies that the atman exists. *See also* anatman.

**Avalokitesvara** (Skt.): "Hearer of the Sounds (Cries) of the World," "Seer of the Sounds of the World," and "Sound that Illuminates the World" are among many possible translations. One of the most important bodhisattvas, Avalokiteshvara appears in many Mahayana sutras and embodies or represents Buddhist teachings from the perspective of compassion. *See also* bodhisattva.

**banpō**: All beings, things, and phenomena (*ban*: ten thousand, myriad or numberless; *pō*: beings or things). In Buddhist teachings banpō is often presented as the opposite of *self* as the subject of experience.

**Bendōwa**: "Talk on Wholehearted Practice of the Way." The first part of Bendōwa presents a discussion of zazen practice, including zazen as *jijuyu-zanmai* (*see below*). This section also discusses Dōgen Zenji's travels in China. The second part is a presentation of eighteen questions and answers in which the practice of zazen is discussed within the context of Buddhist teachings.

**bodhi-mind** (Skt.: *bodhi-citta*; Jap.: *bodaishin*): Sometimes translated as "way seeking mind," this is the aspiration to awaken and one's motivation to practice; the intention to adopt a healthy way of life.

**bodhisattva** (Skt.): Awakening being. A person who lives being guided by the vow to help all beings awaken. The great bodhi-sattvas such as Manjushri and Avalokitesvara of the Mahayana sutras can be seen as embodiments or representations of various aspects of Buddhist teachings and practice. Before the Mahayana Buddhist traditions developed, *bodhisattva* referred only to Shakyamuni Buddha before he attained buddhahood, and the word is still limited to this usage in the Theravada tradition.

**bodhisattva vows:** Vows taken by Mahayana Buddhists as the bases for life and practice. The four vows are:

> Beings are numberless, I vow to free them.
> Delusions are inexhaustible, I vow to end them.
> Dharma gates are boundless, I vow to enter them.
> Buddha's Way is unsurpassable, I vow to realize it.

**Buddha Dharma:** The teachings of the Buddha. Also, in Dōgen Zenji's teaching the term refers to practice, the practitioner, Buddha's teachings, awakening, and the reality awakened to, as one seamless reality. *See also* absolute reality.

**Buddha nature:** In Mahayana teaching, the true nature of all beings that enables them to become buddhas. In Dōgen Zenji's teaching, Buddha nature is manifested in practice and is none other than reality itself. *See also* Tathagata-garbha.

**Buddha Way:** The concrete life experience of practice. In Genjōkōan Dōgen Zenji says, "to study the Buddha Way is to study the self," and this self is the self that includes the entire network of interdependent origination as *jijuyu-zanmai* (*see below*).

**chū** (Ch. [中]): Within, middle. Dōgen used this Chinese character in Shōbōgenzō Tsuki as an allusion to teachings such as Tiantai Zhiyi's Truth of the Middle.

**conventional truth:** *see* Two Truths.

**Denkōroku:** "Transmission of Light." Keizan Jōkin Zenji's compilation of stories of the enlightenment of masters in the Sōtō Zen tradition. The record traces the transmission of Dharma between master and disciple from Shakyamuni Buddha through Koun Ejō.

**dharma** (Skt.): 1. phenomenon or things. 2. objects of thought.

**Dharma** (Skt.): 1. the Buddha's teaching. 2. truth or law.

**dharma position** ( Jap.: *hōi*): In Genjōkōan the term refers to the view of an object as perceived in conventional time, i.e., in terms of past, present, and future.

**dropping off body and mind:** *see* shinjin-datsuraku.

**eightfold noble path:** The fourth noble truth. This is the path to the end of suffering, as taught by Shakyamuni Buddha. It includes: right view, right thought, right speech, right action, right livelihood, right effort, right mindfulness, and right concentration. *See also* Four Noble Truths.

**eighteen elements** ( Jap.: *jūhachi-kai*): The six sense organs, the six objects of each sense organ, and the six individual elements of consciousness associated with each sense organ and its object.

**Eihei Kōroku:** "Dōgen's Extensive Record." A collection of the teachings of Dōgen Zenji written or recorded in Chinese. It includes short, formal discourses presented to his assembly, longer informal talks, selected kōans with his commentary, and short appreciative verses on various topics. Eihei Kōroku is essential to a study of the later teachings of Dōgen since it includes his discourses up to 1252, whereas the Shōbōgenzō includes no writings dating after 1246 except Hachi-dainingaku (Eight Awakenings of Great Beings).

**emptiness** (Skt.: *shunyata*): Buddhist technical term that refers to the inconceivable nature of reality. Emptiness can be defined as interdependent origination or as the qualities of impermanence and lack of inherent, independent existence. *See also* interdependent origination.

**five coverings:** Hindrances that prevent the mind from functioning in a healthy way during meditation: greed, anger, sleepiness or dullness, distraction, and doubt about causes and conditions.

**five desires:** Desires that arise in the mind as a result of contact with objects of the five sense organs.

**five schools:** The five major lines of Chinese Cha'n (Zen) Buddhism that developed through the Sixth Ancestor of Cha'n: Fayan (Jap.: Hōgen), Guiyang (Jap.: Igyō), Caodong (Jap.: Sōtō), Yunmen (Jap.: Unmon), and Linji (Jap.: Rinzai).

**four Dharma seals** (Jap.: *shihōin*): Four aspects that confirm a teaching to be that of Buddhism. The seals are: everything contains suffering; everything is impermanent; everything lacks independent existence; nirvana is tranquility.

**Four Noble Truths:** The foundational teaching of Buddhism as taught by Shakyamuni Buddha. The Four Noble Truths are: all life contains suffering; the cause of suffering is craving or desire; suffering can be brought to an end; the eightfold noble path is the path to the end of suffering. *See also* eightfold noble path.

**Fukanzazengi:** "Universal Recommendations for Zazen." Essay originally written by Dōgen Zenji in 1227. It explains the nature of zazen and gives instructions for its practice.

**genjōkōan:** "Actualization of reality." For Dōgen Zenji, the word *genjōkōan* referred to the unity of practice, realization, and true reality manifesting as the present moment. It is also the title of the first chapter of Shōbōgenzō that presents precisely and concretely Dōgen's basic philosophy that one should approach every activity as bodhisattva practice.

**Goshō:** Short for Okikigakishō, "Record and Notes of What Was heard." Written in the thirteenth century by Senne and Kyōgō, since the seventeenth century it has been considered to be the most authoritative commentary on the seventy-five-chapter version of Shōbōgenzō.

**Heart Sutra** (Skt. *Maha Prajna Paramita Hridaya Sutra*): The shortest of the prajna paramita sutras, the important Mahayana sutras expounding the teachings of emptiness. The Heart Sutra contains the "heart" of the teaching of ultimate wisdom. *See also* prajna paramita.

**henyaku-shōji**: Transforming life-and-death. The term refers to the bodhisattva's practice of returning to samsara. Though these bodhisattvas have been released from the karma that causes transmigration, their vow to save beings from suffering moves them to return to the three worlds lifetime after lifetime.

**Hōkyōki**: "Record in the Hōkyō Era." Written by Dōgen Zenji himself, *Hōkyōki* is a record of dialogues between Dōgen Zenji and his teacher, Tiantong Rujing.

**hongaku**: Original enlightenment. Theory that influenced many Buddhist schools in China through the text *Awakening the Faith in the Mahayana*. It states that in terms of absolute tathata, all living beings are fundamentally identical to *tathata*, being enlightened from the beginning. *See also* Buddha nature, hongaku-hōmon, *and* shikaku.

**hongaku-hōmon**: Dharma gate of original enlightenment. Teaching of the Tendai school that emphasized concrete phenomena as absolute reality. It states that since all living and non-living beings have Buddha nature, they are all from the beginning enlightened buddhas. *See also* Buddha nature, hongaku, *and* shikaku.

**interdependent origination** (Skt. *pratītya-samutpāda*): Teaching that all things and phenomena are the product of an infinite number of causes and conditions. All these causes and conditions are also infinitely interconnected and constantly changing, hence all things are impermanent and lack independent existence: they are empty. *See also* emptiness.

**jijuyu-zanmai**: Self-receiving and self-employing samadhi. Term used by Dōgen Zenji as the foundation for his teachings on zazen practice. The term points to the dropping off of conceptual boundaries such as "self," "other," "myriad beings," and "practice" in zazen or any wholehearted practice. For Dōgen, the true self beyond concepts of individuality or universality is realized as practice in jijuyu-zanmai.

**jiko:** Self. Jiko refers to the reality that the true self is comprised of all beings and all things.

**jin daichi:** Whole great earth. This is an expression Dōgen Zenji used for the self that is together with all beings.

**Jingde Chuandeng Lu** (Ch.; Jap.: "Keitoku Dentōroku"; Transmission of the Dharma Lamp): One of the earliest historical works of Zen literature. Composed in 1004 by the Chinese monk Doayuan, it contains short biographies, anecdotes, and sayings of the early Chinese Zen masters up to Fayan Wenyi, founder of the Hōgen school.

**juhachi-kai:** *see* eighteen elements.

**kanji** (Ch.: *hanzi*): Chinese characters used for writing in several East Asian languages including Japanese.

**karma** (Skt): Deed. Cause and effect, especially in relation to an individual's actions.

**Keitoku Dentōroku:** *see* Jingde Chuandeng Lu.

**kenshō:** Seeing the (Buddha) nature. The term is often used in the Rinzai Zen tradition, where it refers to an enlightenment experience that usually happens during the process of kōan practice.

**kōan:** Commonly an ancient Chinese story illustrating a Zen teaching or understanding of reality. It is thought that Dōgen Zenji used "kōan" as a word to express the reality of both individuality and universality.

**Madhyamika school:** Buddhist teachings formed during the fourth to fifth centuries based on the teachings of Mulamadhyamaka-karika by Nagarjuna. Madhyamika teachings had a great effect on the development of Mahayana Buddhism in India, Tibet, China, and Japan. *See also* Middle Way, Nagarjuna, Two Truths, *and* Truth of the Middle.

**Mahayana** (Skt.): Great vehicle. Branch of Buddhism that arose during the first century CE and developed first in India and later in China as the foundation of many schools of Buddhism including Tendai, Pure Land, and Zen. Mahayana Buddhism, which stresses the possibility of buddhahood for all beings, likely developed in reaction to the highly insular and monastic practices of early Buddhism. Ideal Mahayana practice is embodied in the bodhisattva, a being who practices for the awakening of both self and others.

**Maka Hannya Haramitsu** (Japanese pronunciation of Skt. "Maha Prajna Paramita"): Dōgen Zenji's commentary or teaching on the Heart Sutra. Written in 1233, it is a chapter of Shōbōgenzō. *See also* Heart Sutra.

**manas** (Skt.): Intelligence or mental faculties and activity. In Yogacara philosophy manas is the seventh of the eight layers of consciousness. It is said to cling to the *alaya* consciousness, interpreting life experiences as reality and thus creating the illusion of the existence of an individual "I" or independent self. *See also* alaya consciousness.

**Mana-Shōbōgenzō:** Collection of three hundred kōan stories compiled by Dōgen Zenji.

**mayoi:** Usually translated as "delusion," mayoi actually refers to a psychological state of mind caused by delusion. It carries the connotation of being lost, confused, and unable to see clearly and make sound judgments.

**Middle Way**: In early Buddhism this term originally referred to the practice of the middle path between the extremes of hedonism and asceticism. In Mahayana Buddhism, the term has evolved and now also refers to the bodhisattva path beyond clinging either to conventional or absolute truth. *See also* Truth of the Middle *and* Two Truths.

**myriad dharmas**: *see* banpō.

**narau**: To study. Used in the phrase "to study the self is to forget the self" in Genjōkōan, where the word means to wholeheartedly study by engaging the entire body and mind in practice, beyond the boundaries of the person studying and the object that is studied.

**network of interdependent origination**: The absolute, total, or universal reality of interconnectedness. The term is similar to Indra's Net, an analogy used in Mahayana Buddhism in which all things of the universe are depicted as knots in the limitless net of reality.

**nirvana** (Skt.): The cessation of suffering; liberation from samsara. Nirvana is the way of life based on awakening to the reality of impermanence and lack of independent existence.

**opening the hand of thought**: A term coined by Kōshō Uchiyama Rōshi for letting go of thoughts, concepts, and emotions in zazen. *See also* shikantaza.

**paramita** (Skt.): Perfection, or "(crossing the river) to reach the other shore." In Mahayana Buddhism, the six paramitas are six virtues one develops in bodhisattva practice. They are *dana* ( generosity), *shila* (precepts), *kshanti* (patience), *virya* (energy), *dhyana* (meditation), and *prajna* (wisdom).

**prajna paramita** (Skt.): Perfection of wisdom that "sees" true reality. In the teachings of Dōgen Zenji, prajna paramita is wisdom realized through, and not separate from, practice, rather than a means used by a practitioner to "see" reality. It is the reality of interdependent origination, interconnectedness, impermanence, and lack of independent existence manifested through practice.

**repentance** (Jap.: *sange*): In Buddhism, repentance is recognizing one's diversion from the practice of awakening and returning to that practice. To awaken to the incompleteness of one's practice is repentance. *See also* uposadha *and* vow and repentance.

**Ryōga-shijiki** (Ch.: Lengga-shizi-ji): "The Record of Teachers and Disciples of the Ryoga Tradition." A history of the northern school of Chinese Zen written in the early eighth century.

**samsara** (Skt.): Buddhist term that usually refers to the "cycle of existence," the transmigration or the rebirth of a person through the six realms of existence. Samsara can also be interpreted as the cyclic emotional quality of one's current life.

**sange**: *see* repentance.

**sanzen**: Going to Zen. This term often refers to a personal interview with a Zen master, especially in the Rinzai tradition. In Shōbōgenzō Zazengi, however, Dōgen Zenji wrote, "Sanzen is zazen."

**satori**: Realization, enlightenment, or awakening. Three Chinese words (*go*, *kaku*, and *shō*), each with subtle differences in meaning, are translated as *satori* in Japanese, and *satori* is usually simply translated as "enlightenment" in English.

**shashu**: A position in which the hands are placed at heart level with the left hand enclosing the thumb and the right hand placed around the left. *Shashu* is usually used in a Zen meditation hall when standing or walking.

**shihōin**: *see* four Dharma seals.

**shikaku**: Process of actualization of enlightenment. According to the Buddhist view that emphasizes the teaching of *shikaku*, although from the perspective of ultimate reality all animate and inanimate beings are enlightened from the primordial beginning, in relative actuality all beings are deluded and must practice in order to rediscover their Buddha nature.

**shikantaza:** Just sitting. Word used by Dōgen Zenji for the zazen he practiced and taught. In practicing shikantaza, no mantra or object of meditation is used, and no technique for controlling or eliminating mental activity is employed. The practitioner simply sits in the upright zazen posture, breathing naturally while letting go of thoughts and emotions as they arise and dissipate.

**shinjin-datsuraku:** Dropping off body and mind. A key word in the teachings of Dōgen Zenji, originally used by his teacher, Tendō Nyojō. For Dōgen, dropping off body and mind was synonymous with zazen, where all relative, conceptual definitions and delineations of self, other, and performed activity fall away.

**Shōbōgenzō:** True dharma eye treasury. This word comes from the legendary Zen account of Shakyamuni Buddha's Dharma transmission to Mahakasyapa when the Buddha said he was transmitting "the true Dharma eye treasury, wondrous mind of nirvana (*Shōbōgenzō nehanmyoshin*)." "Shōbōgenzō" refers to the true reality of all beings, and Dōgen Zenji chose it as the name of his great literary work in which he discusses the philosophical foundations for all aspects of Zen practice. Dōgen used the word in naming his collection of three hundred kōan stories, Mana-Shōbōgenzō, as well.

**shohō-jissō:** True reality of all beings. Taken from the Lotus Sutra, this phrase is an essential element in the teachings of Dōgen Zenji. *Shohō-jissō* is actualized in practice when a person meets reality as it is, going beyond concepts of individuality and universality.

**shōji:** Life and death. *Shōji* is the process of life in which we are born, live, and die. As a Buddhist term, *shōji* is used as the equivalent of the Sanskrit words *jatimarana* and *samsara* (*see above*).

*Jatimarana* refers both to the process of being born, living, and dying, and also to the four kinds of suffering, or *duhkha* (birth, aging, sickness, and death).

**Shōyōroku:** "Book of Serenity," a classic Zen text of one hundred kōan stories. Each kōan is supplemented by a verse written by the Sōtō Zen Master Hongzhi Zhengjue (Jap.: Wanshi Shōgaku, 1091–1157) and a commentary by Master Wansong Xingxiu (Jap.: Banshō Gyōshū, 1166–1246).

**shunyata:** *see* emptiness.

**six elements:** The constituents of all beings and things. They are the earth element, the water element, the fire element, the wind element, the space element, and the consciousness element.

**skandha** (Skt.): Aggregate, heap, group. These are the elemental constituents of all experience and being according to Buddhist teaching. They are: *rupa* (form), *vedana* (sensations), *samjna* (perception), *samskara* (mental formations), and *vijnana* (consciousness). Mahayana Buddhism teaches that the five skandhas are empty, i.e. impermanent and lacking independent existence. *See also* anatman, atman, *and* emptiness.

**Sōtō** (Ch.: Caodong): A school of Zen, one of the original Five Houses of Chinese Zen founded by Dongshan Liangjie (Jap.: Tōzan Ryōkai; 807–69) and his student Caoshan Benji (Jap.: Sōzan Honjaku; 840–901). Dōgen Zenji received Dharma transmission in the Sōtō lineage from his teacher, Tiantong Rujing.

**tathagata** (Skt.): The one who has come from thusness or the one who has gone to thusness. One of the ten epithets of a buddha, the term can refer to Shakyamuni Buddha or to any buddha throughout space and time. From an absolute perspective, tathagata refers to the dharmakaya, or Dharma body of Buddha, i.e. reality itself.

**Tathagata-garbha** (Skt): Womb of the Tathagata. The teaching that all beings have Buddha nature and are therefore able to become buddhas. *Tathagata-garbha* philosophy is an important element in Mahayana Buddhism. *See also* Buddha nature.

**tathata** (Skt.): Thusness, suchness, "as-it-is-ness." The ultimate reality of things as they are.

**Tendai** (Ch.: Tiantai): A school of Buddhism based on the teachings of the Lotus Sutra and Nagarjuna. Zhiyi (538–97) was the most important master of the school in China; Saicho (767–822), founder of the monastic order on Mt. Hiei, studied Tendai Buddhism in China and brought the tradition to Japan in the ninth century. Tendai Buddhism had a great influence on the development of many Buddhist schools in Japan.

**ten thousand dharmas:** *see* banpō.

**Tenzo-Kyōkun:** "Instructions for the Cook." Dōgen's writing describing the practice of the head cook of a Zen monastery. Here he presents the attitude Zen practitioners should carry into the daily activities of their lives.

**three poisonous minds:** Greed, hatred, and delusion. As the sources of self-centered focus and suffering, the three poisonous minds perpetuate samsara (*see above*).

**thusness:** *see* tathata.

**transmigration:** *see* samsara.

**Truth of the Middle** (Ch.: zhong, Jap.: chu): Teaching of Tiantai Zhiyi based on the Two Truths of Nagarjuna. The Truth of the Middle refers to seeing the reality of each and every being from both the side of emptiness ("there is not") and the side of temporal being ("there is").

**Two Truths:** Absolute truth (Skt.: *paramārtha-satya*) and conventional truth (Skt.: *samvriti-sataya*). The teaching of the Two Truths forms the basis of Nagarjuna's philosophy, and in turn forms the foundation for most teachings of the Mahayana schools. Absolute truth is the reality of emptiness or interdependent origination that is beyond concepts or words. We can only describe absolute truth in terms of conventional truth, i.e. concepts, ideas, and words that have meaning only in relation to some other concept, idea, or word. Absolute truth can therefore never be grasped by the thinking mind. Seeing reality from the perspective of both of the Two Truths, without clinging to either, is the Middle Way. *See also* Truth of the Middle.

**tsuki:** Moon. Tsuki is the twenty-third chapter of the seventy-five-chapter version of Shōbōgenzō. In it Dōgen Zenji presents the moon as a metaphor for the functioning of the entire network of interdependent origination and its infinite contents.

**twelve links of causation:** Early Buddhist teaching which attempts to describe the process of dependent origination that perpetuates the cycle of birth, suffering, old age, and death. "Ignorance," the first link in the cycle, was considered to be the fundamental cause of suffering in early Buddhism. "Old age and death" is the last link.

**twelve sense fields** (Jap.: *jūnisho*): The six sense organs (eyes, ears, nose, tongue, body, and mind) and each of the six types of sense objects that interact with those sense organs.

**uji:** "Being-time," the chapter of Shōbōgenzō in which Dōgen discusses the nature of time and his profound and unique insight that "time is being and being is time."

**universal reality:** *see* absolute reality.

**uposadha** (Ch.: *busa*; Jap.: *fusatsu*): Repentance, confession, and vow renewal practice of Buddhist monks, usually performed twice a month, often at or near the time of the new moon and full moon. *See also* repentance.

**vow and repentance**: Term coined by Kōshō Uchiyama Rōshi for the practice of a bodhisattva. A bodhisattva's intention is to live guided by the vow to help all beings awaken; when we see that we have strayed from our vow, we repent by simply returning to that vow as the underlying intention for all of our activities. *See also* repentance.

**Yogacara Buddhism**: The "consciousness only" school of Buddhism. The school uses the analysis of consciousness to explain how a life of suffering is created in the individual. Yogacara philosophy teaches that everything that can be experienced is consciousness only.

**zazen**: Sitting absorption (absorption is here an English translation of the Skt. *dhyana*, which is read as *chan* in Ch. and *zen* in Jap.). Traditionally the central "meditation" practice of the so-called Zen schools of Buddhism. Zazen as practiced and taught by Dōgen Zenji is not actually a form of meditation since there is no attempt to direct the mind on any object. One should keep in mind when studying the teachings of Dōgen Zenji that he often used the word "zazen" in a broader sense to indicate the true reality that is manifested in practice. *See also* shikantaza.

**Zazenshin** (Ch.: Zuochanzhen): "Acupuncture Needle of Zazen." This is a famous poem written by Hongzhi Zhengjue (Jap.: Wanshi Shōgaku, 1091–1157) in which the nature of zazen practice is presented. Dōgen Zenji wrote a chapter of the Shōbōgenzō titled "Zazenshin" which is inspired by Hongzhi's poem. Dōgen Zenji offers his own verse titled "Zazenshin" in that chapter as well.

**zenki**: Total dynamic function. This is the title of the twenty-second chapter of the seventy-five-chapter version of Shōbōgenzō in which Dōgen Zenji used the word "zenki" as an expression for the functioning of self and other and subject and object as one seamless reality.

**Zuimonki:** Collection of informal talks Dōgen Zenji presented to his assembly at Kōshōji monastery. Koun Ejō, Dōgen's first disciple and second abbot of Eiheiji, recorded the talks in *Zuimonki*.

## NAMES OF PEOPLE AND PLACES

**Butsuju Myōzen** (1184–1225): Dōgen's first Zen teacher. Dōgen began practicing with Myōzen in the Rinzai Zen tradition at Kenninji monastery, and Dōgen and Myōzen traveled to China together in 1223.

**Chuang Tzu** (fourth to third c. BCE): An important Chinese Taoist philosopher who lived during the warring states period.

**Eiheiji:** Monastery (formerly named Daibutsuji) founded by Dōgen Zenji in 1244. It remains, along with Sōjiji, one of the head monasteries of Japanese Sōtō Zen.

**Hongzhi Zhengjue** (Jap.: Wanshi Shōgaku, 1091–1157): A famous Chinese Sōtō Zen master who served as abbot of Tiantong monastery from 1129 until his death. Hongzhi was well known for the excellence of his poetry, and he composed verses to supplement a hundred kōans. Wansong Xingxiu (Jap.: Banshō Gyōshū, 1166–1246) later wrote commentaries on these verses and created the Congronglu (Jap.: Shōyōroku; Book of Serenity). Dōgen Zenji deeply respected Hongzhi.

**Kenninji:** The first Zen monastery established in Japan, in 1202. Its founder was Myōan Eisai, a Japanese master who traveled to China and transmitted Rinzai Zen to Japan.

**Kōshōji:** The first Sōtō Zen monastery in Japan. Dōgen Zenji founded Kōshōji in 1233 outside Kyoto. He later moved his assembly to Echizen.

**Kyōgō:** A disciple of both Dōgen and Dōgen's disciple Senne.

Together, Senne and Kyōgō wrote important commentaries on Shōbōgenzō. *See also* Goshō *and* Yōkō Senne.

**Linji Yixuan** (Jap.: Rinzai Gigen, d. 866/67): Great Chinese Zen master and founder of the Linji (Rinzai) school of Zen.

**Magu Baoche** (Jap.: Mayoku Hōtetsu): Chinese Zen master who was the disciple and Dharma heir of Mazu Daoyi. It is thought that Magu Baoche was the person named Magu who Linji Yixuan referred to as having a deep influence on him.

**Mazu Daoyi** (Jap.: Baso Dōitsu, 709–88): One of the most important masters in the history of Chinese Zen. Mazu was the teacher of many important masters and had a great influence on the development of Zen Buddhism. His lineage was called the Hongzhou School.

**Myōan Esai** (1114–1215): First master to successfully transmit Rinzai Zen to Japan. He was the teacher of Butsuju Myōzen, Dōgen Zenji's first Zen teacher.

**Nagarjuna** (second to third c.): The great proponent of early Mahayana Buddhism and expounder of the teachings of emptiness, or shunyata. Nagarjuna is considered to be an ancestor in most Mahayana schools that developed subsequent to his teachings. He is considered to be the fourteenth ancestor of Zen Buddhism. *See also* emptiness *and* Two Truths.

**Tiantong**: Chinese monastery where Dōgen practiced for five years and received Dharma transmission from his teacher Tiantong Rujing Zenji.

**Tiantong Rujing** (Jap.: Tendō Nyojō, 1163–1228): Chinese Zen master and abbot of Tiantong monastery. He transmitted the lineage of Sōtō Zen to Dōgen Zenji.

**Wanshi Shōgaku**: *see* Hongzhi Zhengjue.

**Yōkō Senne:** A direct disciple of Dōgen Zenji and founder of Yōkōji temple in Kyōto. Senne and his disciple Kyōgō wrote the first commentary on the seventy-five-chapter version of Shōbōgenzō, commonly called Okikigakishō, or simply Goshō, which has been considered to be the most authoritative commentary on that version of Shōbōgenzō since the Tokugawa period (seventeenth to nineteenth c.).

# Notes

1  The word "repentance" as I use it here is a translation of *sange* (懺悔), the Japanese pronunciation of the Chinese word *chanhui*. *Chanhui* is a translation from Sanskrit of the Buddhist term *ksama*. The *San* (懺) of *sange* is taken from the first part of *chanma* (懺摩), the Chinese transliteration of the Sanskrit word *ksama*, meaning "to repent" or "to regret." The *ge* (Ch.: *hui*, 悔) of *sange* also means "to repent" or "to regret" in the original Chinese.

2  This is a reference to one of the ten epithets of Buddha: Skt.: *purusa-damya-sarathi*; Jap.: *jōgo-jōbu*, "tamer of men."

3  My translation. Unless otherwise noted, all translations are my own.

4  Verse 160. This is my translation from the Chinese version, the Chinese being a translation from the Sanskrit.

5  This unique term coined by Sawaki Rōshi is just as enigmatic in Japanese as it is in English. He created it by adding *suru*, which in Japanese transforms any word into a verb, to "self" (*jibun*), and combining this with a subjective case "self" and an objective case "self" ("self [subject] 'selfing' [verb] the self [object]").

6  *Sanzen* (参禅) often refers to a personal interview with a Zen master, especially in the Rinzai tradition. In Shōbōgenzō Zazengi, however, Dōgen Zenji wrote, "Sanzen is zazen." Here Rujing also uses this word as an equivalent to zazen.

7  Doubt about the law of causality (karma) and the teachings of the Dharma. This doubt also includes insecurity about one's own ability to understand and practice according to the teachings of Buddhism.

8  The *shikan* of Makashikan is a completely different word than the *shikan* of *shikantaza*, although they share the same pronunciation. "Shikan" in "shikantaza" means "just." "Shikan" in "Makashikan" is a translation of "shamatha" and "vipassana": "shi" means "stopping" and "kan" means "seeing."

9  A position in which the hands are placed at heart level with the left hand enclosing the thumb and the right hand placed around the left.

10 My translation from the Chinese.

11 The final stage of attainment in early Buddhism. An arhat is said to have attained complete enlightenment and entered nirvana.

12 One who has attained enlightenment without the aid of a teacher or guide. It is said that pratyekabuddhas do not teach others how to attain enlightenment.

13 An original disciple of Shakyamuni Buddha. In Sanskrit, literally "one who hears" (the voice of Buddha). According to early Mahayana Buddhists, sravakas were considered followers of the "Lesser Vehicle" (Hinayana) since they had not accepted the complete Dharma as it was revealed by Buddha in Mahayana Buddhist sutras.

14 The world in which we exist, a part of the triple world. The triple world consists of the world of desire, the material world, and the immaterial world. Motivated by a vow to save all beings, a bodhisattva practices within the world of desire.

15 The southern continent of the earth, where ordinary human beings reside, according to the cosmology of classical Buddhism.

16 Kazuaki Tanahashi, ed., *Moon in a Dewdrop: Writings of Zen Master Dōgen* (New York: North Point Press, 1985), p. 167.

17 Burton Watson, trans., *The Zen Teachings of Master Lin-chi* (New York: Columbia University Press, 1999), p. 70.

18 The portion of this sentence in quotation marks is a saying of the great Chinese Zen master Mazu Daoyi (Jap.: Baso Doitsu; 709–88).

19 Gudo Nishijima and Chodo Cross, trans., *Master Dōgen's Shobogenzo* (Woking, Surrey: Windbell, 1997), bk. 3, pp. 5–6.

20 See Shohaku Okumura, ed., *Dōgen Zen And Its Relevance For Our Time* (San Francisco: Soto Zen Buddhism International Center), p. 39.

21 Nishijima and Cross, *Master Dōgen's Shobogenzo*, bk. 2, p. 256.

22 Senika, who appears in the Mahayana Mahaparinirvana Sutra, is a non-Buddhist who converses with Shakyamuni about the nature of the mind/body relationship. In the discussion Senika propounds the theory of an eternal self that exists beyond the body, but later accepts the teaching of anatman as it is presented by the Buddha and becomes a Buddhist monk.

23 Shohaku Okumura and Taigen Daniel Leighton, trans., *The Wholehearted Way: A Translation of Eihei Dōgen's Bendōwa*, with commentary by Kōshō Uchiyama Rōshi (Boston: Tuttle, 1997), p. 32.

24 Jap.: Sōkei. This is another name for the Sixth Ancestor; it is the name of the mountain where he taught.

25 Norman Waddel and Masao Abe, trans., *The Heart of Dōgen's Shōbōgenzō* (Albany: State University of New York Press, 2002), p. 51.

26 I chose to use the word "negate" here and throughout this discussion rather than a word such as "change" or "transform" because although the seed's nature includes the potential to become a plant, the seed is nonetheless 100 percent seed when in the dharma position of a seed. This is why, for example we don't call a seed an "underdeveloped plant" and we don't call a plant a "grown seed." Yet "replace" is also not appropriate since it implies that a plant entirely separate and distinct from the seed takes the seed's place,

and this of course is not the case. Although I also don't intend the negative connotations of "reject" or "deny," "negate" seems to me the word closest in meaning to what Dōgen intended in his discussion of dharma positions in Genjokoan.

27  Robert Thurman, trans., *The Holy Teaching of Vimalakirti* (University Park: Pennsylvania State University Press, 1976), p. 31.

28  *Manyōgana*, a method used to phonetically indicate the sounds of Japanese words with Chinese characters, was used before *hiragana* and *katakana* were invented. It was named *manyōgana* because the method was used in creating *Manyōshū*, the oldest collection of Japanese poems compiled in the Nara period (710–94).

29  如如 如水中月 水月 水如 月如 如中 中如 如 如 是; nyo-nyo nyo-sui-chū-getsu sui-getsu sui-nyo getsu-nyo nyo-chū chū-nyo nyo nyo ze.

30  *Nagarjuna: A Translation of His Mulamadhyamakakarika*, with an introductory essay by Kenneth Inada (Tokyo: Hokuseido, 1970), 24/8–10, p. 146; 24/18, p. 148.

31  Andy Ferguson, *Zen's Chinese Heritage; The Masters and Their Teachings* (Boston: Wisdom Publications, 2000), p. 147.

32  一心一切法、一切法一心.

33  Shohaku Okumura, trans., *Shōbōgenzō Zuimonki* (Tokyo: Sotoshu Shumucho, 1988), 5–12, p. 178.

34  Kōshō Uchiyama, *The Zen Teaching of "Homeless" Kōdō* (Tokyo: Sotoshu Shumucho, 1996), pp. 39–40. This book is Uchiyama Rōshi's commentary on some sayings of his teacher, Kōdō Sawaki Rōshi. It contains many of Sawaki Rōshi's quotes.

35  Ibid., p. 40.

36  The mani jewel is a transparent jewel that becomes the color of any object it touches. It is sometimes called the Wish-Fulfilling Jewel. In the Lotus Sutra, Avalokiteshvara Bodhisattva is said to use the mani jewel to offer beings the ultimate fulfillment of the wish for liberation. The jewel is found in many stories and teachings of Mahayana Buddhism, and it can be seen as the symbolic representation of skillful means, Buddhist faith, emptiness, interdependent origination, and so forth.

37  Okumura, *Shōbōgenzō Zuimonki*, 5–16, p. 187.

38  Kōshō Uchiyama, *Opening the Hand of Thought*, trans. and ed. Tom Wright, Jisho Warner, and Shohaku Okumura (Boston: Wisdom Publications, 2004), p. xxxvii.

39  By Audrey Yoshiko Seo (Boston: Weatherhill, 2007).

40  This phrase is a reference to the traditional kōan story of a dialogue between the Sixth Ancestor of Zen, Dajian Huineng (Jap.: Daikan Enō) and his student Nanyue Huairang at their first encounter:

> Huineng said to Nanyue, "Where do you come from?"
> Nanyue said, "I come from Mt. Song."
> Huineng said, "What is it that thus comes?"
> Nanyue could not answer.
> Eight years later, Nanyue attained enlightenment. He told the Sixth Ancestor, "I now understand."
> The Sixth Ancestor said, "What is it?"
> Nanyue said, "To say it exists misses the mark."

> The Sixth Ancestor said, "Then does it exist or not?"
> Nanyue said, "I don't say that it does not exist but that it cannot be defiled."
> The Sixth Ancestor said, 'This cannot be defiled' is what has been confirmed and maintained by all buddhas. You are thus and I am thus."

Dōgen's phrase "there is practice-enlightenment" refers to the Sixth Ancestor's question "Then does it exist or not?"

41  The last sentence of this citation is a reference to a kōan presented by Tōzan Ryōkai named "The Way of Birds." In answer to the question "What is the original face?" Tōzan replied, "Not going the way of birds." This means there is no separation between the birds' way, the activity of birds, and the birds themselves.

42  Okumura and Leighton, *Wholehearted Way*, pp. 22, 23.

43  This is another reference to Tōzan's kōan "The Way of Birds." In the kōan he says that birds fly with "no strings under their feet," or with no support from any fixed object.

44  Burton Watson, trans., *Chuang Tzu: Basic Writings* (New York, Columbia University Press, 1968), p. 23.

45  Ibid., p. 25.

46  Ibid.

47  Ibid., p. 26.

48  See p. 91 at note 16.

49  Taigen Daniel Leighton and Shohaku Okumura, trans., *Dōgen's Pure Standards for the Zen Community* (Albany: State University of New York Press, 1995), p. 34.

50  This story appears in Watson, *Zen Teachings of Master Lin-chi*, p. 12.

51  Ibid., p. 98.

52  Ibid., p. 59.

53  John Daido Loori and Kazuaki Tanahashi, trans., *The True Dharma Eye: Zen Master Dōgen's Three Hundred Koans* (Boston: Shambhala, 2005), p. 164.

54  Okumura, *Shobogenzo Zuimonki*, 6–7, p. 207.

55  John R. McRae, *Seeing through Zen, Encounter, Transformation, and Genealogy in Chinese Chan Buddhism* (Berkeley: University of California Press), p. 61.

56  Ibid., pp. 61–62.

57  "and so forth until" indicates an abbreviation of the list of practical approaches given two paragraphs above. The list begins with "precepts" and ends with "saving various sentient beings."

# ABOUT THE AUTHOR

 SHOHAKU OKUMURA was born in Osaka, Japan in 1948. He is an ordained priest and Dharma successor of Kōshō Uchiyama Roshi in the lineage of Kōdō Sawaki Roshi. He is a graduate of Komazawa University and has practiced at Antaiji with Kōshō Uchiyama Roshi, Zuioji with Narasaki Ikkō Roshi in Japan, and Pioneer Valley Zendo in Massachusetts. He taught at Kyoto Sōtō Zen Center in Japan and Minnesota Zen Meditation Center in Minneapolis. He was the director of the Soto Zen Buddhism International Center (previously called Soto Zen Education Center) in San Francisco from 1997 to 2010.

His previously published books of translation include *Dōgen's Extensive Record: A Translation of the Eihei Kōroku*; *Shikantaza: An Introduction to Zazen*; *Shōbōgenzō Zuimonki: Sayings of Eihei Dōgen Zenji*; *Heart of Zen: Practice without Gaining-mind* (previously titled *Dōgen Zen*); *Zen Teachings of "Homeless" Kōdō*; *Opening the Hand of Thought*; *The Whole Hearted Way: A Translation of Eihei Dōgen's Bendōwa with Commentary by Kōshō Uchiyama Roshi*; and *Dōgen's Pure Standards for the Zen Community: A Translation of Eihei Shingi*. Okumura is also the editor of *Dōgen Zen and Its Relevance for Our Time*; *Soto Zen: An Introduction to Zazen*; and *Nothing Is Hidden: Essays on Zen Master Dōgen's Instructions for the Cook*.

He is the founding teacher of the Sanshin Zen Community, based in Bloomington, Indiana, where he lives with his family.

## About Wisdom Publications

Wisdom Publications is the leading publisher of classic and contemporary Buddhist books and practical works on mindfulness. To learn more about us or to explore our other books, please visit our website at wisdomexperience.org or contact us at the address below.

Wisdom Publications
199 Elm Street
Somerville, MA 02144 USA

We are a 501(c)(3) organization, and donations in support of our mission are tax deductible.

Wisdom Publications is affiliated with the Foundation for the Preservation of the Mahayana Tradition (FPMT).